Microeconomics using Excel

Market and policy analysis is central to microeconomics and there is a growing demand for education and training. Many national and international institutions require analytical capacities for policy impact analysis, strategic development and decision-making support. Students and analysts in this field need to have a sound understanding of the theoretical foundations of microeconomics and spreadsheet modelling.

Microeconomics using Excel will provide students with the necessary tools to better understand microeconomic analysis. This new textbook focuses on solving microeconomic problems by integrating economic theory, policy analysis and spreadsheet modelling. This unique approach will facilitate a more comprehensive understanding of the link between theory and problem-solving.

Microeconomics using Excel discusses both basic and advanced microeconomic problems and emphasises policy orientation. It is divided into four core parts:

- Analysis of price policies
- Analysis of structural policies
- Multi-market models
- Budget policy and priority setting.

The theory behind each problem is explained and each model is solved using Excel. In addition, there is online content available as an accompaniment to the book. *Microeconomics using Excel* will be of great interest to students studying economics as well as to professionals in economic and policy analysis.

Kurt Jechlitschka and **Dieter Kirschke** are at the Humboldt University of Berlin, and **Gerald Schwarz** is at the Macaulay Institute, Aberdeen.

Microeconomics using Excel

Integrating economic theory, policy analysis
and spreadsheet modelling

**Kurt Jechlitschka, Dieter Kirschke
and Gerald Schwarz**

Routledge
Taylor & Francis Group

LONDON AND NEW YORK

First published 2007
by Routledge
2 Park Square, Milton Park, Abingdon, Oxon OX14 4RN

Simultaneously published in the USA and Canada
by Routledge
270 Madison Ave, New York, NY 10016

Routledge is an imprint of the Taylor & Francis Group, an informa business

© 2007 Kurt Jechlitschka, Dieter Kirschke and Gerald Schwarz

Typeset in Baskerville by
RefineCatch Limited, Bungay, Suffolk

British Library Cataloguing in Publication Data
A catalogue record for this book is available from the British Library

Library of Congress Cataloging in Publication Data
Jechlitschka, Kurt.
    Microeconomics using Excel: integrating economic theory, policy analysis and
spreadsheet modelling / Kurt Jechlitschka, Dieter Kirschke, and Gerald Schwarz.
        p. cm.
    Includes bibliographical references and index.
    ISBN-13: 978–0–415–41786–0 (hb)
    ISBN-13: 978–0–415–41787–7 (pb)
    1. Microeconomics. 2. Microsoft Excel (Computer file)   I. Kirschke, Dieter.
II. Schwarz, Gerald. III. Title.
    HB172.J43 2007
    338.50285′554 – dc22
    2006032879

ISBN10: 0–415–41786–4 (hbk)
ISBN10: 0–415–41787–2 (pbk)

ISBN13: 978–0–415–41786–0 (hbk)
ISBN13: 978–0–415–41787–7 (pbk)

Publisher's Note
The publisher has gone to great lengths to ensure the quality of this book but regrets to inform the
customer that previously available online resources are no longer available with this title.

Contents

Preface

This book will give readers a new look at microeconomic analysis. The focus is on integrating economic theory, policy analysis and spreadsheet modelling. The book discusses fundamental problems of price, structural and budget policies in 18 chapters. The theory behind each problem is explained and it is shown how the problem can be modelled and solved using Excel. The models, also available on the accompanying free online content, may be used as prototypes for further analyses and specific needs.

The book is targeted at students of economics and other related disciplines at universities. It may be used as a basic textbook or as a supplement for a variety of courses. The book is also useful for professionals in economic and policy analysis combining theoretical background and computer-based analysis for different questions. The models can also be used and extended for specific problems and needs.

We would like to express our gratitude to a large number of people who contributed to this book. We are, in particular, grateful to Kerstin Oertel, Sabine Plaßmann and Regina Schiffner who helped tirelessly to transform and improve our manuscript. We would also like to thank Christoph Schaefer-Kehnert and GFA Consulting Group for their interest and support. We particularly thank our families for their patience and support.

Given the new concept of the book we would be very grateful for suggestions and criticism from readers. We hope you will enjoy working with the book and your computer.

Kurt Jechlitschka, Dieter Kirschke and Gerald Schwarz
Berlin, March 2007

Symbols

b share of financial contribution (to the common budget)
B government budget (revenue)
B^m government budget (revenue) of a customs union member country
BE (government) budget expenditure
BES (government) budget expenditure for structural policies

c supply constant
C cost
CS consumer surplus
CV compensating variation

d demand constant
D, D^M (Marshallian) demand curve
D^H Hicksian demand curve

E consumer expenditure
EE external effect
ES export supply curve
EV equivalent variation

f (supply) shift parameter
f^d average (supply) shift parameter
FE foreign exchange (revenue)
FE^m foreign exchange (revenue) of a customs union member country

g^c distributional weight for consumers
g^g distributional weight for the government
g^p distributional weight for producers

i interest rate
ID import demand curve
IRR internal rate of return

L	Lagrange function
MC	marginal cost
NB	net government budget (revenue)
NW	net welfare
p	domestic price
p^a	autarky price
p^d	demand price
$\tilde{p}^d(\cdot)$	inverse demand function
p^s	supply price
$\tilde{p}^s(\cdot)$	inverse supply function
p^u	customs union price
p^w	world market price
PS	producer surplus
PV	present value of net welfare effects (of a structural policy)
q^d	quantity demanded
$q^d(\cdot)$	demand function
$q^{d(H)}(\cdot)$	Hicksian demand function
q^{ex}	quantity exported
q^{im}	quantity imported
q^s	quantity supplied
$q^s(\cdot)$	supply function
r	protection rate
R	producer revenue
s	producer subsidy rate
S	supply curve
t	(time) period
T	transfer
TB	total benefit
v	consumer subsidy rate
w	expenditure share of a product
W	welfare
W^a	adjusted welfare (integrating distributional weights)
W^m	welfare of a customs union member country
W^s	social welfare (integrating external effects)
y	income

z objective variable

a weight

ε elasticity
ε^d demand elasticity
$\boldsymbol{\varepsilon^d}$ price elasticity matrix on the demand side
$\boldsymbol{\varepsilon^d}, \boldsymbol{\eta}$ matrix of price and income elasticities on the demand side
ε^s supply elasticity
$\boldsymbol{\varepsilon^s}$ price elasticity matrix on the supply side

$\mathbf{H^d}$ matrix of the derivatives of the Hicksian demand functions with respect to the prices
$\mathbf{H^s}$ matrix of the derivatives of the supply functions with respect to the prices

η income elasticity of demand

λ Lagrange multiplier

Introduction

With this book we want to provide a new look at microeconomic analysis. The focus is on solving microeconomic problems by integrating economic theory, policy analysis and spreadsheet modelling. The approach allows a better understanding of the link between theory and problem-solving; you will learn how to model and solve specific problems with Excel; and you will be able to use and extend the models developed for your own needs.

The book discusses various basic and advanced microeconomic problems and emphasises a policy orientation. It is divided into four parts:

- Analysis of price policies
- Analysis of structural policies
- Multi-market models
- Budget policy and priority setting

In each part we discuss specific problems based on neoclassical microeconomic theory. The methods used focus on equilibrium and optimisation models. In Parts I to III partial equilibrium models are applied, with single-market models being developed and used in Parts I and II and multi-market models in Part III. Part IV is based on linear programming.

Each chapter follows the same structure. Starting with the objective and the theory we then formulate an exercise and explain the solution step by step. At the end of each chapter some relevant literature is listed. The accompanying free online content provides the opportunity to check the models developed by yourself or to use the models on the online content for further questions.

Depending on the knowledge and interest of the reader, the book may be used in different ways. We would suggest that you become familiar with the theoretical background before starting the modelling exercise. But you can also start with the available models on the online content to get an overview of the different modelling approaches.

The chapters build on each other and it is recommended to follow the order suggested by the book. But, of course, you can also develop your own program. Chapters 1 to 4 in Part I are essential for Parts I, II and III. The remaining chapters in Part I and Parts II and III can be worked through quite independently from each other. Part IV is self-contained and can also be dealt with on its own. Moreover, the book presents two modelling frameworks, which may be used for further analyses and specific needs: a framework for a multi-market model covering up to 12 markets (Chapter 15) and a framework for budget policies and priority setting (Chapter 18).

The book may be used for different university courses. It is a basic textbook for microeconomic courses that follow our approach of integrating economic theory, policy analysis and spreadsheet modelling. For more conventional microeconomic courses it would be a useful supplement offering a comprehensive policy and modelling orientation. In addition, the book or specific chapters may be used in a variety of other courses related to trade, policy analysis, modelling and software application. Due to the focus of the book on solving microeconomic problems both theory-oriented and modelling-oriented courses would benefit from our approach.

The book requires some basic knowledge about microeconomics, policy analysis, modelling and spreadsheet programs. The references in each chapter should help to provide some orientation. Given the vast amount of available literature for the different topics addressed, only a selection of publications is listed.

The (solution) steps consist of instructions to develop the different models supported by a large number of figures and tables. The steps are written following recent Excel versions, but most of the Excel files will not work with Excel 95 or an earlier version.

According to the different exercises, file names have been allocated to the models, which can also be identified from the figures. The models build on each other (e.g. exercise4.xls is the basis for exercise12.xls) and not only give the solutions to the problems but also provide basic modelling concepts using Excel. The first models are intentionally kept simple, while the descriptions are rather detailed; in later chapters the models are more complex and the descriptions shorter.

Following the principle of learning by doing the specific exercises allows you to solve the problems and to gain modelling abilities using Excel. In addition to basic techniques (e.g. copy and paste of specific cells and ranges and handling formulas), more advanced techniques and aspects of Excel are introduced; these include: generating data tables and charts, Solver applications, linkages between sheets, VBA programs, protection of models, files and macros. If you follow the steps in the different chapters, you will quickly learn these techniques. The accompanying online content makes all models and model variants (123 altogether) available to the reader; the respective models may be found in the folders Exercise-01 to Exercise-18 according to the chapters of the book.

Part I

Analysis of price policies

1 Supply, demand and price policies

Objective

In Chapter 1 we discuss the basic concepts of supply, demand and price policies, and we formulate an appropriate Excel model. In order to do this, supply and demand functions are defined and the process of price formation on a market without and with government intervention is illustrated. We then discuss how various price policies affect political objectives such as producer revenue, consumer expenditure, foreign exchange or government budget.

Theory

The starting point for the analysis of price policies on a market is the formulation of supply and demand functions. Let us consider the following linear supply function:

$$q^s(p^s) = a + b\,p^s; \qquad a < 0, b > 0 \tag{1.1}$$

where $q^s(\cdot)$ – supply function
  q^s – quantity supplied
  p^s – supply price.

Parameter a describes the hypothetical quantity of supply for a supply price of zero, and the value will be negative since supply will only begin above a certain minimum supply price. Parameter b describes the slope of the supply function and indicates the change in units supplied as a consequence of an increase of the supply price by one unit, exactly: by one infinitesimally small unit. It is common to graphically show supply and demand functions as inverse functions with the price on the y-axis and the quantity on the x-axis. Solving (1.1) with respect to p^s yields the following inverse supply function:

$$\tilde{p}^s(q^s) = -\frac{a}{b} + \frac{1}{b}q^s \tag{1.1$'$}$$

where $\tilde{p}^s(\cdot)$ – inverse supply function.

The function is visualised in Figure 1.1.

Similar to the supply side, the following linear demand function can be formulated:

$$q^d(p^d) = c + d\,p^d; \qquad c > 0, d < 0 \tag{1.2}$$

where $q^d(\cdot)$ – demand function
         q^d – quantity demanded
         p^d – demand price.

Parameter c marks a saturated situation. Parameter d is the slope of the demand function indicating the change in units demanded as a consequence of an increase of the demand price by one unit, exactly: by one infinitesimally small unit.

Solving (1.2) with respect to p^d yields the following inverse demand function illustrated in Figure 1.1:

$$\tilde{p}^d(q^d) = -\frac{c}{d} + \frac{1}{d}q^d \tag{1.2}'$$

where $\tilde{p}^d(\cdot)$ – inverse demand function.

Let us now consider a closed economy without government intervention. For such a policy framework there will be an equilibrium price on the market equalising supply and demand. This is the autarky price p^a in Figure 1.1. Under free

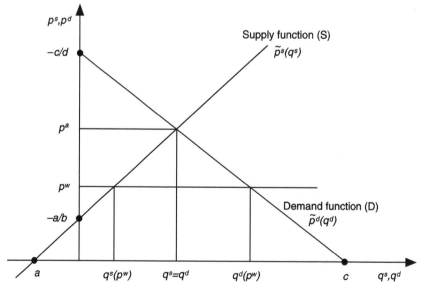

Figure 1.1 Linear supply and demand functions.

trade, instead, the world market price p^w will be the relevant price for domestic supply and demand. We assume that the world market price is given for the domestic market; this is the 'small country assumption' according to which the world market price will not change due to domestic supply and demand changes. According to Figure 1.1, domestic supply and demand will be $q^s (p^w)$ and $q^d (p^w)$ under free trade and imports will be $q^{im} = q^d (p^w) - q^s (p^w)$. Autarky and free trade as discussed here mark the absence of government interventions in a market, but the scenarios may also be interpreted as describing only the specific policy framework: autarky and free trade.

Let us now consider that a country sets the domestic price independently of the world market price according to domestic policy objectives. Such a price policy can be implemented by price and quantity interventions; in market economies the typical intervention is a 'subsidisation' or a 'taxation' of economic activities yielding domestic supply and/or demand prices different from the world market price. In Figure 1.2 a protectionist price policy is visualised that may be implemented by a tariff in an import situation or an export subsidy in an export situation. Formally, policy objectives on this market such as increasing producer revenue or government budget now depend on the world market price and/or the domestic price.

Figure 1.2 presents the case of a protectionist price policy in an import situation. As compared to free trade, the quantity of supply increases to $q^s (p)$ and the quantity of demand decreases to $q^d (p)$. Further relevant policy objectives may be defined for this protectionist price policy. The producer revenue will be:

$$R (p) = q^s (p) \cdot p. \tag{1.3}$$

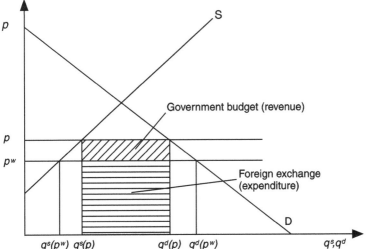

Figure 1.2 Consequences of a protectionist price policy in an import situation.

For consumer expenditure we get:

$$E(p) = q^d(p) \cdot p. \tag{1.4}$$

In the import situation considered here import expenditures occur. In general, covering both an import and an export situation, we define a foreign exchange function as follows:

$$FE(p, p^w) = \left(q^s(p) - q^d(p) \right) p^w. \tag{1.5}$$

Thus, foreign exchange is a function of the two exogenous prices and it has a negative value in the import situation considered. Similarly, we define a government budget function:

$$B(p, p^w) = \left(q^d(p) - q^s(p) \right) \left(p - p^w \right). \tag{1.6}$$

The value of this function is positive for the case considered. It would be negative for a protectionist price policy in an export situation to be established by an export subsidy. Foreign exchange (expenditure) and government budget (revenue) are visualised in Figure 1.2.

The values of the defined functions can now be calculated depending on the values of the exogenous prices and the parameters of the supply and demand functions. In order to assess the impact of the prices on these functions, it is helpful to draw the corresponding graphs of these functions. Foreign exchange will thus be a linear rising function of the domestic price p as the derivative of this function

$$\frac{\partial}{\partial p} FE(p, p^w) = \left(\frac{\partial q^s}{\partial p} - \frac{\partial q^d}{\partial p} \right) p^w \tag{1.5$'$}$$

is a constant. It intersects the price axis at the autarky price p^a. The foreign exchange function is visualised in Figure 1.3.

Figure 1.3 also shows the government budget function with respect to the domestic price. For the linear supply and demand functions considered, we get a strictly concave quadratic budget function, intersecting the price axis at free trade $p = p^w$ and autarky at $p = p^a$. At a domestic price level below the world market price, import subsidies are paid and, hence, budget expenditures occur that decrease with a rising domestic price. For a domestic price level between free trade p^w and autarky p^a, tariffs create budget revenues, with a maximum exactly between p^w and p^a. Finally, with higher domestic prices above the autarky price p^a, increasing budget expenditures occur due to export subsidies.

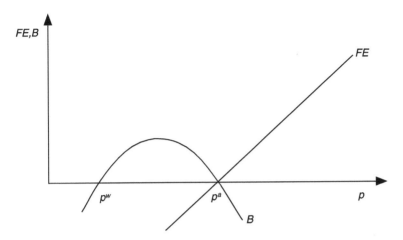

Figure 1.3 Foreign exchange and government budget as a function of the domestic price.

Based on (1.5) and (1.6), analogous foreign exchange and government budget functions could be drawn as functions of the world market price p^w, taking the domestic price as a constant. The equations show that the graph of a function in one price depends on the value of the other price.

Exercise 1

Consider the supply function

$$q^s(p^s) = a + b\,p^s$$

with $a = -30, \quad b = 6$

and the demand function

$$q^d(p^d) = c + d\,p^d$$

with $c = 120, \quad d = -4.$

Set up a linear market model in Excel and solve the following problems:

(a) Consider a free trade situation with a world market price $p^w = 10$. Calculate producer revenue, consumer expenditure and foreign exchange.
(b) The country now pursues a price policy setting the domestic price independently of the world market price. Calculate producer revenue, consumer expenditure, foreign exchange, and government budget for $p = 12$ and $p = 18$.
(c) How do foreign exchange and government budget develop in a domestic

price range $10 \leq p \leq 20$? Show the graph of the functions and discuss the shape.

(d) How do foreign exchange and government budget develop for $p = 12$ and $10 \leq p^w \leq 20$? Show the graph of the functions and discuss the shape. How does the graph change for $p = 18$?

(e) The country considers implementing an autarky policy. Calculate equilibrium price and equilibrium quantity.

Solution

Step 1.1 Enter the value of 10 in cell B4 for the domestic price and the same value in C4 for the world market price. Enter the values of the parameters a, b, c and d in the range B8:E8.

Step 1.2 In cell E4, we now define the supply function by entering the formula = B8 + C8*B4. Respectively, in F4 we define the demand function with = D8 + E8*B4.

Step 1.3 According to (1.3)–(1.6), enter the formula for producer revenue, consumer expenditure, foreign exchange and government budget in H4 to K4 and your linear market model is completed (see Figure 1.4). The values in your model describe the free trade situation with $p^w = 10$. In order to determine the consequences of a protectionist price policy (Exercise 1b), you simply set the domestic price at $p = 12$ and $p = 18$, respectively. You obtain the values of the defined variables for an import and an export situation.

Step 1.4 To solve Exercise 1c you proceed as follows. Enter the value of 10 in G11 and go again to cell G11. Now select the Excel menu 'Edit', 'Fill' and 'Series', take the option 'Series in columns' and enter 20 as the 'Stop value'. In H9 enter the formula = J3 and copy it to the range H9:I10. Now select the table range G10:I21 and select 'Data' and 'Table'. Click into the field 'Column input cell' and then on B4. You will get the values for foreign exchange and government budget for domestic prices from 10 to 20. If you now select the range G9:I21 and then select the 'Chart wizard' icon (e.g. the diagram type 'Line with markers displayed at each data value') you will get, possibly after some editing, a diagram as indicated in Figure 1.5.

	A	B	C	D	E	F	G	H	I	J	K
1		Linear Market Model									
2											
3		Domestic price	World market price		Supply	Demand		Revenue	Expenditure	Foreign exchange	Government budget
4		10	10		30	80		300	800	-500	0
5											
6		Parameter:									
7		a	b	c	d						
8		-30	6	120	-4						

Figure 1.4 Linear market model (exercise1.xls).

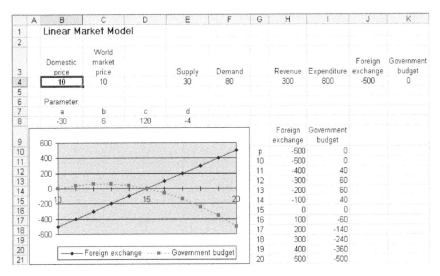

Figure 1.5 Foreign exchange and government budget as a function of the domestic price with a world market price of 10 (exercise 1.xls).

The shape of the foreign exchange function and the government budget function clearly reveal an autarky price $p^a = 15$. The functions underline our discussion on the consequences of a protectionist price policy (compare Figure 1.3).

Similarly you can solve Exercise 1d by selecting the world market price (C4) as 'Column input cell' within the multiple operation 'Data', 'Table'. The focus of this exercise is to find out the consequences of a rising world market price on foreign exchange as well as on the government budget for a given domestic price. With $p = 12$ the country is an importer with an import quantity of 30. According to Figure 1.6, foreign exchange is negative and decreases with a rising world market price. In addition, the government budget decreases with an increasing world market price. The government budget is positive with a higher domestic price than the world market price due to tariff revenues, but it becomes negative for a higher world market price indicating an import subsidisation policy.

Figure 1.7 shows an export situation with an export quantity of 30. With a rising world market price foreign exchange is rising too. Government budget is negative for the situation of a protectionist price policy, but becomes positive for a world market price above 18 indicating budget revenues from an export tax. For the free trade situation with $p^w = 18$, the budget is zero.

Step 1.5 For the determination of the equilibrium price under autarky we use the Excel Solver. To do this, select the Excel menu 'Tools', 'Solver' command. If the Solver is not available, select the 'Tools', 'Add-ins' command. If the Solver still does not show up you need to reinstall

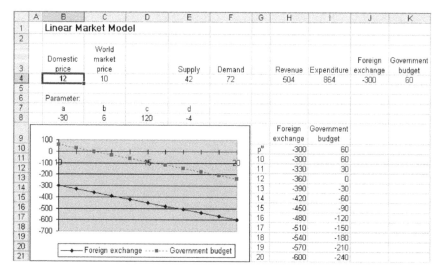

Figure 1.6 Foreign exchange and government budget as a function of the world market price with a domestic price of 12 (exercise1d.xls).

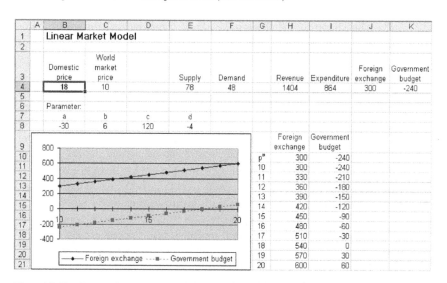

Figure 1.7 Foreign exchange and government budget as a function of the world market price with a domestic price of 18 (exercise1d.xls).

Office or Excel with the Custom option of the original MS-Office CD. Since we do not really have an optimisation problem in Exercise 1e the setting of the target cell does not play an important role – but it should be a cell with a formula (e.g. E4) or you can even select nothing by leaving the space empty. As changing cells you take the domestic price (by writing B4 into the appropriate line or by clicking first on this field and then on cell B4). As a constraint you add E4 = F4 (show or register). Thus the Solver is set (see Figures 1.8 and 1.9).

Since our model is a linear one you should click on 'Options' and activate 'Assume linear model'. Also select 'Assume non-negative'. This ensures that the changing cells – in our case the domestic price – will assume non-negative values (see Figure 1.10). Click 'OK' and 'Solve' and you will get the domestic price of 15 and the equilibrium quantity of 60. For further details of using the Solver see Winston and Venkataramanan (2002) or the Excel Help function.

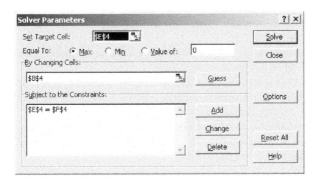

Figure 1.8 Solver dialogue box.

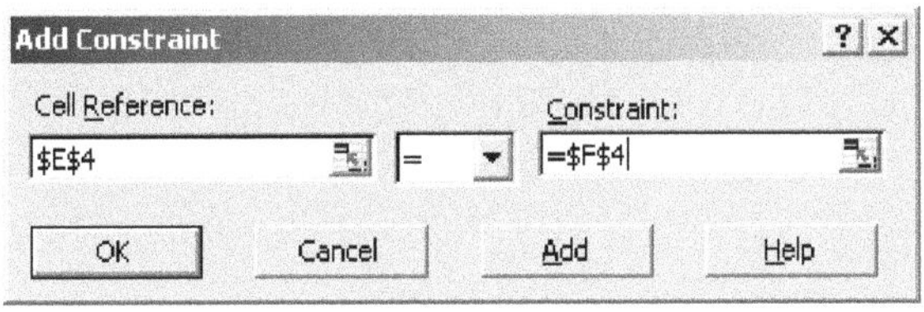

Figure 1.9 Dialogue box for adding constraints.

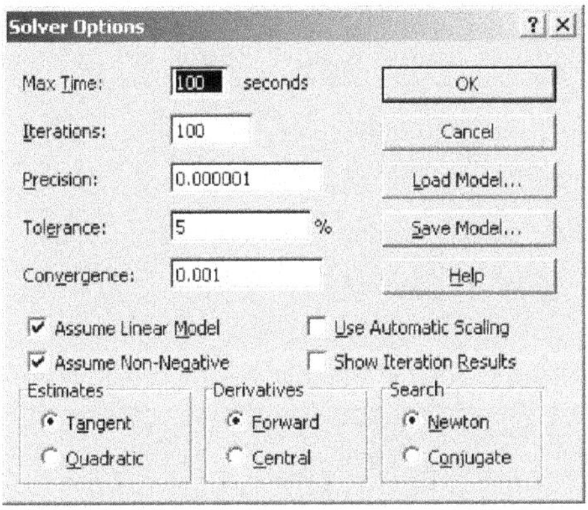

Figure 1.10 Solver options dialogue box.

References

Chiang, A.C. and Wainwright, K. (2005) *Fundamental Methods of Mathematical Economics* (4th edn), Boston, MA: McGraw-Hill, pp. 5–8, 15–34.

Klein, M.W. (2002) *Mathematical Methods for Economics* (2nd edn), Boston, MA: Addison Wesley, pp. 6–18, 75–82.

Koester, U. (2005) *Grundzüge der landwirtschaftlichen Marktlehre* (3rd edn), Munich: Vahlen, pp. 30–7, 89–98, 130–2 (WiSo-Kurzlehrbücher: Reihe Volkswirtschaft).

Mas-Colell, A., Whinston, M.D. and Green, J.A. (1995) *Microeconomic Theory*, New York, Oxford: Oxford University Press, pp. 316–25.

Microsoft, Original Handbooks and Microsoft Excel-help. Online. Available: <http://www.microsoft.com> (accessed 20 July 2006).

Nicholson, W. (2005) *Microeconomic Theory: Basic Principles and Extensions* (9th edn), Mason, OH: Thomson, pp. 279–95.

Pindyck, R.S. and Rubinfeld, D.L. (2005) *Microeconomics* (6th edn), Upper Saddle River, NJ: Pearson Prentice Hall, pp. 19–32.

Powell, S.G. (1995) 'The teachers' forum: six modeling heuristics', *Interfaces*, 25, pp. 114–25.

—— (1997) 'Leading the spreadsheet revolution', *ORMS Today*, 24 (6), pp. 50–4.

Varian, H.R. (2003) *Intermediate Microeconomics: A Modern Approach* (6th edn), New York: W.W. Norton, pp. 266–70, 288–300, Mathematical Appendix.

Winston, W.L. and Venkataramanan, M. (2002) *Introduction to Mathematical Programming*, Belmont, CA: Duxbury Press, pp. 202–10.

2 Welfare and distribution

Objective

In Chapter 2 we introduce further indicators for price policies. Based on the concept of applied welfare economics, welfare functions and their components are defined and welfare and distributional effects of different price policies are explained.

Theory

Following the concept of applied welfare economics, the maximum willingness to pay may be used as a welfare indicator for the consumer. Willingness to pay is defined as the maximum amount a consumer is prepared to pay for a good or service. It is therefore a monetary measure of the satisfaction of consuming a good. In Figure 2.1 willingness to pay, aggregated for all consumers, is illustrated by the area under the demand curve up to the quantity demanded $q^d(p)$. We also call this the total benefit of consumption, defined as:

$$TB(p) = \int_0^{q^d(p)} \tilde{p}^d(v)\, dv \tag{2.1}$$

with TB – total benefit
          v – integration variable, here q^d.

Since goods have to be produced before being consumed, the production of a certain good implies that production and consumption of all other goods will be reduced. A measure of the reduced willingness to pay on other markets is the variable cost of producing a good, because factors cannot be used to produce other goods and cannot create benefit on other markets. Hence, the cost function represents the benefit foregone, or opportunity cost, and, as shown in Figure 2.1, may be visualised by the area under the supply curve up to the quantity supplied $q^s(p)$:

$$C(p) = \int_{0}^{q^{s}(p)} \tilde{p}^{s}(v)\, dv \qquad (2.2)$$

with C – cost

        v – integration variable, here q^{s}.

Furthermore, in an open economy, welfare implications of trade and changes in foreign exchange have to be considered. Foreign exchange revenue from exports increases welfare as the revenue may be seen as a potential demand of foreign goods leading to additional satisfaction. Foreign exchange expenditure for imports, on the other hand, leads to a reduction of the ability to consume other foreign goods, thus decreasing welfare. The case of foreign exchange expenditure is shown in Figure 2.1.

Adding the different welfare components, the example for a protectionist price policy leads to a welfare level indicated by the bold-framed area in Figure 2.1. Thus, the welfare function is defined as:

$$W(p, p^{w}) = TB(p) - C(p) + FE(p, p^{w}) \qquad (2.3)$$

with W – welfare,

and

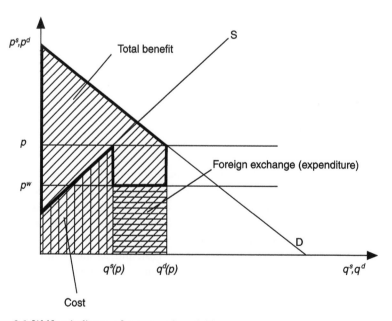

Figure 2.1 Welfare indicators for economic activities.

$$W(p, p^{w}) = \int_{0}^{q^{d}(p)} \tilde{p}^{d}(v)\, dv - \int_{0}^{q^{s}(p)} \tilde{p}^{s}(v)\, dv$$

$$+ \left(q^{s}(p) - q^{d}(p) \right) p^{w}. \tag{2.3$'$}$$

The welfare function as defined in equations (2.3) and (2.3)′ is based on the economic activities of consumption, production and trade. Since welfare is an indicator for the satisfaction of a society from the consumption of goods, welfare may also be defined as an aggregate of the welfare level of different groups: consumers, producers and taxpayers.

Looking at consumers first, they gain benefits from consumption, but have to pay for the goods they consume. The expenditure for a certain good cannot be used to gain satisfaction from the consumption of other goods. Hence, from the consumers' point of view, expenditure is the cost of consuming a good. The difference of total benefit and consumer expenditure is the relevant welfare indicator for consumers, called consumer surplus. Consumer surplus, illustrated in Figure 2.2 as the difference of the area under the demand curve up to the quantity demanded $q^{d}(p)$ and consumer expenditure, is defined as:

$$CS(p) = \int_{0}^{q^{d}(p)} \tilde{p}^{d}(v)\, dv - q^{d}(p)\, p \tag{2.4}$$

with CS – consumer surplus.

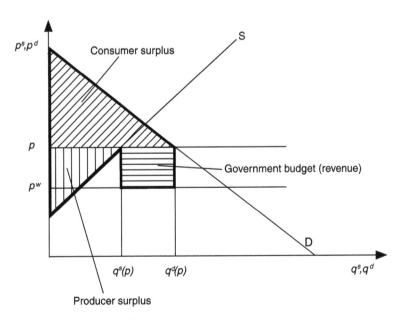

Figure 2.2 Welfare indicators for groups.

Accordingly, producer revenue describes the ability of producers to demand goods and to derive benefit from their consumption, while cost for variable factors reduces the ability to consume goods. Thus, the relevant indicator to describe the welfare of producers is the difference of producer revenue and cost; it is called producer surplus. Producer surplus is displayed in Figure 2.2 and defined as:

$$PS(p) = q^s(p)\,p - \int_0^{q^s(p)} \tilde{p}^s(v)\,dv \qquad (2.5)$$

with PS – producer surplus.

Producer surplus is comparable to gross margin in business management. Using producer surplus as an income and welfare indicator for producers it is important to keep in mind that it does not take into account ownership of fixed factors and does not consider variable factors such as family labour belonging to the producer household.

It is also important to note that the concept of applied welfare economics is based on the assumptions of utility maximisation of consumers, profit maximisation of producers, and perfectly competitive markets. Without these assumptions the welfare indicators cannot be defined. Moreover, the concept is based on an individual welfare concept assuming that preferences are properly revealed on markets. Furthermore, the aggregation of individual welfare does not consider income differences. It applies a so-called 'dollar-democracy', where each dollar provides equal satisfaction for society, no matter if it accrues to consumers, producers or taxpayers. This shows the importance of evaluating distributional effects of policy changes.

In applied welfare economics the consequences of policy changes for taxpayers are analysed through changes in government budget. Government budget revenue, as shown in Figure 2.2, increases the ability of society to consume goods (e.g. through increased transfer payments, reduced taxes or the provision of public goods). In contrast, government budget expenditure reduces the ability of a society to consume.

If we aggregate welfare indicators for the different groups, we can define the welfare of a society as:

$$W(p, p^w) = CS(p) + PS(p) + B(p, p^w) \qquad (2.6)$$

and

$$W(p, p^w) = \int_0^{q^d(p)} \tilde{p}^d(v)\,dv - \int_0^{q^s(p)} \tilde{p}^s(v)\,dv$$

$$+ \left(q^s(p) - q^d(p) \right) p^w. \qquad (2.6)'$$

The welfare functions defined in equations $(2.3)'$ and $(2.6)'$ are the same and the bold-framed areas in Figures 2.1 and 2.2 are identical.

The basic concept of applied welfare economics is widely used and may be applied without problems for the welfare indicators foreign exchange and government budget as well as for cost and producer surplus which are derived from the supply function. But for welfare indicators derived from the demand function such as total benefit and consumer surplus, it is important to note that these indicators represent only an approximation of the relevant welfare indicators and not exact values. However, such approximation is acceptable as long as we restrict the analysis to a small fraction of the economy such as a commodity market. On that basis we can now analyse different problem settings.

One can show, for example, that free trade leads to a maximisation of welfare. This is the theorem of comparative advantage. A domestic price set above or below the world market price through government intervention results in an efficiency loss to society. This welfare loss comprises deadweight losses due to consumption distortion and production inefficiency, which may be identified as 'deadweight loss triangles' in Figures 2.1 and 2.2. Accordingly, one can describe a welfare function which is strictly concave in p with a maximum at $p = p^w$. Furthermore, one can show in Figure 2.1 that a protectionist price policy to reduce foreign exchange expenditure for imports leads to a welfare loss.

Welfare gains from the transition from autarky to free trade depend on the extent of resource reallocation induced by free trade, indicating a comparative advantage or disadvantage. Figure 2.3 shows that with an autarky price equal to the world market price, opening the economy evidently does not cause any change in welfare as no trade takes place. However, both the export case at $p^{w'}$ and the import

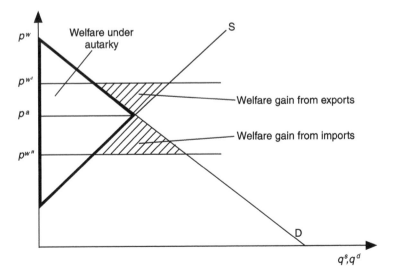

Figure 2.3 Welfare gains from trade.

case at $p^{w''}$ result in welfare gains. Accordingly, for free trade one may describe a welfare function $W(p^w; p = p^w)$ depending on p^w, which is strictly convex with a minimum at the autarky price p^a. This function is also called gains from trade curve.

Exercise 2

Consider the supply function

$$q^s(p^s) = a + b\,p^s$$

with $a = -30, \quad b = 6$

and the demand function

$$q^d(p^d) = c + d\,p^d$$

with $c = 120, \quad d = -4.$

Extend the market model from Exercise 1 by the functions for total benefit, cost and welfare as well as consumer surplus and producer surplus. Solve the following problems:

(a) A country has set the domestic price independently from the world market; the world market price is $p^w = 10$. Show that free trade leads to welfare maximisation.

(b) How do welfare, consumer surplus and producer surplus develop for $p = 12$ and $p = 14$ with $p^w = 10$ compared to free trade?

(c) Depict the graph of the functions for welfare, consumer surplus and producer surplus for $5 \leq p \leq 15$ with $p^w = 10$ and explain the result. How does the graph change with $p^w = 12$?

(d) Show how, starting from free trade with $p^w = 10$, a step-by-step increase in the domestic price $10 \leq p \leq 20$ leads, at the same time, to foreign exchange increases and welfare losses as compared to free trade.

(e) Depict the gains from trade curve for $10 \leq p^w \leq 20$.

Solution

To start with, the indicators of applied welfare economics have to be integrated into the linear market model.

Step 2.1   Let us create, based on exercise1.xls, some space for the cost function, total benefit function and welfare function, which we enter in cells H4 to J4. To do this, you move the function block H3:K4 to K3:N4 (e.g. highlight H3:K4, go with the cursor over the frame – the cursor becomes an arrow – then select with a pressed left mouse button the new area and release the left mouse button).

Step 2.2 We begin with the cost function, which we enter in cell H4. Cost is defined as the area under the inverse supply function. Hence, assuming the supply function $q^s = -30 + 6p$, we can calculate the cost, for example, as the difference of the revenue $p \cdot q^s (p)$ and the triangle $(p - 30/6) \cdot q^s(p)/2$. $30/6 = 5$ is the intersection of the supply function with the price axis, and thus the minimum supply price. The Excel formula in H4 is $=$ B4*E4 – (B4 + B8/C8)*E4/2. Alternatively, we could determine the cost calculating the trapezium $(p + 30/6) \cdot q^s(p)/2$. Both calculations may be explained using Figure 2.4.

Step 2.3 Assuming the linear demand function $q^d (p) = 120 - 4p$, we can calculate benefit as the trapezium $(p + 120/4) \cdot q^d(p)/2$. Hence, we enter in I4 the Excel formula: $=$ (B4 – D8/E8)*F4/2. (Note the negative value of E8 $= -4$.) The calculation may be explained again using Figure 2.4.

Step 2.4 Now, we can easily derive welfare from the formula total benefit – cost + foreign exchange in cell J4. Similarly straightforward are the formulas for producer surplus and consumer surplus in O4 and P4. Producer surplus is the difference of revenue and cost, while consumer surplus is the difference of total benefit and expenditure. Compare the results of your model with the values in Figure 2.5. Choose then for the domestic

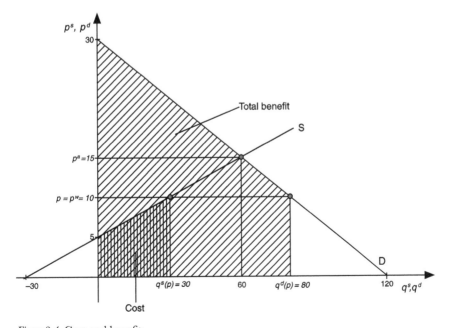

Figure 2.4 Cost and benefit.

	A	B	C	D	E	F	G	H
1	Linear Market Model							
2								
3		Domestic price	World market price		Supply	Demand		Cost
4		10	10		30	80		225
5								
6		Parameter:						
7		a	b	c	d			
8		-30	6	120	-4			

	I	J	K	L	M	N	O	P
1								
2								
3	Total benefit	Welfare	Revenue	Expenditure	Foreign exchange	Government budget	Producer surplus	Consumer surplus
4	1600	875	300	800	-500	0	75	800

Figure 2.5 Linear market model with cost, total benefit, welfare, producer surplus and consumer surplus at a domestic price of 10 (exercise2.xls).

	A	B	C	D	E	F	G	H
1	Linear Market Model							
2								
3		Domestic price	World market price		Supply	Demand		Cost
4		12	10		42	72		357
5								
6		Parameter:						
7		a	b	c	d			
8		-30	6	120	-4			

	I	J	K	L	M	N	O	P
1								
2								
3	Total benefit	Welfare	Revenue	Expenditure	Foreign exchange	Government budget	Producer surplus	Consumer surplus
4	1512	855	504	864	-300	60	147	648

Figure 2.6 Linear market model with cost, total benefit, welfare, producer surplus and consumer surplus at a domestic price of 12.

price in B4 the value 12. By doing so, you obtain the values shown in Figure 2.6. Then choose a domestic price of 14 and you have already solved Exercise 2b. The rise of the domestic price from 10 to 14, at $p^w = 10$, outlines the consequences of an increasing protectionist price policy. That is an increase in producer surplus, but a decline of consumer surplus and welfare.

Step 2.5 In order to solve Exercise 2a you have to carry out the following steps. Assume a domestic price of 14 and a world market price of 10; set the Solver as follows: target cell: J4; welfare to be maximised; target value: max; changing cell: B4; constraints: none. As a result you obtain the welfare-maximising domestic price of 10, in other words, the world market price, following the theorem of comparative advantage.

The result is only an approximation. Since the welfare function is not a linear function of the prices, the optimisation model is not linear either, and the Solver provides, depending on the settings chosen under 'Options', an approximate solution close to 10. Compare the results the Solver provides for different domestic prices.

Step 2.6 To solve Exercise 2c enter the base values for the domestic price (10) and world market price (10) in your market model. Then proceed as follows. Enter in G11 the number 5 and go back to G11. Under 'Edit', 'Fill' and 'Series' choose the option 'Series in columns' and enter 15 as the 'Stop value'. Then write the formula = O3 in H9 and copy H9 in the range H9:I10. Write the formulas = J3 and = J4 in J9 and J10, respectively. Now, select the range G10:J21 and choose 'Data', 'Table', click into the field 'Columns input cell' and then click on B4. In that way, you obtain the values for producer surplus, consumer surplus and welfare at integer domestic prices from 5 to 15; you may depict the functions by using the 'Chart Wizard', as explained in Step 1.4.

Step 2.7 In order to facilitate the interpretation of the shape of the functions, it may be helpful to look at the changes in the indicators from one domestic price to the next. We can show these absolute changes in H25:J34 through intelligent copying of the formula of the difference. If you have in G24:G34 the series 5 to 15 and in H23:J23 the appropriate terminology, you can depict the required diagram by selecting G23:J34 and using the 'Chart Wizard'. Compare your results with Figure 2.7.

Figure 2.7 shows that producer surplus increases under a rising domestic price, while consumer surplus decreases accordingly. In line with the theorem of comparative advantage the welfare maximum is at $p = 10$. The increasing welfare loss under a rising domestic price points to the 'cost' of a protectionist price policy in the context of this political objective.

At a world market price of $p^w = 12$ we get similar results, of course with different values. The welfare maximum is now at $p = 12$, hence smaller

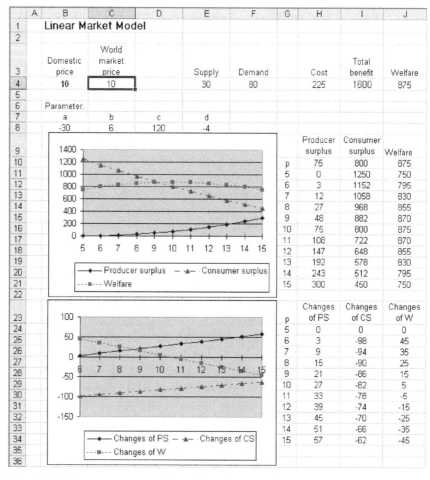

Figure 2.7 Welfare, consumer surplus and producer surplus as functions of the domestic price at a world market price of 10 (exercise2c.xls).

than at $p = p^w = 10$. But it still applies that a country can maximise its welfare through free trade, but the welfare gain from trade is smaller due to less comparative advantage compared to autarky. Compare your results with Figure 2.8.

Step 2.8   To solve Exercise 2d, again implement in your market model a free trade situation with $p = 10$ and $p^w = 10$. Now generate, as carried out in Exercise 2c, a data series for foreign exchange and welfare at prices between 10 and 20 and create the relevant diagrams. Note that the changes to be calculated in this exercise refer to the free trade situation. You will find the result in Figure 2.9.

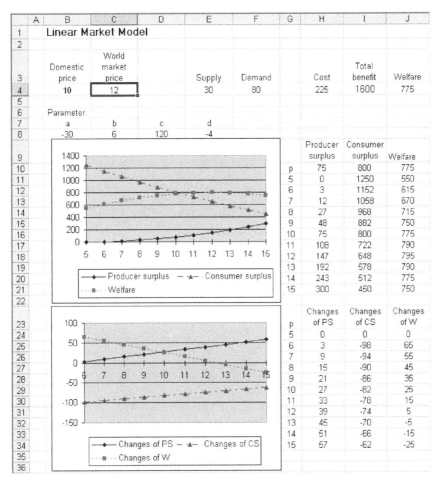

Figure 2.8 Welfare, consumer surplus and producer surplus as functions of the domestic price at a world market price of 12.

Figure 2.9 shows how foreign exchange and welfare change if the domestic price increases from a word market price level at 10 to a price of 20. For an autarky price of 15 there is no foreign exchange expenditure; hence foreign exchange increases by 500 compared to free trade. Welfare at autarky, on the other hand, is at 750, which is a reduction of 125 compared to free trade. In this example this is the welfare gain of free trade, the gains from trade.

Step 2.9   The scale of the gains from trade depends on the difference between the free trade equilibrium and the autarky equilibrium. The bigger the difference between the two equilibria the bigger the gains from trade.

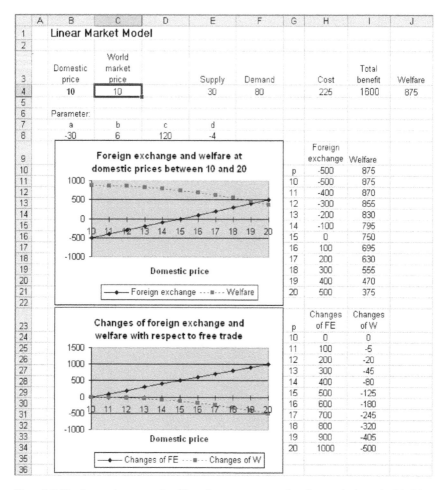

Figure 2.9 Foreign exchange and welfare changes compared to free trade (exercise2d.xls).

Accordingly, you can define a gains from trade function in Exercise 2e, which depicts welfare in free trade situations at different world market prices. To define this function you enter in C4 the formula = B4 and proceed as outlined in Exercise 2c using the data series 10 to 20 and displaying the welfare function. Compare your results with Figure 2.10.

Figure 2.10 shows a strictly convex gains from trade curve with a minimum at the autarky price $p = p^w = 15$. If the world market price is equal to the equilibrium price in autarky, there is obviously no welfare gain from trade, because trade does not take place.

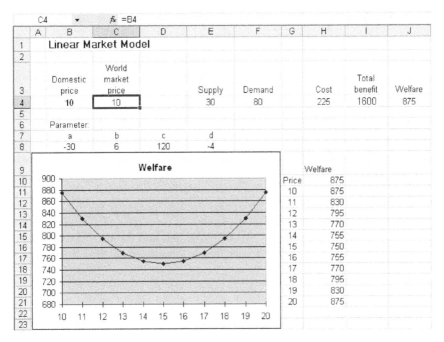

Figure 2.10 Gains from trade curve (exercise2e.xls).

References

Chiang, A.C. and Wainwright, K. (2005) *Fundamental Methods of Mathematical Economics* (4th edn), Boston, MA: McGraw-Hill, pp. 444–64.

Just, R.E., Hueth, D.L. and Schmitz, A. (2004) *The Welfare Economics of Public Policy: A Practical Approach to Project and Policy Evaluation*, Cheltenham, Northampton, MA: Edward Elgar, pp. 49–55, 98–112, 259–84.

Klein, M.W. (2002) *Mathematical Methods for Economics* (2nd edn), Boston, MA: Addison Wesley, pp. 363–73, 389–91.

Koester, U. (2005) *Grundzüge der landwirtschaftlichen Marktlehre* (3rd edn), Munich: Vahlen, pp. 266–88 (WiSo-Kurzlehrbücher: Reihe Volkswirtschaft).

Mas-Colell, A., Whinston, M.D. and Green, J.A. (1995) *Microeconomic Theory*, New York, Oxford: Oxford University Press, pp. 328–34.

Nicholson, W. (2005) *Microeconomic Theory: Basic Principles and Extensions* (9th edn), Mason, OH: Thomson, pp. 317–30.

Pindyck, R.S. and Rubinfeld, D.L. (2005) *Microeconomics* (6th edn), Upper Saddle River, NJ: Pearson Prentice Hall, pp. 128–31, 276–81, 299–310.

Varian, H.R. (2003) *Intermediate Microeconomics: A Modern Approach* (6th edn), New York: W.W. Norton, pp. 249–54, 258–63, 306–9.

3 Price policy instruments

Objective

In Chapter 3 we further differentiate the analysis of price policies. We explain how different price policy instruments can be integrated into the market model and what implications such instruments have for the formulated political objectives.

Theory

In the analysis thus far, for situations where a country deviates from free trade and sets the domestic price independently from the world market, we have differentiated between the world market price and a domestic price. However, government intervention can be more complex, resulting in a separate supply price and demand price for the same good. An example of such a price policy in an import situation is shown in Figure 3.1. In this case the supply price p^s is set significantly higher than the world market price (e.g. to establish a protectionist price policy for

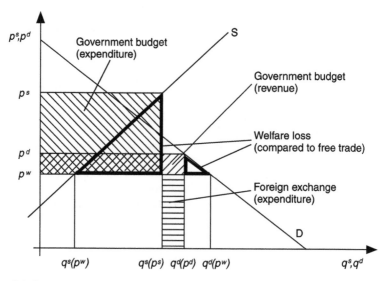

Figure 3.1 Consequences of a differentiated supply price and demand price policy.

producers) while the demand price p^d is also above the world market price, but lower than the supply price. Consequently, a demand price higher than the world market price implies a tax on consumers.

The consequences of such a price policy can be shown by redefining the relevant political objectives as functions of supply price, demand price and world market price. Producer revenue will be:

$$R(p^s) = q^s(p^s) \cdot p^s. \tag{3.1}$$

For consumer expenditure we get:

$$E(p^d) = q^d(p^d) \cdot p^d. \tag{3.2}$$

We define a foreign exchange function as follows:

$$FE(p^s, p^d, p^w) = \left(q^s(p^s) - q^d(p^d) \right) p^w; \tag{3.3}$$

similarly, we define a government budget function:

$$B(p^s, p^d, p^w) = q^d(p^d)\left(p^d - p^w \right) - q^s(p^s)\left(p^s - p^w \right). \tag{3.4}$$

Accordingly, welfare functions and their components explained in Chapter 2 need to be redefined. It follows:

$$TB(p^d) = \int_0^{q^d(p^d)} \tilde{p}^d(v)\, dv \tag{3.5}$$

$$C(p^s) = \int_0^{q^s(p^s)} \tilde{p}^s(v)\, dv \tag{3.6}$$

$$CS(p^d) = \int_0^{q^d(p^d)} \tilde{p}^d(v)\, dv - q^d(p^d)\, p^d \tag{3.7}$$

$$PS(p^s) = q^s(p^s)\, p^s - \int_0^{q^s(p^s)} \tilde{p}^s(v)\, dv \tag{3.8}$$

and

$$W(p^s, p^d, p^w) = \int_0^{q^d(p^d)} \tilde{p}^d(v)\, dv - \int_0^{q^s(p^s)} \tilde{p}^s(v)\, dv$$
$$+ \left(q^s(p^s) - q^d(p^d) \right) p^w. \tag{3.9}$$

The consequences of such a price policy for some political objectives are depicted in Figure 3.1. Government budget is the difference between the two corresponding rectangles (budget revenue and budget expenditure) following the two components $q^d(p^d)(p^d - p^w)$ and $q^s(p^s)(p^s - p^w)$ defined in equation (3.4). The welfare loss compared to free trade is shown by the bold-framed areas, which indicate the deadweight losses due to consumption distortion and production inefficiency. Finally, foreign exchange expenditure is indicated by the hatched area.

Let us now look at the question of how a government implements such a price policy. It will rarely happen in a market economy that a government intervenes directly in the economic activities of production, consumption and trade to set target prices. It is more likely that a government will intervene through subsidisation or taxation of economic activities to reach certain target prices on the domestic market. Taxation of imports and subsidisation of exports, for example, will lead to a domestic price above the world market price, while subsidisation of imports and taxation of exports achieve the opposite effect. From a domestic price obtained through taxation and subsidisation of trade, the supply price can deviate through taxation or subsidisation of producers. Accordingly, the same principle applies for a deviation of the demand price from the domestic price.

If we consider a percentage subsidy or tax based on the value of economic activities, it follows:

$$p = (1 + r)\, p^w \tag{3.10}$$

with r – protection rate

$$p^s = (1 + s)\, p \tag{3.11}$$

with s – producer subsidy rate

$$p^d = (1 - v)\, p \tag{3.12}$$

with v – consumer subsidy rate.

For simplification we assume r, s, v are 'positive': r indicates how many percentage points the domestic price is higher than the world market price (or lower than the world market price if r is negative); s and v denote the percentage by which the supply price or the demand price deviate from the domestic price benefiting producers and consumers, respectively.

If we include (3.10) in (3.11) and (3.12), respectively, it follows:

$$p^s = (1 + s)\,(1 + r)\, p^w \tag{3.13}$$

and

$$p^d = (1 - v)\,(1 + r)\, p^w. \tag{3.14}$$

In the same way we could adjust the functions defined in (3.1) to (3.9), for example, the welfare function $W(s, v, r, p^w)$, and examine the implications of different subsidy rates and tax rates for relevant policy objectives.

Exercise 3

Consider again the supply function

$$q^s(p^s) = a + b\,p^s$$

with $\quad a = -30, \quad b = 6$

and the demand function

$$q^d(p^d) = c + d\,p^d$$

with $\quad c = 120, \quad d = -4.$

Extend the market model from Exercise 2 by differentiating between a supply price and a demand price. Then, solve the following problems:

(a) A country sets the supply price and demand price independently from the world market price; the world market price is $p^w = 10$. Calculate foreign exchange, government budget and welfare for $p^s = 14$ and $p^d = 12$ and for $p^s = 20$ and $p^d = 8$. Explain the results in comparison to free trade.

(b) At what level do the supply price and demand price need to be set to maximise welfare in a closed and open economy?

(c) The government subsidises both supply and demand by 20 per cent. Compare foreign exchange, government budget and welfare for $r = 0$, 20 per cent and −20 per cent.

(d) Assume free trade. Show graphically and discuss the welfare function under a gradual increase of both producer subsidy rate and consumer subsidy rate to 50 per cent.

(e) Again, assume free trade. Show graphically that welfare losses occurring under a gradual increase in the protection rate to 50 per cent are the sum of the welfare losses of a corresponding producer subsidisation and consumer taxation. Does the result differ for $p^w = 12$?

Solution

Step 3.1   We extend the linear market model with only one domestic price from Exercise 2 by entering the value 14 for the supply price p^s in cell A4 and changing the previous domestic price in cell B4 to the demand price $p^d = 12$.

Step 3.2   Check and correct the functional relationships with the differentiated prices. The demand function, total benefit function, welfare function, foreign exchange function, producer surplus function and consumer surplus function are already correct and do not need to be changed. However, you need to adjust the formulas for supply, cost and revenue, i.e. in each case substitute B4 with A4. For government budget, following equation (3.4), enter the Excel formula = F4*(B4 – C4) – E4*(A4 – C4). Check your market model by using the 'Formula auditing' which you will find under 'Tools'. You can remove all traces by using 'Remove all arrows'. For the free trade situation $p^s = p^d = 10$ the model must produce the results given in Exercise 2.

Step 3.3 In order to examine the variables mentioned in Exercise 3a, we only need to enter the relevant price framework in A4 and B4 (cf. Figures 3.2 and 3.3). In Figure 3.2 a protectionist price policy for producers and minor taxation of consumers is shown. On the other hand, Figure 3.3 describes a substantial protectionist price policy for producers and consumers, following examples of a planned economy for agriculture. The latter policy leads to a comparatively low welfare level and large budget expenditure.

Step 3.4 Establish the solutions for Exercise 3b for the same market model by using the Solver (compare with Step 2.5). In this case, free trade with $p^s = p^d = 10$ leads to a maximisation of welfare, while in a closed economy, welfare is maximised at the autarky price level $p^s = p^d = 15$.

Step 3.5 To solve Exercise 3c proceed as follows. Enter the protection and subsidy rates r, s and v in the cells A15, B15 and C15, i.e. the values 0, 0.2 and 0.2, respectively. Next, define the supply price and the demand price as endogenous variables as outlined in (3.13) and (3.14), so that you finally get the formula = (1 + B15)*(1 + A15)*C4 in cell A4 and the formula = (1 – C15)*(1 + A15)*C4 in cell B4. This automatically

	A	B	C	D	E	F	G	H	I
1		Linear Market Model							
2									
3	p^s	p^d	p^w		Supply	Demand		Cost	Total benefit
4	14	12	10		54	72		513	1512
5									
6		Parameter:							
7		a	b	c	d				
8		-30	6	120	-4				

	J	K	L	M	N	O	P
1							
2							
3	Welfare	Revenue	Expenditure	Foreign exchange	Government budget	Producer surplus	Consumer surplus
4	819	756	864	-180	-72	243	648

Figure 3.2 Linear market model at a supply price of 14 and a demand price of 12 (exercise3.xls).

	A	B	C	D	E	F	G	H	I
1		**Linear Market Model**							
2									
3	p^s	p^d	p^w		Supply	Demand		Cost	Total benefit
4	20	8	10		90	88		1125	1672
5									
6		Parameter:							
7		a	b	c	d				
8		-30	6	120	-4				

	J	K	L	M	N	O	P
1							
2							
3	Welfare	Revenue	Expenditure	Foreign exchange	Government budget	Producer surplus	Consumer surplus
4	567	1800	704	20	-1076	675	968

Figure 3.3 Linear market model at a supply price of 20 and a demand price of 8.

adjusts all functions and takes into account the more differentiated price framework. For example, welfare is now defined as a function of the (exogenous) variables r, s, v, p^w (in addition to the parameters a, b, c, d). By clicking on the welfare cell in J4 and then several times on 'Trace precedents' under 'Formula auditing' you can easily trace and display this relationship.

In order to obtain the values for foreign exchange, government budget and welfare for $r = 20$ per cent and -20 per cent, you only need to change the value in cell A15 to 0.2 and -0.2, respectively. The values for these policy objectives are summarised in Figure 3.4. Hence, this

A4		f_x =(1+B15)*(1+A15)*C4								
	A	B	C	D	E	F	G	H	I	J
1		**Linear Market Model**								
2										
3	p^s	p^d	p^w		Supply	Demand		Cost	Total benefit	Welfare
4	12	8	10		42	88		357	1672	855
5										
6		Parameter:								
7		a	b	c	d					
8		-30	6	120	-4					
9										
10										
11										
12										
13		Protection rate / Subsidy rate					r	Foreign exchange	Government budget	Welfare
14		r	s	v			0	-460	-260	855
15	0	0.2	0.2				0.2	-252	-280.8	816.6
16							-0.2	-668	-328.8	848.6

Figure 3.4 Linear market model with protection rate, producer subsidy rate and consumer subsidy rate (exercise3c.xls).

exercise shows the consequences of a protectionist price policy for producers and consumers, where a country differentiates the supply price and demand price from a domestic price, as given by a certain trade policy (e.g. free trade with $r = 0$).

Step 3.6   Exercise 3d aims to examine the impact of a simultaneous increase in the producer subsidy rate and consumer subsidy rate on welfare at a protection rate of 0. To do this, enter the value 0 in cells A15 and B15 and define the value for v as being equal to the value for s, i.e. enter the formula = B15 in cell C15. We can now develop a data series for welfare at different (subsidy) rates in the range G14:H24 by following the same approach as described under Steps 1.4 and 2.6 (choose 'Data table', click on the field 'Columns input cell' and then on B15). Again, you can depict the functions by using the 'Chart wizard'.

The result is displayed in Figure 3.5. Figure 3.5 clearly shows that, in

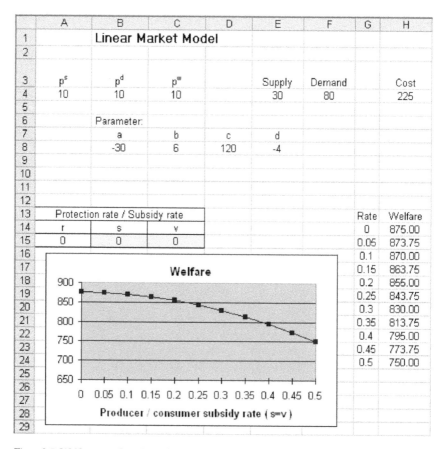

Figure 3.5 Welfare as a function of producer subsidy rate and consumer subsidy rate ($s = v$) (exercise3d.xls).

comparison with free trade, increasing protection for producers and consumers will lead to growing welfare losses.

Step 3.7 We use our model now to solve Exercise 3e. Enter the value 0 (free trade) in the cells A15, B15 and C15. Since we already have the series 0, 0.05 to 0.5 for the rates in G14 to G24 and the link to the welfare function with the formula = J4 in H14, we can, once we have selected the range G14:H24, create a data series for welfare under different protection rates in the cells H14:H24. To do this, choose again 'Data, table' and 'Columns input cell' and, in this case, click on cell A15. Now select the range H14:H24, choose 'Copy', click on cell I14 and choose 'Paste special . . .' with the option 'Values'.

Let us now alter the value for s. Select again the range G14:H24 and follow the same approach as before using 'Data, table' and subsequent steps. We will now paste the new welfare values into the range J14:J24. Since we examine consumer taxation in the third example, we need to adjust the rate series by changing the value in G15 from 0.05 to −0.05, selecting G14:G15 and then moving the thin black '+' cursor in the lower right-hand corner of the two cells towards G24 (until the value −0.5 is reached). For these values of v we again generate the welfare values, as described above, and copy the values in the range K14:K24 using 'Paste special . . .' (cf. Figure 3.6).

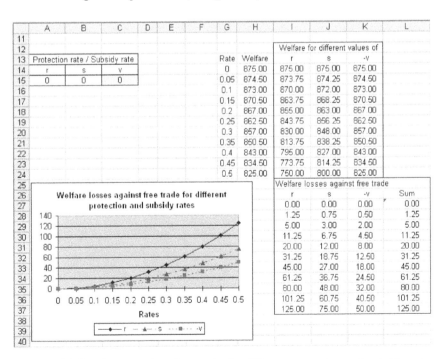

Figure 3.6 Welfare losses against free trade for different protection and subsidy rates (exercise3e.xls).

Since our main interest is to compare the welfare losses of the different price policies against free trade, we enter these welfare losses a little further down on the sheet in the range I27:K37. Enter 0 in the cells I27, J27 and K27, then fill the formula = I$14–I15 in cell I28 and copy the formula into I28:K37. In order to prove our thesis, enter the sum of the cells in the J and K columns in L27:L37 and compare these sums with the welfare losses relating to the protection rate in the I column. With the 'Chart wizard' you can now easily create a diagram that compares graphically the welfare losses from the different policy scenarios. For a different world market price (e.g. $p^w = 12$), the relations regarding the welfare losses remain, although with different numbers. Calculate the relevant numbers. In this way Exercise 3e shows that a protectionist price policy does indeed correspond with an equivalent producer subsidisation and consumer taxation policy.

References

Just, R.E., Hueth, D.L. and Schmitz, A. (2004) *The Welfare Economics of Public Policy: A Practical Approach to Project and Policy Evaluation*, Cheltenham, Northampton, MA: Edward Elgar, pp. 269–84.

Koester, U. (2005) *Grundzüge der landwirtschaftlichen Marktlehre* (3rd edn), Munich: Vahlen, pp. 291–329, 347–50 (WiSo-Kurzlehrbücher: Reihe Volkswirtschaft).

Nicholson, W. (2005) *Microeconomic Theory: Basic Principles and Extensions* (9th edn), Mason, OH: Thomson, pp. 322–30.

Pindyck, R.S. and Rubinfeld, D.L. (2005) *Microeconomics* (6th edn), Upper Saddle River, NJ: Pearson Prentice Hall, pp. 310–33.

Varian, H.R. (2003) *Intermediate Microeconomics: A Modern Approach* (6th edn), New York: W.W. Norton, pp. 294–305.

4 Iso-elastic supply and demand functions

Objective

In Chapter 4 the analysis of price policies will be based on iso-elastic supply and demand functions. We will show how a corresponding market model can be developed and applied for the impact analysis of different policy scenarios.

Theory

It is common in economics to talk about elasticities when we look at inter-dependencies between two variables. An elasticity indicates by how many percentage points an endogenous variable changes if an exogenous variable changes by 1 per cent, whereby, to be exact, an infinitesimally small change is considered. The advantage of elasticities is that they are non-dimensional which allows a relatively straightforward discussion of the relationship between variables. Hence, it follows for any function $y = f(x)$:

$$\varepsilon_{y,x} = \frac{\frac{dy}{y}}{\frac{dx}{x}} = \frac{\frac{dy}{dx}}{\frac{y}{x}} = \frac{dy}{dx}\frac{x}{y} \tag{4.1}$$

with ε – elasticity.

Correspondingly, we can define the own-price elasticity of supply, i.e. supply elasticity ε^s, for a supply function $q^s = q^s(p^s)$. The supply elasticity ε^s indicates by how many percentage points the quantity supplied changes if the supply price increases by 1 per cent. Similarly, the own-price elasticity of demand, i.e. demand elasticity ε^d, for a demand function $q^d = q^d(p^d)$ indicates by how many percentage points the quantity demanded changes if the demand price increases by 1 per cent.

In order to simplify the analysis of markets, it is often assumed that supply and demand functions have constant elasticities and are iso-elastic functions. Power functions with the corresponding elasticities as exponents fulfil this postulate; in economics, according to its developers, such functions are called Cobb–Douglas functions. Let us first consider the following iso-elastic supply function:

$$q^s(p^s) = c(p^s)^{\varepsilon^s}; \quad \varepsilon^s > 0 \tag{4.2}$$

with c – supply constant
         ε^s – supply elasticity.

Apparently, it follows:

$$\frac{dq^s}{dp^s}\frac{p^s}{q^s} = \frac{\varepsilon^s c(p^s)^{\varepsilon^s-1} p^s}{c(p^s)^{\varepsilon^s}} = \varepsilon^s.$$

The function goes through the origin and the supply constant c influences the slope of the function.

Similarly, we can define the following iso-elastic demand curve:

$$q^d(p^d) = d(p^d)^{\varepsilon^d}; \quad \varepsilon^d < 0 \tag{4.3}$$

with d – demand constant
         ε^d – demand elasticity.

Due to the negative demand elasticity this function is a hyperbolic curve, which approaches the axes at infinity; the demand constant d influences the slope of the function.

Because iso-elastic supply and demand functions can be easily interpreted, these functions are widely used in market models. However, the functions considered in the analysis of price policies have to be defined accordingly and some particularities need to be taken into account. In this context, the graphical representation of the iso-elastic supply and demand functions in Figure 4.1 clearly reveals that, besides the desired characteristics discussed above, other characteristics of these functions are not exactly economically sound and require some abstraction. For example, total benefit, defined as the integral below the demand curve, would be infinite and hence not suitable as an indicator for the satisfaction from consuming goods. Similarly, with respect to the supply function we need to prescind from fixed cost.

One approach to dealing with these problems could be to suitably shift the functions and to define an upper price limit for demand and a minimum price for supply, respectively. That, however, would eliminate the main advantage of such functions removing the constant elasticities. Consequently, we proceed as follows. For the definition of total benefit we set an arbitrary upper limit for the demand price p^{d_+} as a quasi-intersection of the demand curve and the price axis. On the supply side, we prescind from fixed cost when we define cost. However, this procedure has to be considered when we interpret the model results. As a

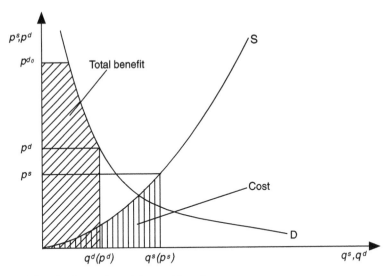

Figure 4.1 Iso-elastic supply and demand functions.

consequence, one should focus on changes in welfare indicators rather than levels.

It is important to note that any definition of supply and demand functions should satisfy two conditions. It should reflect the concrete decision-making of producers and consumers, and it should be founded empirically. The first condition refers to the microeconomic foundation of supply and demand functions and this condition is particularly important in deriving welfare conclusions of policy changes. Since information regarding the real decision-making behaviour of producers and consumers is limited, microeconomic theory provides relevant postulates for assumed behaviour and frameworks on markets (e.g. the marginal cost pricing principle in relation to the supply function of producers, assuming profit maximisation and perfect competition). The microeconomic considerations allow for an assessment of the chosen functional forms and of their limitations for policy evaluation.

While an alternative approach, namely to derive supply and demand functions from a concrete microeconomic optimisation exercise, is possible, it would require adequate knowledge about the decision-making behaviour and may lead to less assessable and comprehensive model specifications compared to the iso-elastic supply and demand functions chosen here. Basically, the model specification chosen is always the result of a consideration between an explicit microeconomic foundation and a (more) pragmatic simplification and abstraction; we will return to this issue again in the discussion of multi-market models.

In any case, every model specification and development should be as empirically based as possible. Using iso-elastic supply and demand functions, the ideal case would be if, for all parameters and elasticities, precise econometric estimations were available. At least, elasticities used in a model should be empirically plausible.

If such plausible data for supply and demand elasticities are available, realistic policy simulations on the basis of iso-elastic supply and demand functions, as shown in (4.2) and (4.3), are relatively straightforward and require only limited additional data on quantities and prices on the relevant markets. To do this, supply and demand functions have to be calibrated to define the respective constants. Following (4.2) we define the supply constant as:

$$c = \frac{q^s}{(p^s)^{\varepsilon^s}}. \tag{4.4}$$

Similarly, we can define the demand constant. It is important to note that a certain elasticity value has to be assumed for the calibration. If one is interested in evaluating the consequences of a certain price policy for different elasticities, the supply and demand functions need to be calibrated for each of these different elasticities.

Generally, the analysis of price policies with the market model based on iso-elastic functions follows the procedure outlined in Chapter 3. The relevant political objectives will be defined as functions of supply price, demand price and world market price or as functions of protection rate, producer subsidy rate and consumer subsidy rate (cf. (3.1) to (3.9)). For the supply function we get in this case:

$$q^s\,(s,\,r,\,p^w) = c\,((1+s)\,(1+r)\,p^w)^{\varepsilon^s}. \tag{4.5}$$

and for the demand function:

$$q^d\,(v,\,r,\,p^w) = d\,((1-v)\,(1+r)\,p^w)^{\varepsilon^d}. \tag{4.6}$$

Exercise 4

Consider the supply function

$$q^s\,(p^s) = c\,(p^s)^{\varepsilon^s}$$

with $\varepsilon^s = 0.3$

and the demand function

$$q^d\,(p^d) = d\,(p^d)^{\varepsilon^d}$$

with $\varepsilon^d = -0.4.$

As in Chapter 3, develop a market model in Excel and solve the following problems:

(a) A country sets supply price and demand price independently from the world market price with $p^s = 15$ and $p^d = 12$; the world market price is $p^w = 10$. At this price setting the country is an importer; the quantity supplied is $q^s = 80$, and the quantity demanded is $q^d = 100$. Calibrate the supply and demand functions.

(b) At what level do supply price and demand price need to be set to maximise welfare in a closed and open economy?

(c) Assume free trade. Show graphically and discuss the impacts on self-sufficiency of a gradual increase of the protection rate, the producer subsidy rate and the consumer subsidy rate to 50 per cent.

(d) Assume again free trade. Show graphically the welfare losses occurring under a gradual increase of the protection rate to 50 per cent.

(e) Change the elasticities to $\varepsilon^s = 0.5$ and $\varepsilon^d = -0.7$ and compare the curve progression with (d).

Solution

Step 4.1 Similar to the linear market model developed in Chapter 3, we now develop a non-linear market model of the Cobb–Douglas type. In order to facilitate our work we take the linear Excel model from Chapter 3 and change, where required, functions and parameters. First, we change the parameters. In cell B8 we enter for the supply constant c the value 1 and assume the same value for the demand constant d in cell C8. We then enter a supply elasticity of 0.3 in cell D8 and a demand elasticity of -0.4 in cell E8 (cf. Figure 4.2).

	A	B	C	D	E	F	G	H
1		Cobb-Douglas Market Model						
2								
3	p^s	p^d	p^w		Supply	Demand		Cost
4	15.00	12.00	10.00		2.25	0.37		7.80
5								
6		Constants			Elasticities			
7		c	d	of supply	of demand			
8		1	1	0.3	-0.4			

	I	J	K	L	M	N	O	P
1								
2					Foreign	Government	Producer	Consumer
3	Total benefit	Welfare	Revenue	Expenditure	exchange	budget	surplus	surplus
4	14.47	25.50	33.80	4.44	18.83	-10.53	26.00	10.03

Figure 4.2 Cobb–Douglas market model without calibration (exercise4.xls).

Step 4.2   Change the supply function in cell E4 to = B8*A4^D8. Through simply copying E4 we can obtain the demand function in cell F4.

Step 4.3   Now we only need to change the cost function in cell H4 and the total benefit function in cell I4. By using integral calculus we can describe the relevant marked areas in Figure 4.1 and, with the supply function (4.2), we get for the cost (cf. Step 2.2):

$$C = p^s \, q^s \, (p^s) - \int_0^{p^s} q^s \, (v) \, dv$$

$$= p^s \, q^s \, (p^s) - \frac{1}{\varepsilon^s + 1} \, c \, (p^s)^{\varepsilon^s + 1}. \tag{4.7}$$

According to (4.7) enter the Excel formula = A4*E4 − B8*A4^(D8+1)/(D8+1) in H4.

With the total benefit function, however, we have the problem that the respective area below the (inverse) Cobb–Douglas demand function would be infinite, as the integral value is ∞. A way out of this dilemma is to define a quasi-intersection of the demand curve with the price axis and to cut off the integral at a sufficiently high price; in this example at $p^{d_0} = 50$. This approach is acceptable, as many questions to be answered with market models focus on the changes in functional values (in this example total benefit), for which the choice of the upper price limit does not cause any problems. But, of course, we have to be careful when we assess the level of total benefit and other functions which are based on total benefit (e.g. consumer surplus and welfare).

Thus we define total benefit in our model as:

$$TB = p^d \cdot q^d \, (p^d) + \int_{p^d}^{50} q^d \, (v) \, dv$$

$$= p^d \cdot q^d \, (p^d) + \frac{d}{\varepsilon^d + 1} \, (50^{\varepsilon^d + 1} - (p^d)^{\varepsilon^d + 1}). \tag{4.8}$$

Following (4.8) you enter the Excel formula = B4*F4+C8/(E8+1)*(50^(E8+1) − B4^(E8+1)) in cell I4. The other functions do not require any changes (cf. Figure 4.2).

Let us look at the outcome of the model at a domestic price of 1. Since we get for $p^s = p^d = 1$ the equilibrium quantity $q = 1$, the role of the constants c and d as shift parameters becomes clear. In this context, try, for example, to get a certain amount of quantity supplied at a given price (e.g. 15) by choosing an adequate value for the parameter c.

Step 4.4   For the calibration, following Exercise 4a, enter the prices $p^s = 15$, $p^d = 12$ and $p^w = 10$. Then enter the values 15, 12, 80 and 100 in the cells A5, B5, E5 and F5, respectively, as our 'parameters of calibration'. Following (4.4), you now enter for the constant c the Excel

	B8	▼		*fx* =E5/A5^D8				
	A	B	C	D	E	F	G	H
1			Cobb-Douglas Market Model with Calibration					
2								
3	p^s	p^d	p^w		Supply	Demand		Cost
4	15.00	12.00	10.00		80.00	100.00		276.92
5	15.00	12.00	Parameters of calibration		80.00	100.00		
6		Constants			Elasticities			
7		c	d	of supply	of demand			
8		35.5028003	270.192008	0.3	-0.4			

	I	J	K	L	M	N	O	P
1								
2								
3	Total benefit	Welfare	Revenue	Expenditure	Foreign exchange	Government budget	Producer surplus	Consumer surplus
4	3908.72	3431.80	1200.00	1200.00	-200.00	-200.00	923.08	2708.72

Figure 4.3 Cobb–Douglas market model with calibration (exercise4a.xls).

formula = E5/A5^D8 in cell B8 and for constant d the formula = F5/B5^E8 in cell C8. Your market model is now calibrated (see Figure 4.3).

Step 4.5 The optimal prices for welfare maximisation can again be computed by the Solver (cf. Step 2.5 or 3.4). In the case of a closed economy you have to take account of the equilibrium constraint E4 = F4 and you get the value $p^s = p^d \approx 18.16$.

Step 4.6 In order to prepare the model for Exercise 4c, we extend our calibrated Cobb–Douglas model by incorporating protection and subsidy rates (as in Exercise 3c). To do this we can either proceed as explained under Step 3.5 or copy the range A13:C15 and the cells A4 and B4 from the corresponding Excel sheet to the actual sheet using 'Copy' and 'Paste'. We set all rates r, s, v equal to zero, which means we simulate free trade. In cell H14 we calculate the self-sufficiency ratio (SSR) using the formula = E4/F4. In G14:G24 we again enter the series (0, 0.05, . . ., 0.5) for different rates. We can now generate a data series for self-sufficiency at different rates for r, s and v, respectively, by choosing 'Data table' and following the procedure as explained earlier. We can then, through clicking on 'Copy', 'Paste special . . .' and 'Values', summarise the values in the range I14:K24 (see Figure 4.4). Again, you can depict the functions by using the 'Chart wizard'.

Figure 4.4 shows that a rise in border protection leads to a significantly larger increase in self-sufficiency than an equivalent percentage increase in the producer subsidy rate. On the other hand, a consumer subsidy decreases self-sufficiency.

Step 4.7 To solve Exercise 4d proceed in the same way as in Exercise 3e or Step 3.7 to get the results shown in Figure 4.5, which show the growing

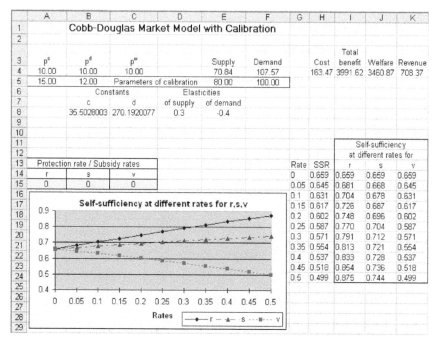

Figure 4.4 Self-sufficiency as a function of protection rate, producer subsidy rate and consumer subsidy rate (exercise4c.xls).

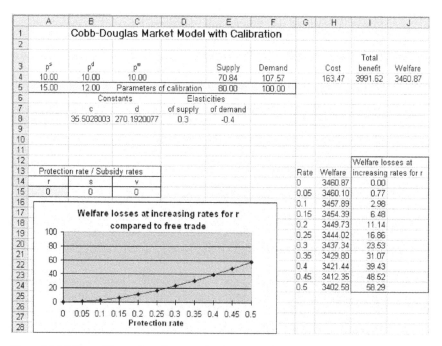

Figure 4.5 Welfare effects of an increase in the protection rate compared to free trade (exercise4d.xls).

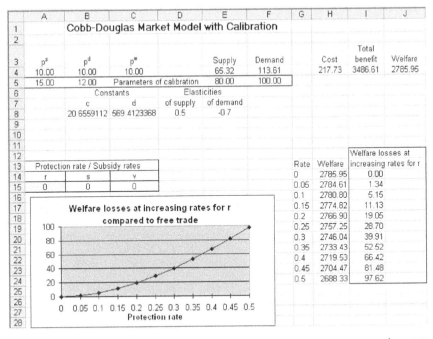

	A	B	C	D	E	F	G	H	I	J
1		Cobb-Douglas Market Model with Calibration								
2										
3	p^s	p^d	p^w		Supply	Demand		Cost	Total benefit	Welfare
4	10.00	10.00	10.00		65.32	113.61		217.73	3486.61	2785.95
5	15.00	12.00	Parameters of calibration		80.00	100.00				
6		Constants		Elasticities						
7		c	d	of supply	of demand					
8		20.6559112	569.4123368	0.5	-0.7					
9										
10										
11										
12										Welfare losses at
13	Protection rate / Subsidy rates						Rate	Welfare	increasing rates for r	
14	r	s	v				0	2785.95	0.00	
15	0	0	0				0.05	2784.61	1.34	
16							0.1	2780.80	5.15	
17		Welfare losses at increasing rates for r					0.15	2774.82	11.13	
18		compared to free trade					0.2	2766.90	19.05	
19	100						0.25	2757.25	28.70	
20	80						0.3	2746.04	39.91	
21	60						0.35	2733.43	52.52	
22	40						0.4	2719.53	66.42	
23	20						0.45	2704.47	81.48	
24	0						0.5	2688.33	97.62	
25										
26	0 0.05 0.1 0.15 0.2 0.25 0.3 0.35 0.4 0.45 0.5									
27	Protection rate									
28										

Figure 4.6 Welfare effects of an increase in the protection rate for $\varepsilon^s = 0.5$ and $\varepsilon^d = -0.7$, compared to free trade (exercise4e.xls).

welfare losses of an increasing protectionist price policy compared to free trade.

Step 4.8   To solve Exercise 4e you must keep in mind that the model again has to be calibrated for $p^s = 15$, $p^d = 12$, $q^s = 80$, $q^d = 100$, $\varepsilon^s = 0.5$ and $\varepsilon^d = -0.7$ by changing only the values at D8 and E8. The results show that higher elasticities increase the welfare losses of a protectionist price policy compared to free trade (compare your results with Figure 4.6).

References

Chiang, A.C. and Wainwright, K. (2005) *Fundamental Methods of Mathematical Economics* (4th edn), Boston, MA: McGraw-Hill, pp. 178–87, 205–10.

Kirschke, D. and Jechlitschka, K. (2003) 'Analyse von Preispolitiken mit Excel', *WiSt-Wirtschaftswissenschaftliches Studium, Zeitschrift für Ausbildung und Hochschulkontakt*, 32 (10), pp. 582–9. Available online at <http://edoc.hu-berlin.de/oa/articles/re3C1xH26k Qwk/PDF/29uPNywMfGpUI.pdf> (accessed 20 July 2006).

Klein, M.W. (2002) *Mathematical Methods for Economics* (2nd edn), Boston, MA: Addison Wesley, pp. 189–95.

Koester, U. (2005) *Grundzüge der landwirtschaftlichen Marktlehre* (3rd edn), Munich: Vahlen, pp. 37–52, 107–16 (WiSo-Kurzlehrbücher: Reihe Volkswirtschaft).

46 *Analysis of price policies*

Nicholson, W. (2005) *Microeconomic Theory: Basic Principles and Extensions* (9th edn), Mason, OH: Thomson, pp. 27–8, 139–41.

Pindyck, R.S. and Rubinfeld, D.L. (2005) *Microeconomics* (6th edn), Upper Saddle River, NJ: Pearson Prentice Hall, pp. 32–46, 122–7.

Varian, H.R. (2003) *Intermediate Microeconomics: A Modern Approach* (6th edn), New York: W.W. Norton, pp. 270–81.

5 Policy formulation and trade-offs

Objective

In this chapter the formulation of price policies will be looked at in more detail. We will show how the developed market model may be used for different questions of policy formulation and how trade-offs between objectives and with respect to the implementation of different instruments can be identified.

Theory

The question of why governments intervene in markets and pursue price policies and, in fact, whether they should do so at all, remains a controversial issue. Here, we assume that governments behave rationally and introduce price policy instruments to achieve certain objectives. Then, the problem of policy formulation may be considered as an optimisation problem. Employing a simplified approach in this manner does not deny the complex reality of policy formulation; it is simply a useful tool that allows us to assess government intervention in a transparent way.

In previous chapters we have looked at some problems of policy formulation. We have seen, for example, that a policy with a domestic price equal to the world market price leads to a maximisation of welfare. From an economic point of view such a policy seems to be adequate; however, at this point we do not want to discuss such assessments. In fact, policy formulation applied by governments is much more multifaceted and complex.

The focus on single components of the welfare function at the expense of others is common practice. For example, in comparison to a free trade situation, a protectionist price policy leads to budget revenue in an import case. Figure 1.3 shows that an optimal (i.e. in this case a budget maximising) domestic price should be between the world market price and the autarky price. In addition, a rise in the domestic price to increase foreign exchange has often been discussed, both as import substitution policy in the import case or as export promotion policy in the export case. Figure 1.3 points out that in this case there is no optimal (here: foreign exchange maximising) price, since every rise in the domestic price leads to a further increase in foreign exchange. Hence, a real optimisation problem only exists if certain constraints are considered (e.g. budget expenditure or welfare losses).

Many government interventions on markets are driven by distributional objectives. If the supply price is to be increased in order to protect producers from competition from abroad, such a policy will usually lead to a burden on government budget and welfare losses to both consumers and society. The specific result of a protectionist policy depends on the instrument applied and the constraints to be considered. Figure 5.1 shows the consequences of a producer subsidy and an export subsidy. For example, for a subsidisation of producers we get a maximum supply price p'', if the resultant budget expenditure may not exceed the hatched area. A relaxation of the budget constraint would of course widen the scope for a supply price increase, for example, to p''', while an additional consideration of a maximum welfare loss would be a binding or non-binding constraint for the optimisation problem depending on the limit chosen. On the other hand, a protectionist price policy, which leads to an increase in the price for producers and consumers, would, under the same budget constraint, result in greater scope for producer protection. Following Figure 5.1 the maximum domestic price would now be p'. Note that for simplification, in Figure 5.1 and in the following diagrams we continue to assume linear supply and demand curves.

For any chosen policy described by instruments implemented and constraints, we can define a trade-off curve between different objectives. Such a trade-off curve, for example, between producer surplus and government budget, depicts the maximum value for producer surplus that may be realised at a certain government budget value or vice versa. Figure 5.2 shows such a trade-off curve for the discussed example of a producer subsidisation. At a maximum level of the budget constraint (i.e. at budget expenditure B'), producer surplus would be PS'.

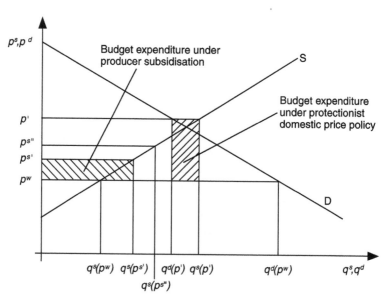

Figure 5.1 Protectionist policy for producers under budget expenditure constraints.

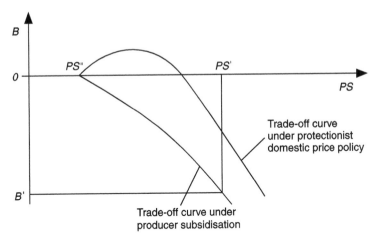

Figure 5.2 Trade-off curve between producer surplus and government budget.

A gradual decrease of the maximum possible budget expenditure would lead to the outlined curve, which at free trade would have the values PS'' and $B = 0$.

As we can see in Figure 5.2, increasing the domestic price would lead to a different trade-off curve. In an import case such a price increase would first result in both a higher producer surplus and government budget, but later lead to a conflict between these two political objectives, although at a higher level. Hence, using trade-off curves allows us to examine the scope for and choice of different policy instruments and constraints. It is, however, important to note that in this example changes in consumer surplus have not been considered.

In order to take into account distributional aspects in policy formulation, the use of distributional weights for different groups in welfare functions has been discussed. Such an approach is theoretically sound, since we surely cannot assume that income distribution in a society is optimal in a way that every euro spent and earned can be weighted equally between individuals. But that is exactly what is assumed in 'classical' welfare economics. In fact, in a society, the marginal utility of income, in other words the additional utility of the last euro, will be higher for poorer groups than for richer groups, providing the basis for different distributional weights. Consequently, by extending (3.9) a welfare function adjusted for distribution may be written as follows:

$$W^a \, (p^s, p^d, p^w; g^c, g^p, g^g) = g^c \, CS(p^d) + g^p \, PS(p^s)$$
$$+ \, g^g \, B \, (p^s, p^d, p^w) \tag{5.1}$$

with W^a – adjusted welfare (integrating distributional weights)
          g^c – distributional weight for consumers
          g^p – distributional weight for producers
          g^g – distributional weight for the government

or

$$W^a\left(p^s, p^d, p^w; g^c, g^p, g^g\right) = g^c \left(\int_0^{q^d(p^d)} \tilde{p}^d(v)\, dv - q^d(p^d)\, p^d\right)$$

$$+ g^p \left(q^s(p^s)\, p^s - \int_0^{q^s(p^s)} \tilde{p}^s(v)\, dv\right)$$

$$+ g^g \left(q^d(p^d)(p^d - p^w) - q^s(p^s)(p^s - p^w)\right). \qquad (5.1)'$$

Now, the objective of government policy formulation could be to maximise the adjusted welfare function. If we imply a bigger distributional weight for producers and set the distributional weight for consumers and the government to 1, we get the following condition for the optimal supply price:

$$p^s\left(1 - \frac{g^p - 1}{\varepsilon^s}\right) = p^w, \qquad (5.2)$$

and for the optimal demand price:

$$p^d = p^w. \qquad (5.3)$$

Thus, in this case, the greater the distributional weight for producers and the more inelastic the supply, the higher the supply price should be set above the world market price. The instrument for such a first-best distribution-oriented policy would be a corresponding producer subsidisation. At an optimal uniform domestic price, on the other hand, welfare losses on the demand side need to be considered. Such a second-best solution for policy formulation would lead to an optimal domestic price between the supply price derived in the first-best solution and the world market price.

As elegant as this extended and distribution-oriented welfare view seems to be, it poses fundamental problems for practical policy formulation. On the one hand, the setting of certain distributional weights is without doubt a rather delicate political issue; on the other hand, the consequence would be a differentiated price system requiring a substantial amount of information to be available to the government in a manner similar to that of a planned economy. In the end, such a policy approach would result in eliminating the information and co-ordination functions of the market mechanism. That is why the 'classical' concept of welfare economics is still central to welfare assessments in policy evaluations; however, the explicit identification of distributional effects is essential to every policy analysis.

The limitations of a distribution-oriented policy formulation also become clear if we examine a typical objective of international agricultural and food policy: to

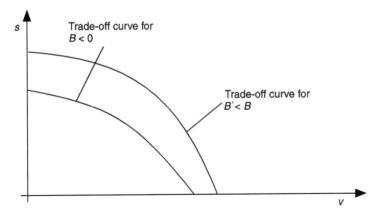

Figure 5.3 Trade-off curve between producer and consumer subsidy rates under subsidisation of producers and consumers and a binding budget constraint.

ensure proper incentive prices for producers and, at the same time, to establish reasonable food prices for consumers. In this case, the obvious suitable policy would be subsidisation of both producers and consumers which, of course, would lead to welfare losses and budget expenditure. Figure 5.3 shows a corresponding trade-off curve between a maximum producer subsidy rate at a given consumer subsidy rate or vice versa in a situation where a budget constraint applies. If higher budget expenditure is an option, the scope for the policy pursued increases and the trade-off curve shifts outside.

Exercise 5

Consider again the supply function

$$q^s(p^s) = c(p^s)^{\varepsilon^s}$$

with $\varepsilon^s = 0.3$

and the demand function

$$q^d(p^d) = d(p^d)^{\varepsilon^d}$$

with $\varepsilon^d = -0.4$.

For the calibration we also use the values from Exercise 4 with $p^s = 15$, $p^d = 12$, $q^s = 80$ and $q^d = 100$; the world market price is $p^w = 10$. Solve the following problems:

(a) At what level does the uniform domestic price need to be set to maximise government budget? And at what level should it be set to maximise foreign exchange, whereas budget expenditure may not exceed 100 (200)?

(b) Assume free trade; a country wants to increase the supply price, but to limit budget expenditure to a maximum of 400. What is the highest possible supply price? What uniform domestic price would be possible instead?

(c) Assume again free trade; show for both policies the trade-off curve between producer surplus and government budget of $-400 \leq B \leq 0$.

(d) For distributional reasons producers get a 20 per cent higher weight than consumers and the government. How should supply and demand prices be set to maximise the adjusted welfare function? At what level should an optimal uniform domestic price be set instead?

(e) Assume free trade again; a country wants to increase the supply price, but, at the same time, also decrease the demand price, again limiting budget expenditure to a maximum of 400. What trade-off curve would we get for the producer and consumer subsidy rates, and how does this trade-off curve change for a budget expenditure constraint of 800?

Solution

Step 5.1   Since we assume the same starting values as in Exercise 4, we can use the model calibrated in Exercise 4a; or we can conduct a new calibration as explained in Step 4.4. Exercise 5a is again a typical Solver application, whereas in the first part we want to get the uniform domestic price (changing cell: A4; in cell B4 is the formula = A4), which maximises government budget (target cell: N4). Compare your result with Figure 5.4. The optimal domestic price is between the world market price $p^w = 10$ and the autarky price $p^a = 18.16$ (cf. Step 4.5). If we now maximise foreign exchange (target cell: M4) under the budget constraint

	A	B	C	D	E	F	G	H
1		Cobb-Douglas Market Model with Calibration						
2								
3	p^s	p^d	p^w		Supply	Demand		Cost
4	13.76	13.76	10.00		77.95	94.68		247.47
5	15.00	12.00	Parameters of calibration		80.00	100.00		
6		Constants			Elasticities			
7		c	d	of supply	of demand			
8		35.5028003	270.192008	0.3	-0.4			

	J	K	L	M	N	O	P
1							
2							
3	Welfare	Revenue	Expenditure	Foreign exchange	Government budget	Producer surplus	Consumer surplus
4	3425.60	1072.38	1302.54	-167.30	62.86	824.91	2537.83

Figure 5.4 Budget maximisation at a uniform domestic price (exercise5a.xls).

(constraint: N4 > = −100 respectively −200), the optimal domestic price is 21.15 respectively 23.42. The budget constraint thus restricts the export subsidy in a surplus situation.

Step 5.2 We also solve Exercise 5b with the Solver (cf. Figure 5.5). Note that a fixed demand price of 10 must be in cell B4 if we want to change only the supply price. If instead the formula = A4 is in cell B4, you get the optimal uniform domestic price with the same Solver parameters.

Not exceeding the budget expenditure constraint of 400 the producer subsidisation leads to a maximum possible supply price of $p^s = 15.00$. With the same budget constraint the uniform domestic price can be raised above the autarky price to a maximum possible value $p = 27.11$.

Step 5.3 To solve Exercise 5c we use the models with the Solver configuration from Exercise 5b, but for all budget constraints between 0, −50, −100 to −400. To do this, put the corresponding values in the range G14:G22 and enter the Solver solutions for producer surplus in H14:H22. We also need to change the right side of our constraint each time (cf. Figure 5.5). Note that choosing the supply price as the target cell produces the same result as choosing producer surplus, because producer surplus is a monotonically increasing function of the supply price.

Now select the two data series and generate with the 'Chart wizard' (Chart type point (XY), with data points connected by smooth lines) the desired trade-off curve (see Figures 5.6 and 5.7) Under 'Chart options' you can determine the title and the names for the axes.

Pursuing a policy with a uniform domestic price (note the formula = A4 in cell B4), the trade-off curve shifts to the right (cf. Figure 5.8),

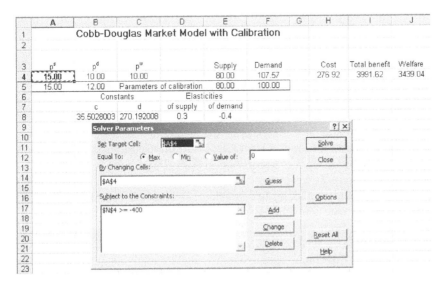

Figure 5.5 Maximum supply price at a budget expenditure constraint of 400 (exercise5b.xls).

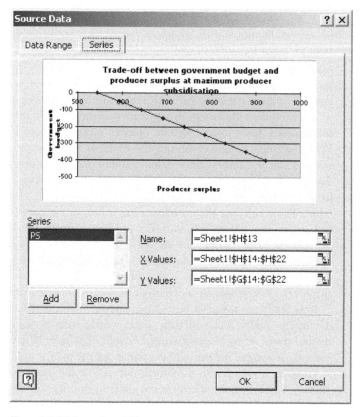

Figure 5.6 Dialogue box 'Chart source data', 'Series' (exercise5c.xls).

which outlines the greater scope of this policy for increasing producer surplus under the budget constraint.

Step 5.4   To solve Exercise 5d simply change the welfare function in cell J4 to = 1.2*O4 + P4 + N4 and run the Solver (cf. Figures 5.9 and 5.10). The first-best policy results in a supply price of $p^s = 30$ and a demand price at world market price level, while the second-best policy produces a uniform domestic price of $p = 13.36$. This example shows the cost of using inappropriate policy instruments in policy formulation.

Step 5.5   In Exercise 5e we discuss the objective of establishing an incentive price for producers and, at the same time, a reasonable price for consumers. In this case the country would have to deviate from free trade subsidising both producers and consumers. This would create a trade-off situation between producer and consumer subsidy rates at a given budget expenditure constraint. We could directly identify the relevant trade-off curve for different values for producer and consumer subsidy rates by maximising the producer subsidy rate for various levels of

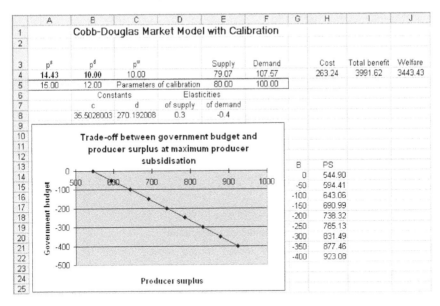

Figure 5.7 Trade-off between government budget and producer surplus at maximum producer subsidisation (exercise5c.xls).

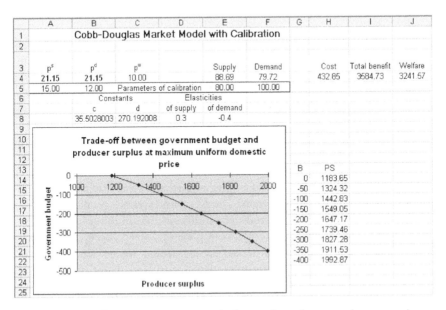

Figure 5.8 Trade-off between government budget and producer surplus at maximum uniform domestic price (exercise5c2.xls).

	J4	▾		f_x =1.2*O4+P4+N4						
	A	B	C	D	E	F	G	H	I	J
1			Cobb-Douglas Market Model with Calibration							
2										
3	p^s	p^d	p^w		Supply	Demand		Cost	Total benefit	Welfare
4	30.00	10.00	10.00		98.49	107.57		681.86	6419.99	6101.96
5	15.00	12.00	Parameters of calibration		80.00	100.00				
6			Constants		Elasticities					
7		c	d		of supply	of demand				
8		35.5028003	270.192008		0.3	-0.4				

Figure 5.9 Supply and demand prices at maximum welfare with a 20 per cent higher weight for producers (exercise5d.xls).

	B4	▾		f_x =A4						
	A	B	C	D	E	F	G	H	I	J
1			Cobb-Douglas Market Model with Calibration							
2										
3	p^s	p^d	p^w		Supply	Demand		Cost	Total benefit	Welfare
4	13.36	13.36	10.00		77.26	95.81		238.12	6284.03	6019.18
5	15.00	12.00	Parameters of calibration		80.00	100.00				
6			Constants		Elasticities					
7		c	d		of supply	of demand				
8		35.5028003	270.192008		0.3	-0.4				

Figure 5.10 Uniform domestic price at maximum welfare with a 20 per cent higher weight for producers (exercise5d2.xls).

consumer subsidy rates or, vice versa, by maximising the consumer subsidy rate for various levels of producer subsidy rates. The procedure would be comparable to Exercise 5c as visualised in Figures 5.7 and 5.8. On the other hand, we could also approach this problem as a vector optimisation problem. Basically, we pursue two objectives: a maximum supply price and a minimum demand price. Such a situation describes a vector optimisation problem, where several objective functions are considered. In our case the two objective functions have a simple structure, with the two prices as variables.

If we now try to find the maximum supply price at a fixed demand price of 10 under the required budget constraint, we get the maximum possible value for the producer subsidy rate. If, on the other hand, we try to find the minimum demand price at a fixed supply price of 10, again under the required budget constraint, we get the maximum possible value for the consumer subsidy rate. If we define both prices as variables (changing cell: A4:B4) we have to accept compromises with respect to the two objectives pursued resulting in the trade-off function. To set up this vector optimisation problem we choose a parameter a, which varies the weights for the two objectives. This means that in each case we maximise the linear combination $a \cdot p^s - (1 - a) p^d$ for different values of $a = 0, 0.1, 0.2, \ldots, 1$. In the target cell (D12) we enter the formula $= C11*A4 - D11*B4$, and the value for the parameter a in C11 and the formula $= 1 - C11$ in D11, i.e. the value for $1 - a$. We have to bear in mind that in addition to the budget constraint the solution is restricted by the limits $p^s \geq 10$ and $p^d \leq 10$. If we start with $a = 0$, we maximise $-p^d$, i.e. minimise p^d and we get the Solver solution $p^s = 10$ and $p^d = 6.81$. We can then copy both values to A14:B14. We now increase the value for a and copy the values for the respective prices to A15:B24.

As a result of the vector optimisation problem and the chosen parametrisation, we get only three different sets of solution values. Hence, we can roughly outline the trade-off curve between a proper incentive price for producers and a reasonable food price for consumers. We can solve the price equations for the subsidy rates s and v following (3.11) and (3.12), and the resultant values provide the basis for the trade-off curve in Figure 5.11. At a maximum budget expenditure of 800 we proceed in the same way and get a trade-off curve with four different solution values shifted slightly to the right.

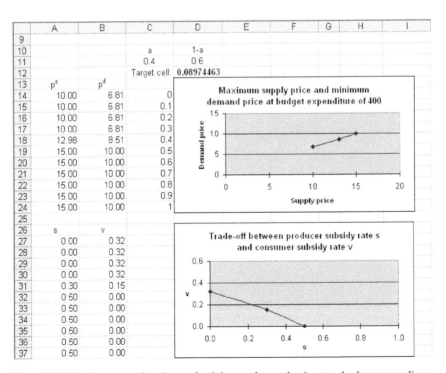

Figure 5.11 Maximum supply price and minimum demand price at a budget expenditure of 400 (exercise5e.xls).

References

Just, R.E., Hueth, D.L. and Schmitz, A. (2004) *The Welfare Economics of Public Policy: A Practical Approach to Project and Policy Evaluation*, Cheltenham, Northampton, MA: Edward Elgar, pp. 8–11.

Kirschke, D. and Jechlitschka, K. (2003) 'Analyse von Preispolitiken mit Excel', *WiSt-Wirtschaftswissenschaftliches Studium, Zeitschrift für Ausbildung und Hochschulkontakt*, 32 (10), pp. 582–9. Available online at <http://edoc.hu-berlin.de/oa/articles/re3C1xH26kQwk/PDF/29uPNywMfGpUI.pdf> (accessed 20 July 2006).

Koester, U. (2005) *Grundzüge der landwirtschaftlichen Marktlehre* (3rd edn), Munich: Vahlen, pp. 253–8 (WiSo-Kurzlehrbücher: Reihe Volkswirtschaft).

Pindyck, R.S. and Rubinfeld, D.L. (2005) *Microeconomics* (6th edn), Upper Saddle River, NJ: Pearson Prentice Hall, pp. 596–8.

Zeleny, M. (1974) *Linear Multiobjective Programming*, Berlin: Springer.

6   External effects

Objective

In Chapter 6 we will discuss how external effects can be considered in the analysis of price policies. We will show what consequences external effects have for the impact analysis and the formulation of price policies.

Theory

External effects, positive or negative, are caused by activities of economic agents which affect the objective function of others (e.g. the utility function of a household or the profit function of a producer) without being reflected in prices. The classical example of a negative external effect is a company polluting a river and thus reducing yield and revenue of a fisherman further downstream. On the other hand, the cultural landscape shaped by farming over centuries is a widely accepted example of a positive external effect.

An external effect results in costs or benefits through economic activities which are not reflected in market prices. In such a situation a market cannot lead to a maximisation of the social objective function; market failure occurs. This implies the question: If and how can government intervention on markets correct market distortions created by external effects? It is a central question in economics, whether and under what conditions direct government intervention is an appropriate mechanism for the internalisation of external effects or whether an internalisation can be achieved through private agreements in a suitable legal framework.

The consequences of external effects for the analysis of price policies are shown in Figure 6.1. In this example we assume a positive external effect through agricultural production (e.g. a contribution of agriculture in maintaining the cultural landscape). The existence of such an external effect requires a differentiation between a 'private' and a 'social' supply curve. The private supply curve reflects the marginal cost (MC) of the producers and thus, under the prevailing assumptions, the marginal cost with respect to welfare. From a social point of view, however, the external benefit in relation to the landscape contribution also needs to be considered. In Figure 6.1 we assume a constant marginal external benefit of

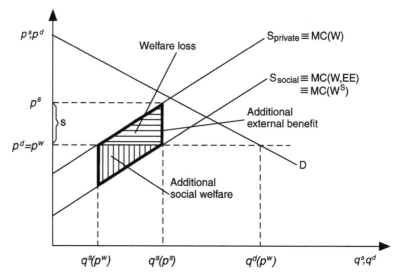

Figure 6.1 Internalisation of a positive external production effect.

the production; hence the 'social' supply curve, which considers the private cost of production and the external benefit, lies below the private supply curve, whereby the distance between the two curves is defined by the marginal external benefit.

External effects thus widen the assessment of market and price policies from a 'classical' welfare perspective to a broader social welfare point of view which also includes external benefits and costs. To differentiate from the classical concept, we define an extended 'social welfare' function. The extension can be formalised in a simple way by defining the external production effect considered as follows:

$$EE(p^s) = f(q^s(p^s))$$ (6.1)

with EE – external effect.

Hence it follows for social welfare from (3.9):

$$W^s(p^s, p^d, p^w) = TB(p^d) - C(p^s) + FE(p^s, p^d, p^w) + EE(p^s)$$ (6.2)

with W^s – social welfare

or

$$W^s(p^s, p^d, p^w) = \int_0^{q^d(p^d)} \tilde{p}^d(v)\, dv - \int_0^{q^s(p^s)} \tilde{p}^s(v)\, dv$$
$$+ \left(q^s(p^s) - q^d(p^d)\right) p^w + f(q^s(p^s)).$$ (6.2)′

In this context Figure 6.1 shows that free trade leads to a maximisation of welfare, but would not maximise social welfare. Instead, a producer subsidisation, as shown in Figure 6.1, would maximise social welfare. Although, in comparison to free trade, the producer subsidisation would lead to a welfare loss of the horizontally hatched area, it would result overall in a social welfare gain of the vertically hatched area, due to the additional external benefit defined by the bold-framed area.

If, instead of a producer subsidisation, we consider a protectionist policy to internalise the external production benefit, the result would be twofold and we would get an increase in social welfare on the supply side, but also a loss on the demand side. We could define an optimal protection rate for the internalisation of the positive external effect, in this case comparing marginal gain and marginal loss under this policy. The protection rate is optimal if marginal gain and marginal loss are equal. Comparing the optimal producer subsidy rate discussed above with such an optimal protection rate, the optimal protection rate would be smaller due to the distortion on the demand side. Hence producer subsidisation would be the first-best policy to internalise the external effect and a protectionist policy would be the second-best policy approach.

The trade-off between welfare and external benefit can also be illustrated graphically. Figure 6.2 shows the trade-off curve under a producer subsidisation and under a protectionist price policy, respectively, while free trade is always our base situation. We can see how the second-best protectionist price policy limits the scope for policy-making compared to a first-best producer subsidisation policy.

The concept of external effects and their internalisation may be extended to other economic activities and, in principle, to any derived variable so long as social welfare effects are plausible. For example, Figure 6.3 assumes a negative external production effect and a positive external consumption effect. Moreover, it implements the assumption of an undervalued exchange rate (the price of foreign exchange) due to an overvalued domestic currency. Thus, the real cost of

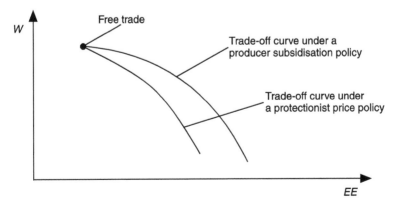

Figure 6.2 Trade-off between welfare and positive external production effect.

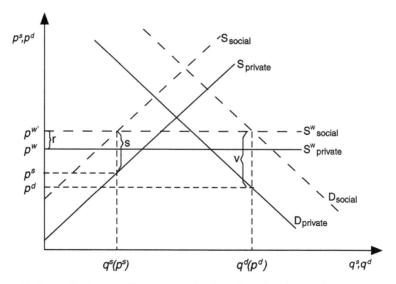

Figure 6.3 Internalisation of different external effects through price policies.

foreign exchange expenditure is higher as shown by the exchange rate, and the shadow price of an imported good is therefore higher than the world market price. Figure 6.3 illustrates how an optimal price policy would be formulated to internalise these external effects. It shows an optimal protection rate, an optimal producer tax rate and an optimal consumer subsidy rate, whereas each of these policy interventions internalises one of the external effects described above. At the end, this combination of policy instruments leads to an optimal supply price and an optimal demand price. However, this result may also be achieved through other combinations of the three policy instruments.

As evident as such policy formulation is, this example also points to the limitations of price policies to internalise external effects. Similar to the definition of distributional weights in Chapter 5, the definition and quantification of external cost and benefit would not be an easy political task. Internalisation would, then, require a differentiated price system which, in the end, would resemble a system somewhat similar to that of a planned economy; in essence, an ambitious policy approach to internalise external effects would result in eliminating the information and co-ordination functions of the market mechanism. A responsible policy formulation in case of external effects therefore implies comparing advantages and disadvantages of government interventions carefully.

Exercise 6

Consider again the supply function

$$q^s\left(p^{s\cdot}\right) = c\left(p^s\right)^{\varepsilon^s}$$

with $\varepsilon^s = 0.3$

and the demand function

$$q^d(p^d) = d(p^d)^{\varepsilon^d}$$

with $\varepsilon^d = -0.4.$

For the calibration of the functions we use the values from Exercise 4 with $p^s = 15$, $p^d = 12$, $q^s = 80$ and $q^d = 100$; the world market price is $p^w = 10$. Solve the following problems:

(a) Assume free trade; the production causes a marginal external benefit of 3 (e.g. with respect to the landscape objectives of a society). Show graphically the welfare function and social welfare function at a gradual increase in the protection rate to 50 per cent.
(b) Compare the optimal producer subsidy rate and the optimal protection rate maximising social welfare.
(c) Assume again free trade; show graphically the trade-off curve between welfare and external production effect at a gradual increase in the producer subsidy rate and the protection rate, respectively, to 50 per cent.
(d) How would the results in (b) and (c) differ with $\varepsilon^s = 0.6$ and $\varepsilon^d = -0.8$, and what would be the consequences of the implementation of a budget expenditure constraint of 150?
(e) Assume again the initial elasticity values. Implement the following assumptions: a negative external production effect of 20 per cent of the supply price, a positive external consumption effect of 30 per cent of the demand price, and a shadow price for foreign exchange which, due to an overvalued domestic currency, is 10 per cent higher than the real exchange rate. Formulate an optimal price policy to internalise these external effects. Compare this policy with an optimal protectionist price policy.

Solution

Step 6.1   We use the model from Exercise 4d as a basis for this exercise (cf. Figure 4.5). In that way, we already have the protection rates and subsidy rates incorporated into the model (see Step 4.6 or 3.5).

We enter value 3 for the marginal external benefit in cell H8. Below, in cell H10, we enter for the external effect $3 \cdot q^s$ the formula $=$ H8*E4 and write for social welfare the formula $=$ J4 $+$ H10 in cell H13. We now only need to produce the welfare function and social welfare function at a changing protection rate r by using 'Data, table ...' and we need to show the results in a diagram (see Figure 6.4); Exercise 6a is now solved.

Figure 6.4 shows that a gradual increase in protection results in welfare losses. Social welfare rises initially above the free trade level due to

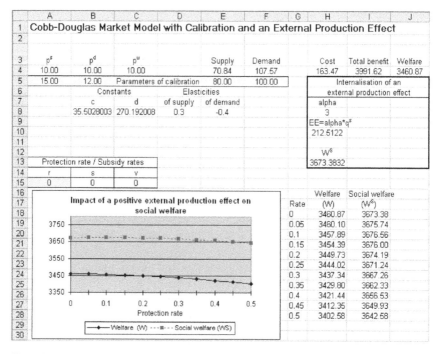

	A	B	C	D	E	F	G	H	I	J
1	Cobb-Douglas Market Model with Calibration and an External Production Effect									
2										
3	p^s	p^d	p^w		Supply	Demand		Cost	Total benefit	Welfare
4	10.00	10.00	10.00		70.84	107.57		163.47	3991.62	3460.87
5	15.00	12.00	Parameters of calibration		80.00	100.00		Internalisation of an		
6		Constants		Elasticities				external production effect		
7		c	d	of supply	of demand			alpha		
8		35.5028003	270.192008	0.3	-0.4			3		
9								EE=alpha*q^s		
10								212.5122		
11										
12								W^s		
13	Protection rate / Subsidy rates							3673.3832		
14	r	s	v							
15	0	0	0							

Rate	Welfare (W)	Social welfare (W^s)
0	3460.87	3673.38
0.05	3460.10	3675.74
0.1	3457.89	3676.56
0.15	3454.39	3676.00
0.2	3449.73	3674.19
0.25	3444.02	3671.24
0.3	3437.34	3667.26
0.35	3429.80	3662.33
0.4	3421.44	3656.53
0.45	3412.35	3649.93
0.5	3402.58	3642.58

Figure 6.4 Impact of a positive external production effect on social welfare (exercise6a.xls).

the external production effect, but then also declines due to the increasing welfare losses at higher protection levels.

Step 6.2   Using the Solver you calculate the optimal producer subsidy rate and the optimal protection rate maximising social welfare. Choose H13 as target cell and B15 and A15 as changing cells. You do not need to define any constraints in this exercise. The results are shown in Figures 6.5 and 6.6.

	A	B	C	D	E	F	G	H	I	J
1	Cobb-Douglas Market Model with Calibration and an External Production Effect									
2										
3	p^s	p^d	p^w		Supply	Demand		Cost	Total benefit	Welfare
4	13.00	10.00	10.00		76.64	107.57		229.91	3991.62	3452.44
5	15.00	12.00	Parameters of calibration		80.00	100.00		Internalisation of an		
6		Constants		Elasticities				external production effect		
7		c	d	of supply	of demand			alpha		
8		35.5028003	270.192008	0.3	-0.4			3		
9								EE=alpha*q^s		
10								229.91477		
11										
12								W^s		
13	Protection rate / Subsidy rates							3682.3505		
14	r	s	v							
15	0	0.29999999	0							

Figure 6.5 Optimal producer subsidy rate for social welfare (exercise6b.xls).

	A	B	C	D	E	F	G	H	I	J
1	Cobb-Douglas Market Model with Calibration and an External Production Effect									
2										
3	p^s	p^d	p^w		Supply	Demand		Cost	Total benefit	Welfare
4	11.04	11.04	10.00		72.97	103.40		185.87	3947.83	3457.66
5	15.00	12.00	Parameters of calibration		80.00	100.00		Internalisation of an		
6		Constants		Elasticities				external production effect		
7		c	d	of supply	of demand			alpha		
8		35.5028003	270.192008	0.3	-0.4			3		
9								EE=alpha*q^s		
10								218.90434		
11										
12								w^s		
13	Protection rate / Subsidy rates							3676.5683		
14	r	s	v							
15	0.1038288	0	0							

Figure 6.6 Optimal protection rate for social welfare (exercise6b2.xls).

The optimal producer subsidy rate results in a supply price above the world market price, whereas the difference between the two prices is defined by the marginal external benefit. On the other hand, the optimal protection rate is significantly lower, due to the demand distorting effect of this second-best policy to internalise the external production effect.

Step 6.3   To solve Exercise 6c you can directly use the model from Exercise 6a. You only need to substitute social welfare with the external effect and display the data in a trade-off curve. You then get the trade-off curve for different values of the protection rate r (cf. Step 5.3 and see Figure 6.7); whereas to get the trade-off at a changing producer subsidy rate s (see Figure 6.8), you simply need to alter the 'Data, table' operation ('Columns input cell' B15).

To facilitate a graphical comparison, it is useful to include both curves in the same diagram (with 'Chart source data' and adding a data series: see Figure 6.9). We can see that a producer subsidisation policy provides greater scope for policy-making with respect to welfare and the external benefit considered than a protectionist price policy.

Step 6.4   In Exercise 6d we want to work with other elasticity values. Before doing Steps 6.2 and 6.3 again, you need to calibrate the model for the new values (cf. Step 4.4). To do this, you simply enter the new elasticities in cells D8 and E8, and the calibration constants, the quantities in E4 and F4, and all other functions adjust automatically.

Compare your results with Figures 6.10 to 6.12. You will see that higher elasticity values do not influence the result for the optimal producer subsidy rate, but lower the optimal protection rate. This implies that welfare distortions of this second-best policy are greater if demand

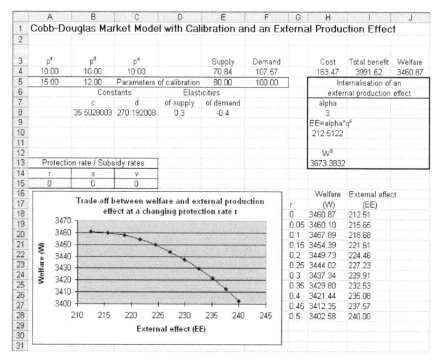

	A	B	C	D	E	F	G	H	I	J
1	Cobb-Douglas Market Model with Calibration and an External Production Effect									
2										
3	p^s	p^d	p^w		Supply	Demand		Cost	Total benefit	Welfare
4	10.00	10.00	10.00		70.84	107.57		163.47	3991.62	3460.87
5	15.00	12.00	Parameters of calibration		80.00	100.00		Internalisation of an		
6		Constants		Elasticities				external production effect		
7		c	d	of supply	of demand			alpha		
8		35.5028003	270.192008	0.3	-0.4			3		
9								EE=alpha*q^s		
10								212.5122		
11										
12								w^s		
13	Protection rate / Subsidy rates							3673.3832		
14	r	s	v							
15	0	0	0							
16									Welfare	External effect
17								r	(W)	(EE)
18								0	3460.87	212.51
19								0.05	3460.10	215.65
20								0.1	3457.89	218.68
21								0.15	3454.39	221.61
22								0.2	3449.73	224.46
23								0.25	3444.02	227.23
24								0.3	3437.34	229.91
25								0.35	3429.80	232.53
26								0.4	3421.44	235.08
27								0.45	3412.35	237.57
28								0.5	3402.58	240.00
29										
30										
31										

Figure 6.7 Trade-off between welfare and external production effect at a changing protection rate (exercise6c.xls).

is more elastic. Another consequence is that the difference between the trade-off curves for first-best and second-best policies is bigger in Figure 6.12 than in Figure 6.9. However, a comparison of the two figures needs to take into account different functional values.

If we limit budget expenditure to a maximum of 150, we get an optimal producer subsidy rate of 0.213 (Solver constraint N4 > = −150; see Figure 6.13). Thus, in this example, budget expenditure for a producer subsidisation policy is a binding constraint for the internalisation of the external production effect. In contrast, the budget expenditure constraint does not affect the result for the optimal protection rate, since the calculated protection rate does not stimulate exports and thus does not cause budget expenditure. In Figure 6.12 the calculated values for budget expenditure show that with a budget constraint of 150 the trade-off curve for the producer subsidisation policy would truncate after the first five values.

Step 6.5   In Exercise 6e we want to consider multiple external effects at the same time. To do this, we enter the values −0.2, 0.3 and 0.1 in the cells I9, I10

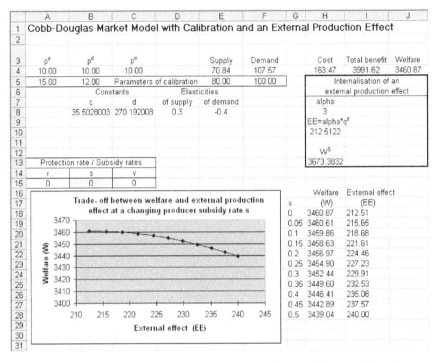

Figure 6.8 Trade-off between welfare and external production effect at a changing producer subsidy rate (exercise6c2.xls).

and I11, respectively. For the sum of the external effects it follows the formula: $EE = a \cdot \text{Cost} + \beta \cdot \text{Total benefit} + \gamma \cdot \text{Foreign exchange}$. In comparison to the previously discussed constant marginal external benefit of production we now consider a percentage supplement or reduction of the supply curve (as marginal cost), of the demand curve (as marginal total benefit) and of the world market price (as marginal foreign exchange expenditure). We enter the appropriate Excel formula = I9*H4 + I10*I4 + I11*M4 in cell H15 and social welfare in cell H18 (see Figure 6.14).

First, we implement free trade as our base situation ($r = 0, s = 0, v = 0$). To determine optimal price policies we again use the Solver. If we begin with the optimal protectionist price policy, we need to define the protection rate r (cell A15) as changing cell; target cell is H18. We get the solution with $r \approx -0.13$ and a domestic price of 8.67. If we now go back to the base situation (free trade, $r = 0, s = 0, v = 0$) and define all three rates as changing cells (i.e. the range A15:C15), we get the optimal values displayed in A20:C20 and E20 and F20 of Figure 6.14.

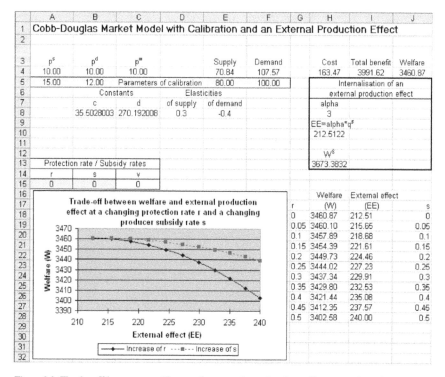

	A	B	C	D	E	F	G	H	I	J
1	Cobb-Douglas Market Model with Calibration and an External Production Effect									
2										
3	p^s	p^d	p^w		Supply	Demand		Cost	Total benefit	Welfare
4	10.00	10.00	10.00		70.84	107.57		163.47	3991.62	3460.87
5	15.00	12.00	Parameters of calibration		80.00	100.00		Internalisation of an		
6		Constants		Elasticities				external production effect		
7		c	d	of supply	of demand			alpha		
8		35.5028003	270.192008	0.3	-0.4			3		
9								EE=alpha*q^s		
10								212.5122		
11										
12								W^s		
13	Protection rate / Subsidy rates							3673.3832		
14	r	s	v							
15	0	0	0							

	Welfare	External effect	
r	(W)	(EE)	s
0	3460.87	212.51	0
0.05	3460.10	215.65	0.05
0.1	3457.89	218.68	0.1
0.15	3454.39	221.61	0.15
0.2	3449.73	224.46	0.2
0.25	3444.02	227.23	0.25
0.3	3437.34	229.91	0.3
0.35	3429.80	232.53	0.35
0.4	3421.44	235.08	0.4
0.45	3412.35	237.57	0.45
0.5	3402.58	240.00	0.5

Figure 6.9 Trade-off between welfare and external production effect at a changing protection rate *r* and producer subsidy rate *s* (exercise6c3.xls).

	A	B	C	D	E	F	G	H	I	J
1	Cobb-Douglas Market Model with Calibration and an External Production Effect									
2										
3	p^s	p^d	p^w		Supply	Demand		Cost	Total benefit	Welfare
4	13.00	10.00	10.00		73.42	115.70		357.91	3353.83	2573.06
5	15.00	12.00	Parameters of calibration		80.00	100.00		Internalisation of an		
6		Constants		Elasticities				external production effect		
7		c	d	of supply	of demand			alpha		
8		15.7556103	730.03721	0.6	-0.8			3		
9								EE=alpha*q^s		
10								220.25334		
11										
12								W^s		
13	Protection rate / Subsidy rates							2793.3144		
14	r	s	v							
15	0	0.29999999	0							

Figure 6.10 Optimal producer subsidy rate for social welfare at $\varepsilon^s = 0.6$ and $\varepsilon^d = -0.8$ (exercise6d1.xls).

	A	B	C	D	E	F	G	H	I	J
1	Cobb-Douglas Market Model with Calibration and an External Production Effect									
2										
3	p^s	p^d	p^w		Supply	Demand		Cost	Total benefit	Welfare
4	10.95	10.95	10.00		66.22	107.62		271.87	3269.28	2583.45
5	15.00	12.00	Parameters of calibration		80.00	100.00		Internalisation of an		
6		Constants		Elasticities				external production effect		
7		c	d	of supply	of demand			alpha		
8		15.7556103	730.03721	0.6	-0.8			3		
9								EE=alpha*q^s		
10								198.67418		
11										
12								W^s		
13	Protection rate / Subsidy rates							2782.1233		
14	r	s	v							
15	0.09473311	0	0							

Figure 6.11 Optimal protection rate for social welfare with $\varepsilon^s = 0.6$ and $\varepsilon^d = -0.8$ (exercise6d2.xls).

If we choose different initial values (e.g. $r = 0.5$, $s = 0$ and $v = 0$), we get a different solution for r, s and v (cf. A21:C21 in Figure 6.14), but the same values for p^s, p^d and for the maximum social welfare. We also get these optimal values if we fix one rate and define the other two rates as changing cells (cf. A23:C25 in Figure 6.14).

Thus it is clear that different combinations of these price policy instruments produce the same first-best result with a supply price of $p^s = 9.17$ and a demand price of $p^d = 8.46$. The optimal supply price is 20 per cent of the value 9.17 lower than the adjusted world market price of 11, as shown in Figure 6.3. Similarly, the optimal demand price is 30 per cent of the value 8.46 below the adjusted world market price.

The above example shows the scope for formulating a first-best price policy with various combinations of price policy instruments. If the number of available policy instruments is restricted, one has to consider the following consequences. With two available instruments there is only one solution which produces the first-best prices; with only one available instrument a first-best solution is not possible in the case considered above. Figure 6.14 shows that, if policy formulation is limited to the protection rate, the optimal domestic price is $p = 8.67$, which is between the supply and the demand price of a first-best policy.

Cobb-Douglas Market Model with Calibration and an External Production Effect

	p^s	p^d	p^w		Supply	Demand		Cost	Total benefit	Welfare
	10.00	10.00	10.00		62.72	115.70		235.22	3353.83	2588.82
	15.00	12.00	Parameters of calibration		80.00	100.00		Internalisation of an		
		Constants		Elasticities				external production effect		
		c	d	of supply	of demand			alpha		
		15.7556103	730.03721	0.6	-0.8			3		
								EE=alpha*q^s		
								188.17264		
								W^s		
Protection rate / Subsidy rates								2776.9939		
	r	s	v							
	0	0	0							

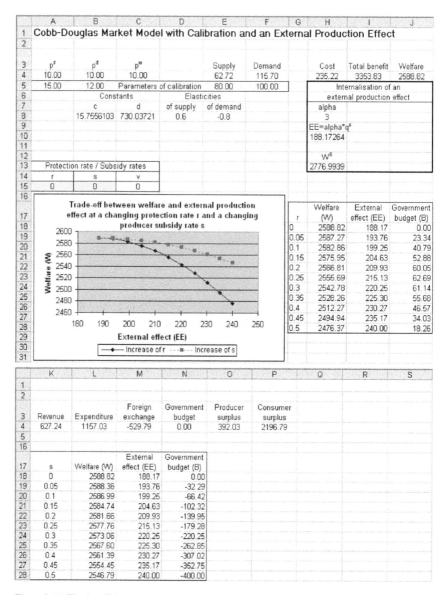

r	Welfare (W)	External effect (EE)	Government budget (B)
0	2588.82	188.17	0.00
0.05	2587.27	193.76	23.34
0.1	2582.86	199.25	40.79
0.15	2575.95	204.63	52.88
0.2	2566.81	209.93	60.05
0.25	2555.69	215.13	62.69
0.3	2542.78	220.25	61.14
0.35	2528.26	225.30	55.68
0.4	2512.27	230.27	46.57
0.45	2494.94	235.17	34.03
0.5	2476.37	240.00	18.26

	K	L	M	N	O	P	Q	R	S
3	Revenue	Expenditure	Foreign exchange	Government budget	Producer surplus	Consumer surplus			
4	627.24	1157.03	-529.79	0.00	392.03	2196.79			

s	Welfare (W)	External effect (EE)	Government budget (B)
0	2588.82	188.17	0.00
0.05	2588.36	193.76	-32.29
0.1	2586.99	199.25	-66.42
0.15	2584.74	204.63	-102.32
0.2	2581.66	209.93	-139.95
0.25	2577.76	215.13	-179.28
0.3	2573.06	220.25	-220.25
0.35	2567.60	225.30	-262.85
0.4	2561.39	230.27	-307.02
0.45	2554.44	235.17	-352.75
0.5	2546.79	240.00	-400.00

Figure 6.12 Trade-off between welfare and external production effect at a changing protection rate r and a changing producer subsidy rate s with $\varepsilon^s = 0.6$ and $\varepsilon^d = -0.8$ (exercise6d5.xls).

	A	B	C	D	E	F	G	H	I	J
1	Cobb-Douglas Market Model with Calibration and an External Production Effect									
2										
3	p^s	p^d	p^w		Supply	Demand		Cost	Total benefit	Welfare
4	12.13	10.00	10.00		70.43	115.70		320.36	3353.83	2580.72
5	15.00	12.00	Parameters of calibration		80.00	100.00		Internalisation of an		
6		Constants			Elasticities			external production effect		
7		c	d	of supply	of demand			alpha		
8		15.7556103	730.03721	0.6	-0.8			3		
9								EE=alpha*q^s		
10								211.28524		
11										
12								W^s		
13		Protection rate / Subsidy rates						2792.0078		
14	r	s	v							
15	0	0.21298223	0							

Figure 6.13 Optimal producer subsidy rate for social welfare with $\varepsilon^s = 0.6$ and $\varepsilon^d = -0.8$ and budget expenditure constraint of 150 (exercise6d6.xls).

	A	B	C	D	E	F	G	H	I	J
1	Cobb-Douglas Market Model with Calibration, Protection Rate, Subsidy Rates									
2	and Multiple External Effects									
3	p^s	p^d	p^w		Supply	Demand		Cost	Total benefit	Welfare
4	9.17	8.46	10.00		69.01	115.00		145.99	4060.01	3454.16
5	15.00	12.00	Parameters of calibration		80.00	100.00				
6		Constants			Elasticities					
7		c	d	of supply	of demand			Internalisation of		
8		35.5028003	270.192008	0.3	-0.4			multiple external effects		
9								alpha	-0.2	
10								beta	0.3	
11								gamma	0.1	
12										
13		Protection rate / Subsidy rates						EE := alpha*Cost+beta*Total benefit		
14	r	s	v					+gamma*Foreign exchange		
15	0.20879122	-0.2416667	0.3					1142.8202		
16										
17		Optimal price policies			p^s	p^d		W^s		
18	-0.1332543	r at optimal protectionist price policy			8.67	8.67		4596.9823		
19	r	s	v		p^s	p^d				
20	-0.0866906	0.00367592	0.07352991		9.17	8.46				
21	0.30572681	-0.2979646	0.35196706							
22										
23	0.1	-0.1666667	0.23076921							
24	-0.2361114	0.2	-0.1076929							
25	0.20879122	-0.2416667	0.3							

Figure 6.14 Optimal price policies considering multiple external effects (exercise6e.xls).

References

Corden, W.M. (1997) *Trade Policy and Economic Welfare* (2nd edn), New York, Oxford: Oxford University Press, pp. 7–17.

Just, R.E., Hueth, D.L. and Schmitz, A. (2004) *The Welfare Economics of Public Policy: A Practical Approach to Project and Policy Evaluation*, Cheltenham, Northampton, MA: Edward Elgar, pp. 527–49.

Koester, U. (2005) *Grundzüge der landwirtschaftlichen Marktlehre* (3rd edn), Munich: Vahlen, pp. 272–6 (WiSo-Kurzlehrbücher: Reihe Volkswirtschaft).

Mas-Colell, A., Whinston, M.D. and Green, J.A. (1995) *Microeconomic Theory*, New York, Oxford: Oxford University Press, pp. 350–9.

Nicholson, W. (2005) *Microeconomic Theory: Basic Principles and Extensions* (9th edn), Mason, OH: Thomson, pp. 586–95.

Pindyck, R.S. and Rubinfeld, D.L. (2005) *Microeconomics* (6th edn), Upper Saddle River, NJ: Pearson Prentice Hall, pp. 641–58.

Varian, H.R. (2003) *Intermediate Microeconomics: A Modern Approach* (6th edn), New York: W.W. Norton, pp. 602–22.

7 Integrated markets

Objective

In Chapter 7 we extend the analysis of price policies to integrated markets. We will show how transfers occur in integrated markets and what consequences such transfers have for the analysis and formulation of price policies.

Theory

There are a number of examples where countries in a certain region integrate their markets, protecting them together against the rest of the world. Regional integration can take place in different forms: in a free trade zone internal trade is free of barriers, but the member states usually keep different tariffs against the rest of the world; in a customs union (e.g. the European Union), member states typically protect their markets through a common tariff. In addition to free internal trade with commodities, a common market is often characterised by free exchange of production factors between the different countries. Further integration concepts are known from discussions surrounding the European Union: an economic and monetary union with a common economic and monetary policy or a political union integrating further policy fields of member countries.

Figure 7.1 shows a customs union such as the European Union, but with only two member states. The common market price p^u in this customs union is above the world market price p^w. As in the case of a single country, this price policy is implemented through a tariff in an import case and an export subsidy in an export case. However, compared to a situation without a customs union, there is one major difference. Due to financial solidarity in a customs union trade policies no longer affect the national but the common budget, and member countries have to finance the common budget through financial contributions. Consequently, trade transfers between the member states arise, which affects the impact and assessment of price policies.

Following Figure 7.1 we see that in a customs union the import country loses the tariff revenue. The country has to pay the higher market price for imports from another member state, leading to a negative trade transfer. Moreover, it has

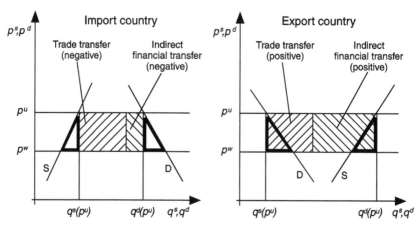

Figure 7.1 Transfers in a customs union.

to transfer the tariff revenue for imports from the rest of the world to the common budget of the customs union, resulting in a negative indirect financial transfer. The reverse situation applies for an export country. The export country does not need to finance export subsidies any more; it receives a positive trade transfer for exports to other member countries due to the higher international price and a positive indirect financial transfer from the common budget for exports to third countries (i.e. the rest of the world).

The assumed net-trade situation for the customs union is overall positive, i.e. the price policy shown in Figure 7.1 leads to a financial burden of the common budget in terms of export subsidies. Depending on the share in the financial contribution to the common budget, a negative direct financial transfer occurs for both countries, which further deteriorates the transfer situation of the import country and reduces the positive transfer situation of the export country. For the customs union as a whole, however, such transfer effects represent a 'zero-sum game' (in other words, the sum of all, positive and negative, transfers in a customs union is 0), so that the protectionist policy shown in Figure 7.1 leads to an overall welfare loss for the union and, hence, for the member countries together depicted by the bold-framed triangles.

The transfer problem for a member country in a customs union may be generalised and formalised in a simple way. For transfers in a member country it follows:

$$T_i\left(p_1^s, \ldots, p_n^s, p_1^d, \ldots, p_n^d, p^u, p^w, b_i\right) = \left(q_i^s(p_i^s) - q_i^d(p_i^d)\right)(p^u - p^w)$$

$$- b_i \sum_{j=1}^{n} \left(q_j^s(p_j^s) - q_j^d(p_j^d)\right)(p^u - p^w) \qquad (7.1)$$

with T_i – transfer
         p^u – customs union price
         b_i – share of financial contribution (to the common budget)
         i – defines the member country considered, while $j = 1, \ldots, i, \ldots, n$ is
                  the index for all member countries in a customs union.

Equation (7.1) shows that the transfer of a member state is a function of the supply prices and demand prices of all member countries as well as the customs union price, the world market price and the share of the financial contribution. If the member states do not pursue a national price policy, which is the basic idea behind a customs union, it then follows $p_i^s = p_i^d = p^u$, and the transfer is thus a function of p^u, p^w and b_i. Equation (7.1) also shows that, overall, the sum of all transfers in a customs union is 0 because we can write:

$$\sum_{i=1}^{n} T_i = \sum_{i=1}^{n} \left(q_i^s(p_i^s) - q_i^d(p_i^d) \right) (p^u - p^w)$$

$$- \sum_{i=1}^{n} b_i \sum_{j=1}^{n} \left(q_j^s(p_j^s) - q_j^d(p_j^d) \right) (p^u - p^w) = 0. \tag{7.2}$$

The transfer for a member state in a customs union changes the foreign exchange and government budget functions of the country and, hence, also the welfare function. For the foreign exchange function it follows based on (3.3):

$$FE_i^m = FE_i + T_i \tag{7.3}$$

or

$$FE_i^m(p_1^s, \ldots, p_n^s, p_1^d, \ldots, p_n^d, p^u, p^w, b_i) = \left(q_i^s(p_i^s) - q_i^d(p_i^d) \right) p^u$$

$$- b_i \sum_{j=1}^{n} \left(q_j^s(p_j^s) - q_j^d(p_j^d) \right) (p^u - p^w) \tag{7.3'}$$

with FE_i^m – foreign exchange (revenue) of a customs union member country.

Similarly, for the government budget function following (3.4), we can write:

$$B_i^m = B_i + T_i \tag{7.4}$$

or

$$B_i^m (p_1^s, \ldots, p_n^s, p_1^d, \ldots, p_n^d, p^u, p^w, b_i) = q_i^d (p_i^d) (p_i^d - p^u) - q_i^s (p_i^s) (p_i^s - p^u)$$

$$- b_i \sum_{j=1}^{n} \left(q_j^s (p_j^s) - q_j^d (p_j^d) \right) (p^u - p^w) \quad (7.4)'$$

with B_i^m – government budget (revenue) of the customs union member country.

Hence, for the welfare function it follows based on (3.9):

$$W_i^m = W_i + T_i \tag{7.5}$$

or

$$W_i^m = TB_i - C_i + FE_i^m, \tag{7.5}'$$

or also

$$W_i^m = CS_i + PS_i + B_i^m \tag{7.5}''$$

and finally

$$W_i^m (p_1^s, \ldots, p_n^s, p_1^d, \ldots, p_n^d, p^u, p^w, b_i) = \int_0^{q_i^d(p_i^d)} \tilde{p}_i^d (v_i) \, dv_i - \int_0^{q_i^s(p_i^s)} \tilde{p}_i^s (v_i) \, dv_i$$

$$+ \left(q_i^s (p_i^s) - q_i^d (p_i^d) \right) p^u$$

$$- b_i \sum_{j=1}^{n} \left(q_j^s (p_j^s) - q_j^d (p_j^d) \right) (p^u - p^w)$$

$$(7.5)'''$$

with W_i^m – welfare of a customs union member country.

Equation (7.5) illustrates that the formulation of total benefit and cost as well as consumer surplus and producer surplus does not change for a member country in a customs union. If we finally aggregate the welfare functions of all member countries, we can formulate the welfare level of the customs union in a way which is comparable to a non-member country (see (3.9)).

In order to understand the transfer problem in a customs union, it is helpful to define the transfers for the different member countries as a function of the customs union price. Figure 7.2 shows some examples of transfer functions.

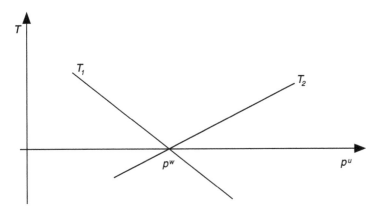

Figure 7.2 Transfer for member countries in a customs union.

Since the transfer is 0 for $p^u = p^w$, in both cases the transfer function intersects the abscissa at p^w. For country 1 the transfer function is decreasing monotonically, meaning that any increase in the customs union price would further deteriorate the transfer situation. Vice versa, any decrease in the internal price in the customs union would improve the situation. This implies that for this country a customs union price at world market price level would not lead to welfare maximisation. Instead, the optimal outcome would be a lower price at which the 'marginal transfer gain' would match the 'marginal welfare loss' as visualised by the welfare loss triangles (cf. Figure 7.1). In a similar way, country 2 would achieve a maximisation of welfare at a customs union price, which is higher than the world market price. Product-tied transfers within a customs union thus result in conflicts between the member countries with respect to a common price policy and create incentives for policy distortions from a union's point of view.

Furthermore, the cost of national policies can also be shifted to other member countries and the union as a whole. For example, a producer subsidisation implemented in one member country could, at a given customs union price, increase export refunds of the customs union and deteriorate the transfer, foreign exchange and budget situation in the other member countries. The extent of such externalisation opportunities in integrated markets depends, of course, on the share of financial contribution to the common budget of the member countries. A hypothetical share of 0, for example, would not affect the national budget as a consequence of an 'externalisation policy'. In this case, the customs union price would be the relevant 'shadow price' for the member country guiding the country's allocation of resources and not the world market price. In an export case and from a national perspective the country should advocate an increasing customs union price at the expense of the union. The other extreme, a hypothetical share of the financial contribution to the common budget of 1, would lead to a totally different outcome. In this case, the country, and only this country, has to bear all the consequences of not only its own national policy, but also of policies implemented in other member countries.

Overall, the integration of markets leads to totally different conditions for an individual country to analyse and formulate price policies. The new policy framework can broaden the scope for formulating and realising policy objectives (e.g. increase in producer surplus and limiting budget expenditure), but it can also restrict the scope for policy-making.

Exercise 7

Consider for both member countries of a customs union the following supply functions:

$$q_i^s(p_i^s) = c_i (p_i^s)^{\varepsilon_i^s}, \qquad i = 1, 2$$

with $\varepsilon_1^s = \varepsilon_2^s = 0.3$

and the demand functions

$$q_i^d(p_i^d) = d_i (p_i^d)^{\varepsilon_i^d}, \qquad i = 1, 2$$

with $\varepsilon_1^d = \varepsilon_2^d = -0.4.$

The customs union sets the customs union price independently from the world market price at $p^u = 12$; the world market price is $p^w = 10$. Under this price setting the first member country is an importer with $q_1^s = 80$ and $q_1^d = 100$, and the second member country is an exporter with $q_2^s = 200$ and $q_2^d = 160$. The share of financial contribution is $b_1 = 0.5$ for the first member country and $b_2 = 0.5$ for the second. Formulate and calibrate the corresponding model and solve the following problems:

(a) Show graphically how the transfers for the two member countries change under a gradual increase of the customs union price from 10 to 20.
(b) At what level does the customs union price need to be set to maximise welfare for the individual member states and what price level is required to maximise welfare for the customs union as a whole?
(c) Describe and explain the reasons for the shape of the welfare function for both countries for $5 \leq p^u \leq 30$. How does the shape change with $b_1 = 0.2\,(0.8)$?
(d) Assume that the customs union price is the relevant price for producers and consumers in both member countries. Show graphically how a gradual increase in the producer subsidy rate to 50 per cent in country 2 affects transfer, foreign exchange and government budget in country 1. How does the result change with $b_1 = 0.2\,(0.8)$?
(e) How does the trade-off between producer surplus and government budget in

country 1 change, if, following a national protectionist policy, a common protectionist policy is pursued in the customs union?

Solution

Step 7.1 We can again use the model from Exercise 4a (or Exercise 5a) calibrated for $p^s = 15$, $p^d = 12$ and $p^w = 10$, $\varepsilon^s = 0.3$ and $\varepsilon^d = -0.4$. Click on cell A1 and add a new first column ('Insert', 'Columns'). You can now enter the customs union price in cell A4. For the second member country of the customs union we copy the market model from the first eight rows of the Excel sheet into rows 9–16.

Step 7.2 Set both the supply price and the demand price equal to the customs union price (= A4 and = A12). Write the formula = A4 in cell A12 and the formula = D4 in cell D12. In that way, prices and elasticities are correct and the model can be calibrated for both countries (importer and exporter) (see also Step 4.4, but note the different parameters of calibration, and see Figure 7.3).

Step 7.3 In this step we want to add the transfer T_i (see (7.1)) to the customs union model. To do this, enter the share of financial contribution $b_1 = 0.5$ in cell A8 and write the formula = 1 − A8 for b_2 in cell A16. If you now calculate customs union expenditure = (F4 − G4)*(A4 − D4) + (F12 − G12)*(A12 − D12) in cell A19, you get the transfer for country 1 defined as = (F4 − G4)*(A4 − D4) − A8*A19 in cell B8 and the transfer for country 2 written as = (F12 − G12)*(A12 − D12) − A16*A19 in B16 (cf. Figure 7.3).

Following (7.3) and (7.4) we have to add the transfers of countries 1 and 2 to their respective foreign exchange and government budget formulas in the cells N4 and O4 (country 1) and N12 and O12 (country 2).

The values in Figure 7.3 show the consequences of membership in a customs union. As importer, country 1 loses tariff revenue and, in addition, has to contribute to the export subsidies of the customs union. Under the described price policy scenario country 1 has a budget revenue of 40 as a non-member of the customs union. Being a member of the customs union leads to a deteriorating budget situation and a budget expenditure of 20. Moreover, foreign exchange expenditure increases from 200 to 260. On the other hand, for country 2 the consequences of joining the customs union are exactly the opposite to those described for country 1.

Step 7.4 We can now solve Exercise 7a. We assume free trade as our base situation and enter the value 10 for p^u in cell A4. We produce the transfer data for both member countries under a gradual increase of the customs union price by using 'Data, table' (as explained in Step 1.4) and depict the values in a diagram (see Figure 7.4). Figure 7.4 shows that an increase in the customs union price above the world market price leads to a growing transfer from country 1 to country 2.

	B8	▾	*fx* =(F4-G4)*(A4-D4)-A8*A19					
	A	B	C	D	E	F	G	H
1				**Cobb-Douglas Market Model for a Customs Union**				
2	**Country 1**							
3	Customs union price	Supply price	Demand price	World market price		Supply	Demand	
4	12.00	12.00	12.00	10.00		80.00	100.00	
5		12.00	12.00	Parameters of calibration		80.00	100.00	
6	Share of financial		Constants		Elasticities			
7	contribution	Transfer	c	d	of supply	of demand		
8	0.5	-60	37.9608225	270.192008	0.3	-0.4		
9								
10	**Country 2**							
11	Customs union price	Supply price	Demand price	World market price		Supply	Demand	
12	12.00	12.00	12.00	10.00		200.00	160.00	
13		12.00	12.00	Parameters of calibration		200.00	160.00	
14	Share of financial		Constants		Elasticities			
15	contribution	Transfer	c	d	of supply	of demand		
16	0.5	60	94.9020561	432.307212	0.3	-0.4		
17	Customs union							
18	expenditure							
19	40							

	I	J	K	L	M	N	O	P	Q
1									
2									
3	Cost	Total benefit	Welfare	Revenue	Expenditure	Foreign exchange	Government budget	Producer surplus	Consumer surplus
4	221.54	3908.72	3427.19	960.00	1200.00	-260.00	-20.00	738.46	2708.72
5									
11	Cost	Total benefit	Welfare	Revenue	Expenditure	Foreign exchange	Government budget	Producer surplus	Consumer surplus
12	553.85	6253.96	6160.11	2400.00	1920.00	460.00	-20.00	1846.15	4333.96

Figure 7.3 Model for a customs union (exercise7.xls).

Step 7.5   We solve Exercise 7b using the Solver. For country 1 we get an optimal customs union price of $p^u \approx 8.36$, and for country 2 of $p^u \approx 19.73$. From the customs union point of view (target cell here is a cell with the formula = K4 + K12 as the union's welfare) the optimal price is the world market price.

While different national political objectives in the various member states of a customs union may always result in differences in the assessment of a common policy, this example demonstrates that just the institutional framework of a customs union can lead to conflicting interests.

Step 7.6   In Exercise 7c we get the welfare functions in the same way as in Step 7.4 using 'Data, table'. The way we have built our models for the customs union allows us to analyse the situations at different shares of financial contributions by simply changing the value for b_1 in cell A8 (see exercise7c.xls).

	A	B	C	D	E	F	G	H	I
1			Cobb-Douglas Market Model for a Customs Union						
2	**Country 1**								
3	Customs union price	Supply price	Demand price	World market price			Supply	Demand	Cost
4	10.00	10.00	10.00	10.00			75.74	107.57	174.79
5		12.00	12.00	12.00	Parameters of calibration		80.00	100.00	
6	Share of financial		Constants		Elasticities				
7	contribution	Transfer	c	d	of supply	of demand			
8	0.5	0	37.9608225	270.192008	0.3	-0.4			
9									
10	**Country 2**								
11	Customs union price	Supply price	Demand price	World market price			Supply	Demand	Cost
12	10.00	10.00	10.00	10.00			189.35	172.10	436.97
13		12.00	12.00	12.00	Parameters of calibration		200.00	160.00	
14	Share of financial		Constants		Elasticities				
15	contribution	Transfer	c	d	of supply	of demand			
16	0.5	0	94.9020561	432.307212	0.3	-0.4			
17	Customs union								
18	expenditure								
19	0								
20									
21		p^u	Transfer 1	Transfer 2					
22		10	0.00	0.00					
23		11	-27.39	27.39					
24		12	-60.00	60.00					
25		13	-97.21	97.21					
26		14	-138.54	138.54					
27		15	-183.58	183.58					
28		16	-232.02	232.02					
29		17	-283.57	283.57					
30		18	-338.02	338.02					
31		19	-395.16	395.16					
32		20	-454.81	454.81					

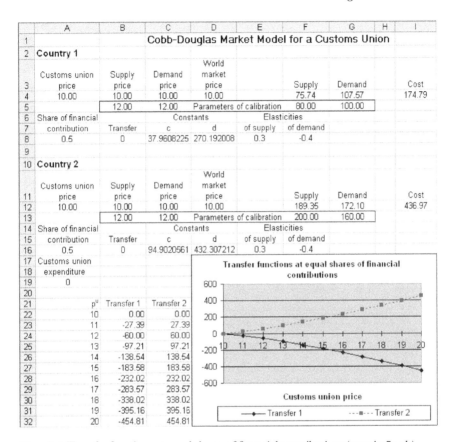

Figure 7.4 Transfer functions at equal shares of financial contributions (exercise7a.xls).

At a share of financial contribution of $b_1 = b_2 = 0.5$ the welfare functions reach their maximum at $p^u \approx 8$ for country 1 and $p^u \approx 20$ for country 2, in line with the result of Exercise 7b. However, at shares of financial contributions of $b_1 = 0.2$ and $b_2 = 0.8$ country 2 has a greater 'financial responsibility' in the customs union; the welfare-maximising customs union price for country 2 is now only slightly above the world market price. On the other hand, at shares of financial contribution of $b_1 = 0.8$ and $b_2 = 0.2$ we get a rather paradoxical situation where any increase in the customs union price makes sense for country 2, but at the expense of the other member country, country 1 (cf. Figure 7.5).

Step 7.7 To solve Exercises 7d and 7e we need to include the protection rate and subsidy rates in the model for both countries (e.g. as in Exercise 6e). In order to create some space for these parameters, we move country 2 from rows 10–19 to rows 13–22. To do this, highlight the rows 10–19 and move the contents to the new range (compare with Step 2.1). The

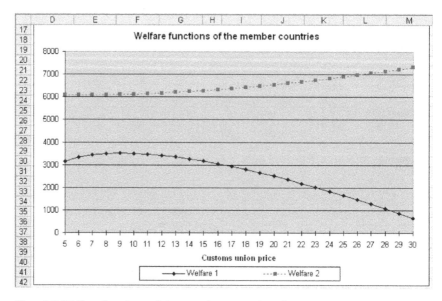

Figure 7.5 Welfare functions of the member countries of a customs union at shares of financial contributions of $b_1 = 0.8$ and $b_2 = 0.2$ (exercise7c.xls).

lower space of the Excel sheet would be better blank (operations such as 'Data, table' or a diagram could interfere). Alternatively, you can use the model exercise7.xls. In the same way, move customs union expenditure (A20:A22) to D24:D26. Besides the inclusion of the rates, do not forget to endogenise supply and demand prices, defined as dependent on the customs union price and not on the world market price (cf. Step 3.5 or 4.6 and see Figure 7.6).

Step 7.8   We can now generate transfer, foreign exchange and government budget data for country 1 for different producer subsidy rates s_2 in country 2 by again using 'Data, table' and create a diagram (see Figure 7.6). We recommend a separate presentation of the individual curves. You can vary the share of financial contribution in cell A8 (in cell A19 we have the formula $= 1 - A8$).

Depending on the shares of financial contributions, higher production in country 2 due to producer subsidisation in this country leads to an increase in the negative transfer for country 1 and a rise in government budget and foreign exchange expenditures. This spill-over effect from country 2 to country 1 is particularly high with a larger share of financial contribution coming from country 1.

Step 7.9   Let us proceed to Exercise 7e. In order to formulate a common protectionist price policy in the customs union, we add a protection rate for the customs union (*r union*) with a preliminary value of 0 in cell A26, and link this cell with the world market price defining the customs union

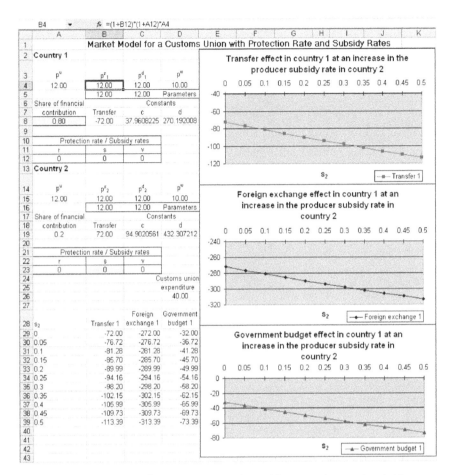

| B4 | ▼ | fx =(1+B12)^(1+A12)^A4 |

Figure 7.6 Market model for a customs union with protection and subsidy rates (exercise7d.xls).

price; hence, in cell A4 we get the formula = (1 + A26)*D4. Moreover, we assume the same share of financial contribution in both member countries ($b_1 = b_2 = 0.5$) and no national price policies ($r_i = s_i = v_i = 0$). We can now generate transfer, government budget and producer surplus data for country 1 at a changing protection rate (r union) again by using 'Data, table'. Finally, we depict government budget and producer surplus as trade-off function (cf. Figure 7.7 and Step 5.3).

Step 7.10 In the next step, we want to simulate a protectionist price policy in country 1 without being a member of the customs union, show the resulting trade-off curve between producer surplus and government budget and compare the trade-off curve with the previous trade-off curve from Step 7.9. To do this we first fix the values generated through

	A	B	C	D	E	F	G
1	**Market Model for a Customs Union with Protection Rate and Subsidy Rates**						
2	**Country 1**						
3	p^u	p^s_1	p^d_1	p^w		Supply	Demand
4	10.00	10.00	10.00	10.00		75.74	107.57
5		12.00	12.00	Parameters of calibration		80.00	100.00
6	Share of financial		Constants		Elasticities		
7	contribution	Transfer	c	d	of supply	of demand	
8	0.50	0.00	37.960822	270.19201	0.3	-0.4	
9							
10	Protection rate / Subsidy rates						
11	r	s	v				
12	0	0	0				
13	**Country 2**						
14	p^u	p^s_2	p^d_2	p^w		Supply	Demand
15	10.00	10.00	10.00	10.00		189.35	172.10
16		12.00	12.00	Parameters of calibration		200.00	160.00
17	Share of financial		Constants		Elasticities		
18	contribution	Transfer	c	d	of supply	of demand	
19	0.5	0.00	94.902056	432.30721	0.3	-0.4	
20							
21	Protection rate / Subsidy rates						
22	r	s	v				
23	0	0	0				
24				Customs union			
25	r union			expenditure			
26	0.00			0.00			
27							
28	r union	Transfer 1	Government budget 1	Producer surplus 1			
29	0	0.00	0.00	582.63			
30	0.05	-13.00	1.31	620.78			
31	0.1	-27.39	-1.79	659.48			
32	0.15	-43.09	-8.99	698.71			
33	0.2	-60.00	-20.00	738.46			
34	0.25	-78.06	-34.58	778.71			
35	0.3	-97.21	-52.50	819.44			
36	0.35	-117.39	-73.56	860.65			
37	0.4	-138.54	-97.60	902.32			
38	0.45	-160.61	-124.45	944.43			
39	0.5	-183.58	-153.97	986.99			

Figure 7.7 Trade-off between producer surplus and government budget of a country under a common protectionist price policy in the customs union (exercise7e1.xls).

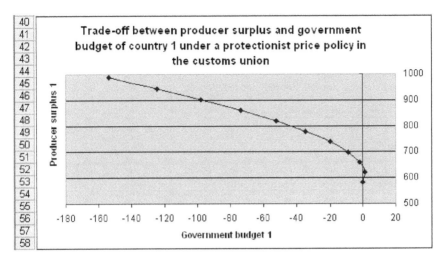

| 40 |
| 41 |
| 42 |
| 43 |
| 44 |
| 45 |
| 46 |
| 47 |
| 48 |
| 49 |
| 50 |
| 51 |
| 52 |
| 53 |
| 54 |
| 55 |
| 56 |
| 57 |
| 58 |

Figure 7.7 continued.

'Data, table' in the range B30:D39 and related to protection in the customs union ('Copy, paste special, values'). Next, substitute the customs union price for the world market price in the formulas of the supply and the demand price and the customs union protection rate by the national protection rate, i.e. p^s and p^d are now dependent on the national rates and p^w. Keep also in mind that government budget may no longer include the transfer (cf. G29). Finally, generate government budget and producer surplus for country 1 at different national protection rates r_1, again by using 'Data, table', and add the relevant data series as the second trade-off function to the diagram (cf. Figure 7.8 and exercise7e2.xls).

Figure 7.8 shows that a protectionist price policy in a non-member country does not lead initially to a conflict between producer surplus and government budget, but would do so if the country becomes a member of the customs union. This emphasises how trade-offs between political objectives and the scope for policy-making of a country can change significantly, if a country becomes a member of a customs union.

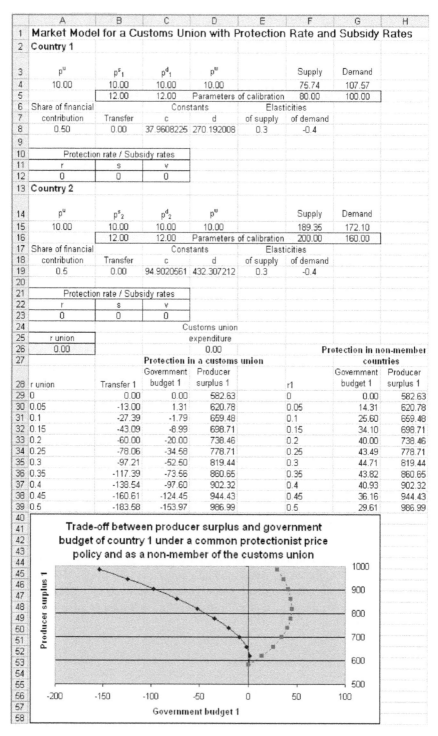

	A	B	C	D	E	F	G	H
1	Market Model for a Customs Union with Protection Rate and Subsidy Rates							
2	Country 1							
3	p^u	p^s_1	p^d_1	p^w			Supply	Demand
4	10.00	10.00	10.00	10.00			75.74	107.57
5		12.00	12.00	Parameters of calibration			80.00	100.00
6	Share of financial		Constants			Elasticities		
7	contribution	Transfer	c	d		of supply	of demand	
8	0.50	0.00	37.9608225	270.192008		0.3	-0.4	
9								
10	Protection rate / Subsidy rates							
11	r	s	v					
12	0	0	0					
13	Country 2							
14	p^u	p^s_2	p^d_2	p^w			Supply	Demand
15	10.00	10.00	10.00	10.00			189.35	172.10
16		12.00	12.00	Parameters of calibration			200.00	160.00
17	Share of financial		Constants			Elasticities		
18	contribution	Transfer	c	d		of supply	of demand	
19	0.5	0.00	94.9020561	432.307212		0.3	-0.4	
20								
21	Protection rate / Subsidy rates							
22	r	s	v					
23	0	0	0					
24				Customs union				
25	r union			expenditure				
26	0.00			0.00			Protection in non-member	
27			Protection in a customs union				countries	
28	r union	Transfer 1	Government budget 1	Producer surplus 1		r1	Government budget 1	Producer surplus 1
29	0	0.00	0.00	582.63		0	0.00	582.63
30	0.05	-13.00	1.31	620.78		0.05	14.31	620.78
31	0.1	-27.39	-1.79	659.48		0.1	25.60	659.48
32	0.15	-43.09	-8.99	698.71		0.15	34.10	698.71
33	0.2	-60.00	-20.00	738.46		0.2	40.00	738.46
34	0.25	-78.06	-34.58	778.71		0.25	43.49	778.71
35	0.3	-97.21	-52.50	819.44		0.3	44.71	819.44
36	0.35	-117.39	-73.56	860.65		0.35	43.82	860.65
37	0.4	-138.54	-97.60	902.32		0.4	40.93	902.32
38	0.45	-160.61	-124.45	944.43		0.45	36.16	944.43
39	0.5	-183.58	-153.97	986.99		0.5	29.61	986.99

Figure 7.8 Trade-off between producer surplus and government budget of a country under a common protectionist price policy and as a non-member of the customs union (exercise7e2.xls).

References

Bowen, H.P., Hollander, A. and Viaene, L-M. (1998) *Applied International Trade Analysis*, Basingstoke, London: Macmillan, pp. 503–10.

Koester, U. (2005) *Grundzüge der landwirtschaftlichen Marktlehre* (3rd edn), Munich: Vahlen, pp. 406–13 (WiSo-Kurzlehrbücher: Reihe Volkswirtschaft).

Krugman, P.R. and Obstfeld, M. (2003) *International Economics, Theory and Policy* (7th edn), Boston, MA: Addison Wesley, pp. 186–206.

8 World market and third country effects

Objective

In Chapter 8 we will examine international interdependencies and linkages. We will show how a price policy implemented in one country can affect the world market price and political objectives in third countries.

Theory

In the discussions thus far we have assumed that price policies in a certain country do not affect the world market price; hence we have assumed in this context a 'small country'. However, in many cases, particularly in the case of integrated markets, price policies are implemented by large countries or regions which have a considerable share in world trade; policies in such large countries or regions will then, of course, have an impact on the world market and third countries.

Figure 8.1 shows how a national protectionist price policy leads to a lower world market price. For the sake of simplification, we assume that the considered

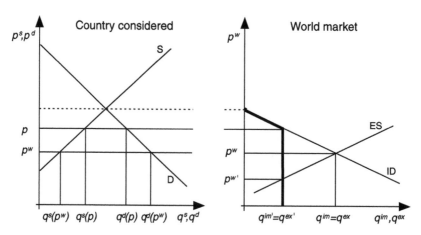

Figure 8.1 Impact of a protectionist price policy on the world market price.

country is the only importer (or consumer) on the world market. The import demand function ID is the difference between the quantities demanded and supplied in the country at the relevant domestic price. The import demand is satisfied through export supply (ES) of the rest of the world. At free trade, the world market is in equilibrium at p^w.

If this country now increases the domestic price to p, the import demand kinks at $q^{im'}$ and becomes totally inelastic. As a consequence of this policy the world market price declines to $p^{w'}$. Similarly, in an export situation a national protectionist price policy will lower the world market price. Generally, the impact on the world market price is larger the more inelastic demand and supply abroad and the bigger the share of the considered country in world trade. On the other hand, the described price effect also depends of course on the specific protectionist policy instrument applied.

In general, for the calculation of the world market price it applies that in the equilibrium the world market must be cleared. Hence, in contrast to the assumption of a small country, we need to endogenise the world market price. It follows:

$$\left(q^s(p^s) - q^d(p^d) \right) + \left(q_r^s(p^w) - q_r^d(p^w) \right) = 0 \qquad (8.1)$$

where r denotes the rest of the world from the point of view of the considered country.

Similar to (3.13) and (3.14) we can also write the following for different price policies:

$$\left(q^s(s, r, p^w) - q^d(v, r, p^w) \right) + \left(q_r^s(p^w) - q_r^d(p^w) \right) = 0 \qquad (8.1)'$$

and for free trade:

$$\left(q^s(p^w) - q^d(p^w) \right) + \left(q_r^s(p^w) - q_r^d(p^w) \right) = 0. \qquad (8.1)''$$

The changes in world market prices due to price policy interventions in the considered large country affect different political objectives in third countries. Figure 8.2 shows the example of an export country. In this case, changes in welfare, foreign exchange and producer surplus are negative; thus, the rest of the world loses, measured by these political objectives, as a consequence of the national protectionist price policy in the large country.

In the import case the consequences of a protectionist price policy are not that clear. In this case welfare increases and foreign exchange expenditure can increase or decrease depending on the size of the price and quantity effects, and these effects depend on the supply and demand elasticities. From the producers' point of

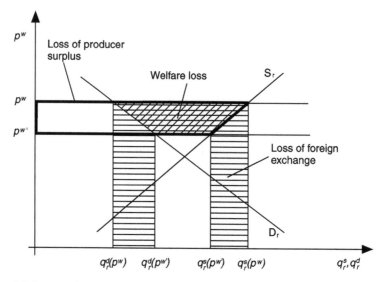

Figure 8.2 Impact of a protectionist price policy on political objectives in third countries.

view, however, also in this case a reduction of producer surplus occurs, as is shown by the bold-framed area in Figure 8.2; the producers in third countries are thus in any case the losers of a protectionist price policy in the considered large country.

However, we have to keep in mind that in our discussion on third country effects of price policies we assume corresponding domestic price changes in third countries due to the world market price changes. But that does not necessarily need to be the case, since these countries could also pursue a price policy independent from the world market price.

The considered large country could finally use its market power on the world market to influence the world market price to achieve its own objectives. Figure 8.3 shows the classical optimal tariff argument. If the large country increases the domestic price to p, this not only causes welfare losses as described for a small country by the welfare loss triangles, but also leads to terms of trade gains through the reduced world market price. The optimal protection rate, the optimal tariff, is where the marginal welfare loss is equal to the marginal welfare gain from the improved terms of trade. The country maximises its welfare as monopsonist on the world market.

The optimal tariff argument may be applied to an export situation. In this case the country could act as a monopolist and use its market power on the world market. By lowering the domestic price below the world market price, the latter could be increased and the welfare level improved. Similar to the optimal tariff argument, it would be possible to derive an optimal export taxation rate. It is tempting to further discuss the relevance and moral of such policies at the expense of other countries, but we do not extend this discussion here.

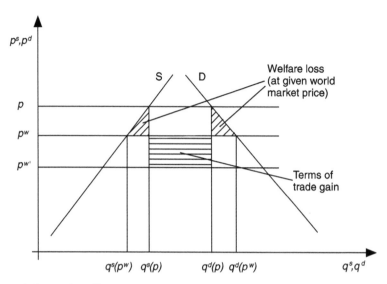

Figure 8.3 Optimal tariff argument.

Exercise 8

For a large country and for the rest of the world the supply functions are:

$$q^s(p^s) = c(p^s)^{\varepsilon^s}$$

with $\qquad \varepsilon^s = 0.3$

and

$$q_r^s(p^w) = c_r(p^w)^{\varepsilon_r^s}$$

with $\qquad \varepsilon_r^s = 0.3$

and the demand functions

$$q^d(p^d) = d(p^d)^{\varepsilon^d}$$

with $\qquad \varepsilon^d = -0.4$

and

$$q_r^d(p^w) = d_r(p^w)^{\varepsilon_r^d}$$

with $\qquad \varepsilon_r^d = -0.4.$

The country sets the domestic price at $p = 15$; the world market price is $p^w = 10$. Under this price policy the country is an importer with a quantity supplied of $q^s = 80$ and quantity demanded of $q^d = 100$. For the rest of the world the quantity supplied is $q_r^s = 200$ and the quantity demanded is $q_r^d = 180$. Formulate and calibrate the corresponding model and solve the following problems:

(a) What is the world market price at free trade?
(b) Assume free trade. Show graphically how the world market price changes with a gradual increase of the country's protection rate to 50 per cent.
(c) Show graphically how welfare, foreign exchange and producer surplus in the rest of the world change at the same gradual increase of the country's protection rate.
(d) Determine the optimal tariff for the considered country.
(e) Compare the optimal tariff, calculated under (d), with the optimal tariff at $\varepsilon^s = 0.5$ and $\varepsilon^d = -0.7$ as well as with the optimal tariff at $\varepsilon_r^s = 0.5$ and $\varepsilon_r^d = -0.7$.

Solution

Step 8.1 In this exercise you may use the model from exercise4a.xls and proceed as in Steps 7.1 and 7.2, copying the first eight rows, inserting a new column G, in which you enter the formula for the excess supply and their sum for the two countries, and then calibrating the model accordingly (cf. Figure 8.4).

Step 8.2 To solve Exercise 8a you will need to define the price linkages at free trade in a way that only the world market price in cell C12 is set as exogenous. You then maximise (e.g. the welfare of the country in the target cell),

	A	B	C	D	E	F	G	H	I
1	Cobb-Douglas Market Model for a Large Country and the Rest of the World								
2	Large country								
3	p^s	p^d	p^w			Supply	Demand	Excess supply	Cost
4	15	15	10			80	100	-20	276.92308
5	15	15	Parameters of calibration			80	100		
6		Constants			Elasticities				
7		c	d	of supply	of demand				
8		35.5028003	295.417694	0.3	-0.4				
9									
10	Rest of the world								
11	p^s	p^d	p^w			Supply	Demand	Excess supply	Cost
12	10	10	10			200	180	20	461.53846
13	10	10	Parameters of calibration			200	180		
14		Constants			Elasticities				
15		c	d	of supply	of demand			Sum	
16		100.237447	452.139558	0.3	-0.4			0	

	J	K	L	M	N	O	P	Q
1								
2								
3	Total benefit	Welfare	Revenue	Expenditure	Foreign exchange	Government budget	Producer surplus	Consumer surplus
4	4148.34042	3671.4173	1200	1500	-200	100	923.076923	2648.34042
5								
11	Total benefit	Welfare	Revenue	Expenditure	Foreign exchange	Government budget	Producer surplus	Consumer surplus
12	6679.58341	6418.045	2000	1800	200	0	1538.46154	4879.58341

Figure 8.4 Market model for a large country and the rest of the world (exercise8.xls).

whereas the world market needs to be cleared (constraint: sum G16 = 0); C12 is defined as changing cell. You obtain a world market price of 11.44.

In this example a liberalisation in the large country compared to the base situation would thus lead to an increase in the world market price of 14.4 per cent.

Step 8.3 As in Step 7.7 you implement the protection and subsidy rates and link the prices with the rates (cf. Figure 8.5). Then, using the Solver, you calculate the world market prices clearing the world markets at different protection rates. You can summarise their values in the range B26:B36 and produce a diagram as in Figure 8.5.

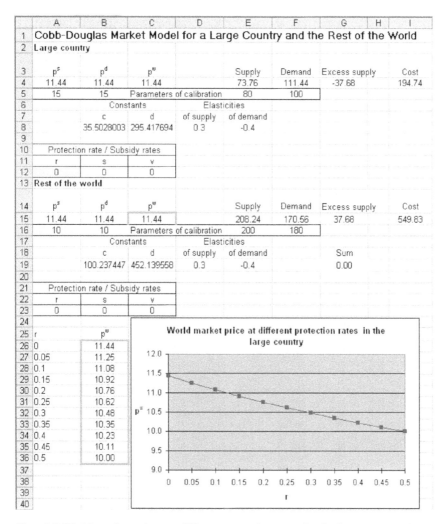

Figure 8.5 World market prices at different protection rates in the large country (exercise8b.xls).

Figure 8.5 shows how the world market price changes with increasing protection in the large country. In comparison to the world market price at free trade ($p^w = 11.4$) the protectionist policy pursued by the large country reduces the world market price (note that this price reduction effect is declining with an increasing protection rate) up to a protection rate of 50 per cent, with the world market price of $p^w = 10$ which is the initial value for the world market price in Exercise 8.

Step 8.4   Since the three political objectives for the rest of the world from Exercise 8c are functions of the world market prices calculated in Exercise 8b, we can use the 'Data, table' operations to enter their values in the range B26:E36, taking C15 as 'Column input cell' (cf. Figure 8.6 and exercise8c.xls). Because of the large differences between the values

	A	B	C	D	E	F	G	H	I
1	Cobb-Douglas Market Model for a Large Country and the Rest of the World									
2	Large country								
3	p^s	p^d	p^w		Supply	Demand	Excess supply		Cost
4	11.44	11.44	11.44		73.76	111.44	-37.68		194.74
5	15	15	Parameters of calibration		80	100			
6		Constants			Elasticities				
7		c	d	of supply	of demand				
8		35.5028003	295.417694	0.3	-0.4				
9									
10	Protection rate / Subsidy rates								
11	r	s	v						
12	0	0	0						
13	Rest of the world								
14	p^s	p^d	p^w		Supply	Demand	Excess supply		Cost
15	11.44	11.44	11.44		208.24	170.56	37.68		549.83
16	10	10	Parameters of calibration		200	180			
17		Constants			Elasticities				
18		c	d	of supply	of demand		Sum		
19		100.237447	452.139558	0.3	-0.4		0.00		
20									
21	Protection rate / Subsidy rates								
22	r	s	v						
23	0	0	0						
24									
25	r	p^w	Welfare	Foreign exchange	Producer surplus				
26	0	11.44	6459.92	431.15	1832.78				
27	0.05	11.25	6453.09	399.90	1794.00				
28	0.1	11.08	6447.07	371.05	1757.94				
29	0.15	10.92	6441.75	344.30	1724.29				
30	0.2	10.76	6437.05	319.43	1692.79				
31	0.25	10.62	6432.88	296.23	1663.22				
32	0.3	10.48	6429.17	274.53	1635.39				
33	0.35	10.35	6425.88	254.18	1609.14				
34	0.4	10.23	6422.96	235.04	1584.31				
35	0.45	10.11	6420.36	217.02	1560.79				
36	0.5	10.00	6418.04	200.00	1538.46				

Figure 8.6 Welfare, foreign exchange and producer surplus of the rest of the world at different protection rates in the large country (exercise8c.xls).

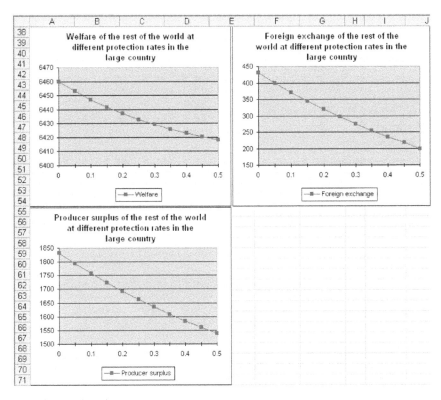

Figure 8.6 continued.

of the three variables it is better to produce a separate graphical presentation of the three functions.

The graphs confirm the theory that a protectionist price policy of a large country has negative consequences for export countries (based on the political objectives considered). On the other hand, consumers in the rest of the world gain due to lower prices.

Step 8.5 To determine the optimal tariff for the large country (Exercise 8d) we set the Solver with the national welfare K4 as target cell, the protection rate of the country in cell A12 and the world market price in cell C15 as changing cells (select non-continuous cells or blocks by holding down the control key), and the market-clearing condition G19 = 0 as constraint. Compare the solution with Figure 8.7. The result confirms that the large country can maximise its welfare, compared to free trade, through a tariff of *r* = *22* per cent.

Step 8.6 Let us now solve Exercise 8e. When you change the elasticities used in exercise8d.xls, the model will automatically be calibrated for the new values. Depending on the changes of the elasticities for the large country, the rest of the world or both, you get different solutions for the optimal tariff, i.e. for the values of *r* and p^w (cf. Figures 8.8 to 8.10).

Figure 8.7

	A	B	C	D	E	F	G	H	I
1	Cobb-Douglas Market Model for a Large Country and the Rest of the World								
2	Large country								
3	p^s	p^d	p^w			Supply	Demand	Excess supply	Cost
4	13.06	13.06	10.70			76.75	105.69	-28.94	231.34
5	15	15	Parameters of calibration		80	100			
6		Constants			Elasticities				
7		c	d	of supply	of demand				
8		35.5028003	295.417694	0.3	-0.4				
9									
10	Protection rate / Subsidy rates								
11	r	s	v						
12	0.22	0	0	Optimal tariff					
13	Rest of the world								
14	p^s	p^d	p^w			Supply	Demand	Excess supply	Cost
15	10.70	10.70	10.70			204.12	175.18	28.94	504.14
16	10	10	Parameters of calibration		200	180			
17		Constants			Elasticities				
18		c	d	of supply	of demand		Sum		
19		100.237447	452.139558	0.3	-0.4		0.00		
20									
21	Protection rate / Subsidy rates								
22	r	s	v						
23	0	0	0						

	J	K	L	M	N	O	P	Q
3	Total benefit	Welfare	Revenue	Expenditure	Foreign exchange	Government budget	Producer surplus	Consumer surplus
4	4227.99	3686.89	1002.49	1380.53	-309.75	68.28	771.15	2847.46
5								
14	Total benefit	Welfare	Revenue	Expenditure	Foreign exchange	Government budget	Producer surplus	Consumer surplus
15	6629.67	6435.28	2184.62	1874.87	309.75	0.00	1680.48	4754.80

Figure 8.7 Calculation of the optimal tariff (exercise8d.xls).

Figure 8.8

	A	B	C	D	E	F	G	H	I
1	Cobb-Douglas Market Model for a Large Country and the Rest of the World								
2	Large country								
3	p^s	p^d	p^w			Supply	Demand	Excess supply	Cost
4	13.53	13.53	10.91			75.99	107.47	-31.49	342.77
5	15	15	Parameters of calibration		80	100			
6		Constants			Elasticities				
7		c	d	of supply	of demand				
8		20.6559112	665.677505	0.5	-0.7				
9									
10	Protection rate / Subsidy rates								
11	r	s	v						
12	0.24	0	0	Optimal tariff					
13	Rest of the world								
14	p^s	p^d	p^w			Supply	Demand	Excess supply	Cost
15	10.91	10.91	10.91			205.31	173.82	31.49	517.01
16	10	10	Parameters of calibration		200	180			
17		Constants			Elasticities				
18		c	d	of supply	of demand		Sum		
19		100.237447	452.139558	0.3	-0.4		0.00		
20									
21	Protection rate / Subsidy rates								
22	r	s	v						
23	0	0	0						

Figure 8.8 Optimal tariff at $\varepsilon^s = 0.5$ and $\varepsilon^d = -0.7$ (exercise8e1.xls).

	A	B	C	D	E	F	G	H	I
1	**Cobb-Douglas Market Model for a Large Country and the Rest of the World**								
2	Large country								
3	p^s	p^d	p^w		Supply	Demand	Excess supply		Cost
4	12.20	12.20	10.62		75.19	108.62	-33.42		211.69
5	15	15	Parameters of calibration		80	100			
6		Constants			Elasticities				
7		c	d	of supply	of demand				
8		35.5028003	295.417694	0.3	-0.4				
9									
10	Protection rate / Subsidy rates								
11	r	s	v						
12	0.15	0	0	Optimal tariff					
13	Rest of the world								
14	p^s	p^d	p^w		Supply	Demand	Excess supply		Cost
15	10.62	10.62	10.62		206.06	172.63	33.42		729.10
16	10	10	Parameters of calibration		200	180			
17		Constants			Elasticities				
18		c	d	of supply	of demand		Sum		
19		63.2455532	902.137021	0.5	-0.7		0.00		
20									
21	Protection rate / Subsidy rates								
22	r	s	v						
23	0	0	0						

Figure 8.9 Optimal tariff at $\varepsilon_r^s = 0.5$ and $\varepsilon_r^d = -0.7$ (exercise8e2.xls).

	A	B	C	D	E	F	G	H	I
1	**Cobb-Douglas Market Model for a Large Country and the Rest of the World**								
2	Large country								
3	p^s	p^d	p^w		Supply	Demand	Excess supply		Cost
4	12.73	12.73	10.86		73.70	112.17	-38.47		312.72
5	15	15	Parameters of calibration		80	100			
6		Constants			Elasticities				
7		c	d	of supply	of demand				
8		20.6559112	665.677505	0.5	-0.7				
9									
10	Protection rate / Subsidy rates								
11	r	s	v						
12	0.17	0	0	Optimal tariff					
13	Rest of the world								
14	p^s	p^d	p^w		Supply	Demand	Excess supply		Cost
15	10.86	10.86	10.86		208.40	169.93	38.47		754.24
16	10	10	Parameters of calibration		200	180			
17		Constants			Elasticities				
18		c	d	of supply	of demand		Sum		
19		63.2455532	902.137021	0.5	-0.7		0.00		
20									
21	Protection rate / Subsidy rates								
22	r	s	v						
23	0	0	0						

Figure 8.10 Optimal tariff at $\varepsilon^s = 0.5$, $\varepsilon^d = -0.7$ and $\varepsilon_r^s = 0.5$, $\varepsilon_r^d = -0.7$ (exercise8e3.xls).

Elastic supply and demand in the large country leads to a stronger decline in the import demand and thus to a larger reduction of the world market price, resulting in a comparably higher optimal tariff. If, however, supply and demand in the rest of the world are elastic, then the opposite is the case, since a protectionist price policy now has a smaller impact on the world market.

References

Bowen, H.P., Hollander, A. and Viaene, L-M. (1998) *Applied International Trade Analysis*, Basingstoke, London: Macmillan, pp. 138–42, 182–4, 511–13.

Corden, W.M. (1997) *Trade Policy and Economic Welfare* (2nd edn), New York, Oxford: Oxford University Press, pp. 82–8.

Just, R.E., Hueth, D.L. and Schmitz, A. (2004) *The Welfare Economics of Public Policy: A Practical Approach to Project and Policy Evaluation*, Cheltenham, Northampton, MA: Edward Elgar, pp. 280–4, 395–405.

Koester, U. (2005) *Grundzüge der landwirtschaftlichen Marktlehre* (3rd edn), Munich: Vahlen, pp. 167–9, 266–72, 281–2, 303–5 (WiSo-Kurzlehrbücher: Reihe Volkswirtschaft).

Krugman, P.R. and Obstfeld, M. (2003) *International Economics, Theory and Policy* (7th edn), Boston, MA: Addison Wesley, pp. 186–217.

Part II

Analysis of structural policies

9 Shifts of the supply curve

Objective

In Chapter 9 we will further extend the market model to analyse structural policies. We will explain how structural policies lead to a shift of supply curves and we will show how such a shift of the supply curve affects political objectives.

Theory

Differentiating between price policies and structural policies, in price policy analysis it is usually assumed that supply and demand curves are given, while structural policies lead to a shift of supply curves. Figure 9.1 emphasises this differentiation: price policies are thus characterised by movements on given supply and demand curves, in contrast to structural policies, which move (i.e. shift) the supply curves to a new position.

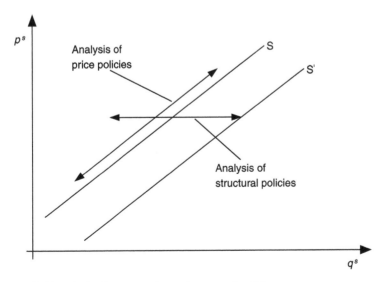

Figure 9.1 Differentiation between price and structural policies.

There are a number of different types of structural policies. For example, research and extension can lead to an enhancement of productivity and hence to a rightward shift of the supply curve. Similarly, policies to improve technical and social infrastructure or to decrease transaction cost in marketing can have the same effect. Generally, such structural policies aim explicitly to improve productivity and the production base which then leads to the described rightward shift of the supply curve. But other structural policies are also possible: for example, environmentally targeted production restrictions increase the production cost and such a structural policy would thus shift the supply curve to the left. Finally, it is important to note that structural policies are not always dependent on, and financed through, a government budget. For example, it is possible that changes in relevant legislation alter the production conditions without resulting in government expenditure or revenue. Given the large variety of structural policies we want to concentrate on the classical case of a structural policy, which is financed through budget expenditure and leads to a rightward shift of the supply curve.

Let us formulate a suitable supply function. The iso-elastic supply function (4.2) is now defined as:

$$q^s(p^s) = c(1+f)(p^s)^{\varepsilon^s}; \qquad \varepsilon^s > 0 \tag{9.1}$$

with　　f – shift parameter.

Equation (9.1) shows that analysing structural policies, practically, means to introduce and incorporate a shift parameter in the supply function. The impact of a structural policy may then be evaluated by comparing relevant political objectives with and without shift parameter. However, we have to take into account that the budget expenditure caused by a structural policy needs to be considered in all political objectives which include budget effects and requires a revision of the formulation of those objectives. For a better differentiation we define net variables for the political objectives, which include the additional budget expenditure for the structural policy. Thus, based on (3.4), we change government budget to net government budget defined as:

$$NB = B - BES \tag{9.2}$$

with　　NB – net government budget

　　　　BES – government budget expenditure for structural policies

and, based on (3.9), welfare to net welfare as:

$$NW = W - BES \qquad \text{or} \tag{9.3}$$

$$NW = CS + PS + NB \tag{9.3}'$$

with　　NW – net welfare.

Figure 9.2 shows welfare and distributional effects of a structural policy in a closed economy, without price policy interventions by the government. The figure emphasises that structural policies lead to an increase in the quantity supplied and also to a lower market price. Because of this spill-over effect of the supply curve shift, consumers benefit from the structural policy through an increase in consumer surplus, which is denoted by the bold line. For producers we can identify two opposite effects: a loss of producer surplus due to the lower price and, on the other hand, a gain in producer surplus due to higher productivity and the associated cost reduction. These effects are shown by the broken line.

Overall, welfare increases by the hatched area. This welfare increase may be divided into two different effects of the structural policy considered: a cost reduction for quantity q produced at the old equilibrium and the welfare effect from the production expansion $(q' - q)$ due to improved production conditions and enhanced productivity. The overall net welfare effect of the structural policy is positive, if the shown welfare effect in the figure is bigger than government budget expenditure for this policy.

Furthermore, welfare and distributional effects of a structural policy depend on the price policy framework in a market. At free trade no price reduction would occur, consumer surplus would remain unchanged and only producers would benefit and get the whole welfare increase. A price policy implementing a fixed domestic price independent of demand would also have a similar effect. In a closed economy without price interventions by the government the distributional effects of a structural policy depend on the elasticities. The more inelastic the demand is, the more consumers benefit from the structural policy due to a high price reduction at the expense of producers.

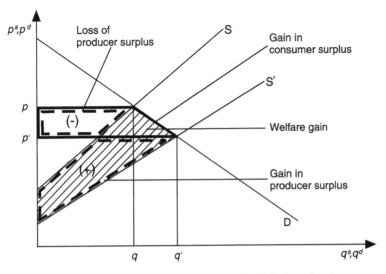

Figure 9.2 Welfare and distributional effects of structural policies in a closed economy.

Structural policies of a government raise a number of interesting questions on policy-making, which can only briefly be outlined in this book. A central question is: should structural policies be pursued at all by governments; in other words, should structures be changed by the government? Doubts are expressed in many cases if government institutions really know better how to develop structures in an economy than private businesses and companies. In other cases, for example, in transition countries, suitable structural policies can clearly promote the competitiveness of businesses. While structural policies often aim explicitly at facilitating adjustment processes of producers and enhancing productivity, the price policy framework should not be ignored and possible price reductions as a consequence of a structural policy should be taken into account. In the context of developing countries, the idea of supporting agricultural development without opening up the markets should be reflected critically. In particular, integration into international markets may reduce the price pressure of national structural policies. It thus seems questionable if the idea of enhancing productivity in the agricultural sector by structural policies in a closed economy is a suitable concept to help producers.

Structural policies are often criticised for increasing the negative consequences of a protectionist price policy; but this argument too has limitations. Without doubt, a protectionist price policy leads to a welfare loss and, in an export case, to government budget expenditure as shown in Figure 9.3. It is also correct to say that, in this case, a structural policy increases government budget expenditure, but, of course, the structural policy would also lead to a welfare gain. Hence the evaluation of a structural policy in a certain price policy framework depends on the political objectives considered. This again shows that looking only at government budget effects can mislead the evaluation of structural policies and

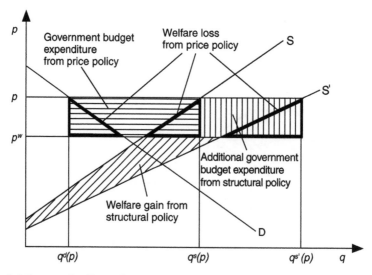

Figure 9.3 Structural policy under a protectionist price policy in an export case.

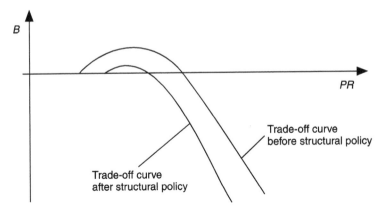

Figure 9.4 Changes in the trade-off between producer surplus and government budget under a protectionist price policy through a structural policy (cf. Figure 5.2).

that self-sufficiency is certainly not a convincing indicator to assess whether a structural policy should be applied or not.

Generally, structural policies change the trade-off between relevant political objectives and thus the scope for policy-making. If, as discussed in Chapter 5, the aims are to increase producer surplus through a protectionist price policy and, at the same time, to limit budget expenditure, a trade-off curve for these two objectives can be developed (Figure 9.4). The structural policy would shift the trade-off curve to the left, hence limiting the scope for the price policy. But structural policies can also lead to an increase in the scope for policy-making. For example, it is clear that the welfare gain from a structural policy increases the scope for distribution to producers and consumers. A trade-off curve between producer surplus and consumer surplus would thus shift to the right. Again, the results depend on the political objectives considered and the changes in trade-offs between these objectives can greatly differ.

Exercise 9

Consider the supply function

$$q^s(p^s) = c(1 + f)(p^s)^{\varepsilon^s}$$

with $\varepsilon^s = 0.3$ and
          f – shift parameter

and the demand function

$$q^d(p^d) = d(p^d)^{\varepsilon^d}$$

with $\varepsilon^d = -0.4.$

For the calibration of the functions we take the values from Exercise 4: $p^s = 15$, $p^d = 12$, $q^s = 80$ and $q^d = 100$; the world market price is $p^w = 10$. Solve the following problems:

(a) A structural policy, with a budget expenditure of 100, shifts the supply curve by 10 per cent to the right. How do consumer surplus, producer surplus, welfare and net welfare change?

(b) What impact would the considered structural policy (a) have on the political objectives at free trade and autarky?

(c) Compare the effects of the considered structural policy at autarky on consumer surplus and producer surplus as under (b) with the results at (absolute) high elasticity values ($\varepsilon^s = 0.5$, $\varepsilon^d = -0.7$) and at (absolute) low elasticity values ($\varepsilon^s = 0.1$, $\varepsilon^d = -0.2$).

(d) Assume the initial elasticities. Compare the impact of the considered structural policy under a protectionist price policy on welfare and government budget for $p = 12$ and $p = 20$ at $p^w = 10$.

(e) Assume the base situation under a protectionist price policy. Compare the trade-off between producer surplus and government budget ($-400 \leq B \leq 0$) before and after the structural policy (compare with Exercise 5c).

Solution

Step 9.1   We can again use the calibrated model from exercise4a.xls. We enter the new shift parameter with a preliminary value of 0 in cell F8 and add the factor (1 + F8) to the formulas for the quantity supplied (E4) and cost (H4) (cf. Figure 9.5 and exercise9.xls).

Step 9.2   In order to solve Exercise 9a we now only need to enter the value 0.1 in cell F8 and display the changes in the relevant variables as shown in Figure 9.6. Under the considered price policy the structural policy leads to a welfare increase for producers. Since the budget expenditure for the structural policy is greater than the welfare gain, the overall net welfare effect is negative.

Step 9.3   For Exercise 9b set the prices at 10 to simulate free trade (cf. Figure 9.7) and, in the autarky case, use the Solver twice (as in Exercise 1e)

H4		f_x =A4*E4-B8*A4^(D8+1)/(D8+1)*(1+F8)							
A	B	C	D	E	F	G	H	I
1 Cobb-Douglas Market Model with Calibration and Supply Shift Parameter								
2								
3 p^s	p^d	p^w		Supply	Demand		Cost	Total benefit
4 15.00	12.00	10.00		80.00	100.00		276.92	3908.72
5 15.00	12.00	Parameters of calibration		80.00	100.00			
6	Constants			Elasticities		Shift parameter		
7	c	d	of supply	of demand	f			
8	35.50280027	270.1920077	0.3	-0.4	0			

Figure 9.5 Cobb–Douglas market model with calibration and shift parameter (exercise9.xls).

	A	B	C	D	E	F	G	H	I
1	Cobb-Douglas Market Model with Calibration and Supply Shift Parameter								
2									
3	p^s	p^d	p^w		Supply	Demand		Cost	Total benefit
4	15.00	12.00	10.00		88.00	100.00		304.62	3908.72
5	15.00	12.00	Parameters of calibration		80.00	100.00			
6		Constants			Elasticities		Shift parameter		
7		c	d	of supply	of demand		f		
8		35.50280027	270.1920077	0.3	-0.4		0.1		
9									
10		CS	PS	W	NW	BES			
11	f = 0,1	2708.72	1015.38	3484.11	3384.11	100			
12	f = 0	2708.72	923.08	3431.80	3431.80				
13	Delta	0.00	92.31	52.31	-47.69				

Figure 9.6 Impact of a structural policy (exercise9a.xls).

	A	B	C	D	E	F	G	H	I
1	Cobb-Douglas Market Model with Calibration and Supply Shift Parameter								
2									
3	p^s	p^d	p^w		Supply	Demand		Cost	Total benefit
4	10.00	10.00	10.00		77.92	107.57		179.82	3991.62
5	15.00	12.00	Parameters of calibration		80.00	100.00			
6		Constants			Elasticities		Shift parameter		
7		c	d	of supply	of demand		f		
8		35.50280027	270.1920077	0.3	-0.4		0.1		
9									
10		CS	PS	W	NW	BES			
11	f = 0,1	2915.97	599.39	3515.36	3415.36	100			
12	f = 0	2915.97	544.90	3460.87	3460.87				
13	Delta	0.00	54.49	54.49	-45.51				

Figure 9.7 Impact of a structural policy at free trade (exercise9b1.xls).

	A	B	C	D	E	F	G	H	I
1	Cobb-Douglas Market Model with Calibration and Supply Shift Parameter								
2									
3	p^s	p^d	p^w		Supply	Demand		Cost	Total benefit
4	15.85	15.85	10.00		89.47	89.47		327.24	3763.37
5	15.00	12.00	Parameters of calibration		80.00	100.00			
6		Constants			Elasticities		Shift parameter		
7		c	d	of supply	of demand		f		
8		35.50280027	270.1920077	0.3	-0.4		0.1		
9									
10		CS	PS	W	NW	BES			
11	f = 0,1	2345.33	1090.80	3436.13	3336.13	100			
12	f = 0	2144.12	1183.61	3327.80	3327.80				
13	Delta	201.21	-92.81	108.33	8.33				

Figure 9.8 Impact of a structural policy at autarky (exercise9b2.xls).

(cf. Figure 9.8). At free trade producers are the only beneficiaries of the structural policy and the welfare gain is equal to the increase in producer surplus; however, the net welfare effect remains negative. At autarky consumers clearly gain from the price reduction, while the welfare level of the producers even declines. Interestingly in this case, the considered structural policy leads to a positive net welfare effect. This may be explained by a significant higher price level under autarky compared to the base situation and free trade.

Step 9.4   If you want to assess the impact of the structural policy at autarky for different elasticities, as required in Exercise 9c, you need to enter these elasticities in cell D8 and cell E8 (cf. Figures 9.9 and 9.10), set a uniform domestic price (formula = A4 in cell B4) and use the Solver for *f* = *0* and *f* = *0.1* (with A4 as changing cell and E4 = F4 as constraint).

At comparably high elasticity values the negative effects for producers and positive effects for consumers are reduced. On the other hand, at comparably low elasticities the redistributional effect from producers to consumers is even greater than at the initial elasticity values. The different total welfare effects are a consequence of the different price levels resulting from the model calibration.

Step 9.5   For Exercise 9d follow the same procedure as in Exercise 9a and take into

	A	B	C	D	E	F	G	H	I
1	Cobb-Douglas Market Model with Calibration and Supply Shift Parameter								
2									
3	p^s	p^d	p^w		Supply	Demand		Cost	Total benefit
4	14.65	14.65	10.00		86.97	86.97		424.67	3164.87
5	15.00	12.00	Parameters of calibration		80.00	100.00			
6		Constants			Elasticities		Shift parameter		
7		c	d	of supply	of demand	f			
8		20.65591118	569.4123368	0.5	-0.7	0.1			
9									
10		CS	PS	W	NW	BES			
11	f = 0,1	1890.86	849.34	2740.20	2640.20	100			
12	f = 0	1788.45	869.82	2658.28	2658.28				
13	Delta	102.40	-20.48	81.92	-18.08				

Figure 9.9 Impact of a structural policy at autarky at ε^s = *0.5* and ε^d = −*0.7* (exercise9c1.xls).

	A	B	C	D	E	F	G	H	I
1	Cobb-Douglas Market Model with Calibration and Supply Shift Parameter								
2									
3	p^s	p^d	p^w		Supply	Demand		Cost	Total benefit
4	19.79	19.79	10.00		90.47	90.47		162.81	4250.38
5	15.00	12.00	Parameters of calibration		80.00	100.00			
6		Constants			Elasticities		Shift parameter		
7		c	d	of supply	of demand	f			
8		61.02121646	164.375183	0.1	-0.2	0.1			
9									
10		CS	PS	W	NW	BES			
11	f = 0,1	2459.48	1628.09	4087.57	3987.57	100			
12	f = 0	1811.67	2099.22	3910.89	3910.89				
13	Delta	647.81	-471.13	176.68	76.68				

Figure 9.10 Impact of a structural policy at autarky at ε^s = *0.1* and ε^d = −*0.2* (exercise9c2.xls).

	A	B	C	D	E	F	G	H	I
1	Cobb-Douglas Market Model with Calibration and Supply Shift Parameter								
2									
3	p^s	p^d	p^w		Supply	Demand		Cost	Total benefit
4	12.00	12.00	10.00		82.30	100.00		227.91	3908.72
5	15.00	12.00	Parameters of calibration		80.00	100.00			
6		Constants			Elasticities	Shift parameter			
7		c	d	of supply	of demand	f			
8		35.50280027	270.1920077	0.3	-0.4	0.1			
9									
10		CS	PS	B	W	NW	BES		
11	f = 0,1	2708.72	759.71	35.40	3503.83	3403.83	100		
12	f = 0	2708.72	690.65	50.36	3449.73	3449.73			
13	Delta	0.00	69.06	-14.96	54.10	-45.90			

Figure 9.11 Impact of a structural policy at $p = 12$ and $p^w = 10$ (exercise9d1.xls).

	A	B	C	D	E	F	G	H	I
1	Cobb-Douglas Market Model with Calibration and Supply Shift Parameter								
2									
3	p^s	p^d	p^w		Supply	Demand		Cost	Total benefit
4	20.00	20.00	10.00		95.93	81.52		442.76	3621.80
5	15.00	12.00	Parameters of calibration		80.00	100.00			
6		Constants			Elasticities	Shift parameter			
7		c	d	of supply	of demand	f			
8		35.50280027	270.1920077	0.3	-0.4	0.1			
9									
10		CS	PS	B	W	NW	BES		
11	f = 0,1	1991.41	1475.88	-144.13	3323.16	3223.16	100		
12	f = 0	1991.41	1341.71	-56.92	3276.20	3276.20			
13	Delta	0.00	134.17	-87.21	46.96	-53.04			

Figure 9.12 Impact of a structural policy at $p = 20$ and $p^w = 10$ (exercise9d2.xls).

account the protectionist price policy setting and revised budget values (cf. Figures 9.11 and 9.12).

Under the considered price policy in Exercise 9d the structural policy leads to a greater increase in producer surplus and a greater reduction of the budget at the high price level. Consumer surplus remains unchanged and the net welfare effect is negative, at similar levels, in both cases.

Step 9.6   Let us now solve Exercise 9e. The situation before the structural policy is exactly depicted by the Excel model in exercise5c2.xls (cf. Figure 5.8). You get the relevant trade-off for the situation after the structural policy for $f = 0.1$ as described in Step 5.3. By adding the new data series to the chart, you can compare the two curves as shown in Figure 9.13.

Figure 9.13 shows that the structural policy decreases the scope for the price policy to increase producer surplus at a given budget expenditure. The structural policy thus shifts the trade-off curve to the left.

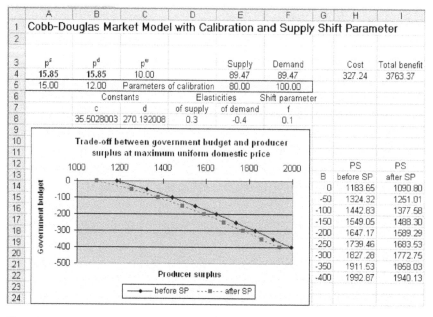

	A	B	C	D	E	F	G	H	I
1	Cobb-Douglas Market Model with Calibration and Supply Shift Parameter								
2									
3	p^z	p^d	p^w		Supply	Demand		Cost	Total benefit
4	15.85	15.85	10.00		89.47	89.47		327.24	3763.37
5	15.00	12.00	Parameters of calibration		80.00	100.00			
6		Constants			Elasticities		Shift parameter		
7		c	d	of supply	of demand		f		
8		35.5028003	270.192008	0.3	-0.4		0.1		
9									

Trade-off between government budget and producer surplus at maximum uniform domestic price

	B	PS before SP	PS after SP
	0	1183.65	1090.80
	-50	1324.32	1251.01
	-100	1442.83	1377.58
	-150	1549.05	1488.30
	-200	1647.17	1589.29
	-250	1739.46	1683.53
	-300	1827.28	1772.75
	-350	1911.53	1858.03
	-400	1992.87	1940.13

Figure 9.13 Trade-off between government budget and producer surplus under a protectionist price policy before and after a structural policy (exercise9e.xls).

References

Koester, U. (2005) *Grundzüge der landwirtschaftlichen Marktlehre* (3rd edn), Munich: Vahlen, pp. 116–25 (WiSo-Kurzlehrbücher: Reihe Volkswirtschaft).

Nicholson, W. (2005) *Microeconomic Theory: Basic Principles and Extensions* (9th edn), Mason, OH: Thomson, pp. 289–91.

Pindyck, R.S. and Rubinfeld, D.L. (2005) *Microeconomics* (6th edn), Upper Saddle River, NJ: Pearson Prentice Hall, pp. 19–32.

10 Implications of structural policies over time

Objective

In Chapter 10 we incorporate the time dimension in the analysis of structural policies. We will show how the impact of structural policies can be depicted and compared over time.

Theory

So far, we have not considered the time dimension in the formulation of market models. The analysis was comparative-static, i.e. we have analysed the implications of a policy regarding its impact on equilibrium values without considering the time horizon in which these changes happen. But the analysis of structural policies requires, at least to some extent, to take into account the time dimension. A supply curve shift induced by a structural policy is likely to occur over several time periods and the analysis should therefore try to capture this time dimension. Furthermore, supply shifts on markets will also occur without structural policies and the impact of a structural policy would then be the difference between two development paths, with and without structural policy, for the political objectives considered.

Figure 10.1 shows such an impact analysis of a structural policy over a specific period of time. A structural policy in the base period results in a change in the development path of welfare over the considered time span of 15 years. The difference between the two development paths describes the impact of the structural policy at each point of time. In Figure 10.1 budget expenditure occurring for the structural policy is not included. A development path of net welfare would have a lower value in the base period, if budget expenditure would occur in that period and, similarly, the value would also be lower than shown in Figure 10.1 over the years 1 to 15, if budget expenditure for the structural policy would also occur in those years.

To describe such development paths, shift parameters and budget expenditures of a structural policy need to be determined for each period of time which then provides the basis for the calculation of the political objectives considered in these periods. It may also be plausible to use a simplified assumption such as an average

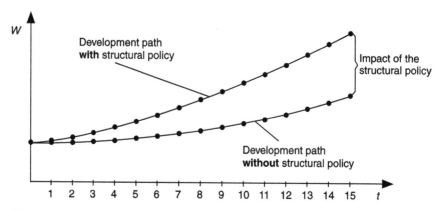

Figure 10.1 Impact of structural policies over time.

shift parameter for each resultant period. The supply function in (9.1) would then be defined as:

$$q_t^s(p^s) = c(1 + f^d)^t (p^s)^{\varepsilon^s}; \qquad \varepsilon^s > 0 \tag{10.1}$$

with
  q_t^s – quantity supplied in period t
  f^d – average shift parameter (from one period to the following)
  t – time period ($t = 0, \ldots, n$).

This formulation allows us to compare equilibriums at different periods and the respective values of their political variables, applying a comparative-static analysis in a time context. This is not a dynamic analysis, since this would entail that variables in a certain period would be dependent on variables of previous periods and require, for example, the formulation of suitable differential equations. Hence our 'comparative-dynamic approach' is not truly dynamic, but allows, to some extent, the incorporation of the time dimension into the analysis in a straightforward way.

Since the analysis of the impact of structural policies on net welfare is comparable to a cost–benefit analysis of projects, the analytical tool of cost–benefit analysis may also be applied for the analysis of structural policies. In a cost–benefit analysis of a project, incoming and outgoing cash flows are compared over time whereby the net receipts of a project are comparable to the net welfare effects of structural policies. In fact, the evaluation of net welfare effects of structural policies could also be described as a cost–benefit analysis of a 'big project'.

Figure 10.2 depicts the impact of a structural policy on net welfare over time. The development path of net welfare results from the difference of the welfare paths depicted in Figure 10.1 and also takes into account the budget expenditure for the structural policy in the base period. In cost–benefit analysis it is common practice to discount all future benefits and costs to their present value to allow for comparison of cash flows occurring over different periods of time. The net

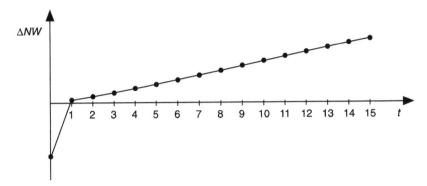

Figure 10.2 Net welfare effects of a structural policy over time.

present value describes the difference between the present value of all cash inflows (benefit) and the present value of all cash outflows (cost). Applying the method to our case, we would calculate the (discounted) present value of all net welfare effects of a structural policy considered. We can write:

$$PV = \sum_{t=0}^{n} \frac{1}{(1+i)^t} (\Delta NW_t) \tag{10.2}$$

with PV – present value of net welfare effects (of a structural policy at
          the base period $t = 0$)
          i – interest rate.

Discounting future net welfare effects implies that net welfare effects are more valuable the sooner they occur. A preference for the presence seems plausible; we typically assume that the interest rate on a perfect capital market would exactly reflect the time preference of a society. In practical applications the interest rate for long-term bonds is often used as an approximation for the time preference of a society. Overall, the present value of net welfare effects is an indicator of the assessment if, and to what extent, a structural policy is worth pursuing and implementing. If the present value of net welfare effects of a certain structural policy is negative, this policy should not be implemented and alternative options should be explored. On the other hand, it implies that positive effects of a structural policy are expected to be greater the higher its present value.

Another important indicator is the internal rate of return, which indicates at which interest rate the present value of net welfare of a structural policy becomes zero. We can write:

$$\sum_{t=0}^{n} \frac{1}{(1+IRR)^t} (\Delta NW_t) = 0 \tag{10.3}$$

with   *IRR*   – internal rate of return.

This implies that a structural policy is only economically viable if the internal rate of return is at least as high as the interest rate characterising the time preference of a society. If this is the case, then, of course, a higher internal rate of return indicates higher potential benefits from an intended structural policy.

The market model formulated in this chapter may be used for the analysis of different types of structural policies so long as the relevant budget expenditures for the structural policy and shift effects of the supply curve can be determined for the considered time periods. Moreover, the formulated market model may be applied for the analysis of other policy interventions, which lead to shifts of supply curves. The infant industry argument provides an example where a protectionist price policy would lead to a shift of the supply curve through the introduction of a temporary tariff. Figure 10.3 shows the impact of such a temporary protection. The tariff leads initially to a static welfare loss, indicated by the bold-framed area. Then, it is argued, temporary protectionism would allow the 'infant industry' to grow and develop. Domestic producers would increase their productivity and become more competitive, leading to an increase in supply from $q^s(p)$ to $q^{s'}(p)$. Thus we get a price policy-induced shift of the supply curve, which leads to a 'dynamic' welfare gain indicated by the hatched area.

A critical evaluation of the infant industry argument should first assess the main assumption that a protectionist price policy leads to an increase in productivity. In fact, it seems plausible to assume that price protection could also lead to the opposite effect. Less competition could mean that production becomes more inefficient which would result in a leftward shift of the supply curve. If the latter

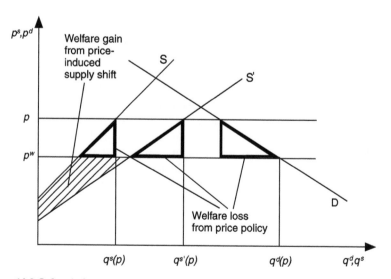

Figure 10.3 Infant industry argument.

applies, that, of course, would be another argument against any protectionist price policy, temporary or not.

But even if the main assumption of the infant industry argument applies, this would not automatically justify the implementation of price protection. What would rather be required is to compare the 'dynamic' welfare gain (from the price-induced supply shift) with the 'static' welfare loss (from the protectionist price policy). In fact, this is a typical case for the application of cost–benefit analysis if the present value of net welfare following the infant industry argument is positive in comparison to free trade. Moreover, it is also possible that other policy options, such as a targeted structural policy, could achieve the desired shift effect more efficiently than a temporary price protection. In this context, Figure 10.3 shows that, for example, a producer subsidy would be superior to infant industry protection and would lead to a higher present value of net welfare, since such a policy would not cause a welfare loss on the demand side.

Exercise 10

Consider the supply function for the period t:

$$q_t^s(p^s) = c\,(1 + f^{d})^t\,(p^s)^{\varepsilon^s}$$

with $\varepsilon^s = 0.3$

and the demand function

$$q^d(p^d) = d\,(p^d)^{\varepsilon^d}$$

with $\varepsilon^d = -0.4.$

For the calibration we again take the values from Exercise 4: $p^s = 15, p^d = 12, q^s = 80$ and $q^d = 100$; the world market price is $p^w = 10$. Solve the following problems:

(a) Show how self-sufficiency and budget expenditure develop over 15 years at a supply shift of 2.5 per cent per year.

(b) A structural policy with a budget expenditure of 100 in the base period $(t = 0)$ increases the supply shift to 3.5 per cent per year. Compare the development of welfare with and without the structural policy over time.

(c) What present value at $i = 0.1$ and what internal rate of return can be calculated for this structural policy?

(d) Infant industry protection with a tariff of 40 per cent leads to an increase in the supply shift from 1 per cent to 2 per cent in comparison to free trade. Show the impact of infant industry protection on welfare over time. What present value of welfare at $i = 0.1$ and what internal rate of return can be calculated following the infant industry argument?

(e) Compare the result from (d) with the respective impact of a producer subsidy of 40 per cent.

Solution

Step 10.1 Add an average shift parameter f^d of 0.025 to the supply function in cell H10, using the model exercise9.xls. Produce a series for the years (periods) 0, 1, 2, ..., 15 in the cells G11:G26. Enter now the formula $= (1 + \$H\$10)^\wedge G11 - 1$ (compound interest formula) in H11 and copy the formula to H12:H26. You can add the $ symbols with the F4 key to fix the cell references in the formulas. By using 'Data, table' (regarding H10:J26 and F8 as input cell) and 'Chart wizard' in the usual way we get the graph for self-sufficiency and budget expenditure (cf. Figure 10.4 and exercise10a.xls).

The graph shows that, at the assumed growth rate of supply, the country becomes an exporter after 10 years and budget expenditure nearly doubles over the 15 years.

Step 10.2 To compare the development of welfare for $f^d = 2.5$ per cent and $f^d = 3.5$ per cent proceed as in Step 10.1 (compare with Figure 10.5 and exercise10b.xls). Be aware that you need to apply 'Data, table' twice.

Step 10.3 In order to provide the data to solve Exercise 10c, we expand the model by adding ΔNW in the cells L11:L26 defined as the difference of the respective 'welfare cells' in columns I and K and deducting budget expenditure for the structural policy. Since only in the base period budget expenditure for the structural policy of $BES = 100$ occurs, we just need to subtract this expenditure from the value in cell L11; i.e. we change the formula in cell L11 to $= I11 - K11 - 100$. We now enter the

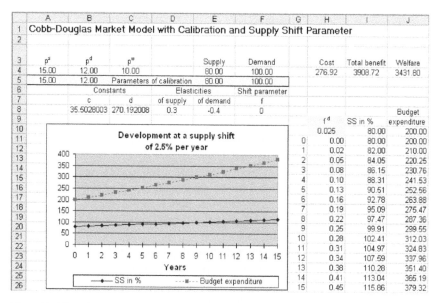

Figure 10.4 Development of self-sufficiency and budget expenditure at a supply shift of 2.5 per cent per year (exercise10a.xls).

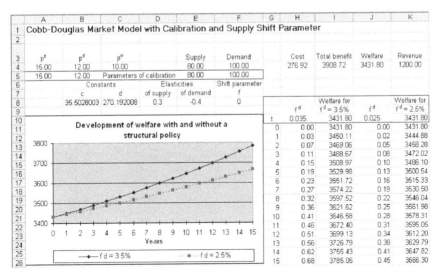

Cobb-Douglas Market Model with Calibration and Supply Shift Parameter

p^s	p^d	p^w		Supply	Demand		Cost	Total benefit	Welfare	Revenue
15.00	12.00	10.00		80.00	100.00		276.92	3908.72	3431.80	1200.00
15.00	12.00	Parameters of calibration		80.00	100.00					
	Constants			Elasticities		Shift parameter				
	c	d		of supply	of demand	f				
	35.5028003	270.192008		0.3	-0.4	0				

t	f^d 0.035	Welfare for $f^d = 3.5\%$	f^d 0.025	Welfare for $f^d = 2.5\%$
0	0.00	3431.80	0.00	3431.80
1	0.03	3450.11	0.02	3444.88
2	0.07	3469.06	0.05	3458.28
3	0.11	3488.67	0.08	3472.02
4	0.15	3508.97	0.10	3486.10
5	0.19	3529.98	0.13	3500.54
6	0.23	3551.72	0.16	3515.33
7	0.27	3574.22	0.19	3530.50
8	0.32	3597.52	0.22	3546.04
9	0.36	3621.62	0.25	3561.98
10	0.41	3646.58	0.28	3578.31
11	0.46	3672.40	0.31	3595.05
12	0.51	3699.13	0.34	3612.20
13	0.56	3726.79	0.38	3629.79
14	0.62	3755.43	0.41	3647.82
15	0.68	3785.06	0.45	3666.30

Development of welfare with and without a structural policy

(chart: Years 0–15; series $f d = 3.5\%$ and $f d = 2.5\%$)

Figure 10.5 Development of welfare with and without a structural policy (exercise 10b.xls).

present value of net welfare at $i = 0.1$ and the internal rate of return in cell L28 and cell L29, respectively, following (10.2) and (10.3). To do this, click on 'Insert function', choose the category 'Financial' and select the functions NPV and IRR (cf. Figure 10.6 and exercise 10c.xls). Note that in cell L28 we have to enter the formula $=$ NPV $(10\%, L12:L26) +$ L11 since the Excel function NPV calculates the present value for the periods $t = 1, \ldots, 15$ with respect to the preceding period $t = 0$.

The considered structural policy apparently seems to be quite successful. The present value of the welfare gain is twice as high as the budget expenditure and the internal rate of return is as high as 26 per cent.

Step 10.4 To solve Exercise 10d you use the model from the previous exercise (exercise 10c.xls). Since we want to compare the impact of infant industry protection with free trade, we need first to set all prices at 10. Remove the budget expenditure for the structural policy (–100) from the formula in cell L11 (ΔNW in the base period), so that the formula now reads as $=$ I11 – K11. Next, update the values for f^d to 0.02 in cell H10 and to 0.01 in cell J10 and the characters in cells I9 and K9, respectively. The welfare values at free trade now need to be defined as base values. To do this, you select the whole range K11:K26, click on 'Copy' followed by 'Paste special' with the option 'Values'. To implement infant industry protection with a tariff of 40 per cent, you now only need to change the supply price and the demand price from 10 to 14 and you automatically get the desired welfare curve in the chart. Simultaneously, you get an internal rate of return of 4 per cent in cell L29 and a negative present value of –60.68 (cf. Figure 10.7 and exercise 10d.xls). Hence, the assessment of the shift effect induced by infant industry

	L28	▼	=	=NPV(10%,L12:L26)+L11	
	G	H	I	J	K	L

	G	H	I	J	K	L
8			Welfare for		Welfare for	
9		f^d	f^d = 3.5%	f^d	f^d = 2.5%	
10	t	0.035	3431.80	0.025	3431.80	Delta NW
11	0	0.00	3431.80	0.00	3431.80	-100.00
12	1	0.03	3450.11	0.02	3444.88	5.23
13	2	0.07	3469.06	0.05	3458.28	10.78
14	3	0.11	3488.67	0.08	3472.02	16.65
15	4	0.15	3508.97	0.10	3486.10	22.86
16	5	0.19	3529.98	0.13	3500.54	29.44
17	6	0.23	3551.72	0.16	3515.33	36.39
18	7	0.27	3574.22	0.19	3530.50	43.73
19	8	0.32	3597.52	0.22	3546.04	51.47
20	9	0.36	3621.62	0.25	3561.98	59.65
21	10	0.41	3646.58	0.28	3578.31	68.27
22	11	0.46	3672.40	0.31	3595.05	77.35
23	12	0.51	3699.13	0.34	3612.20	86.92
24	13	0.56	3726.79	0.38	3629.79	97.00
25	14	0.62	3755.43	0.41	3647.82	107.61
26	15	0.68	3785.06	0.45	3666.30	118.76
27						
28					PV:	218.35
29					IRR:	26%

Figure 10.6 Present value and internal rate of return of a structural policy (exercise10c.xls).

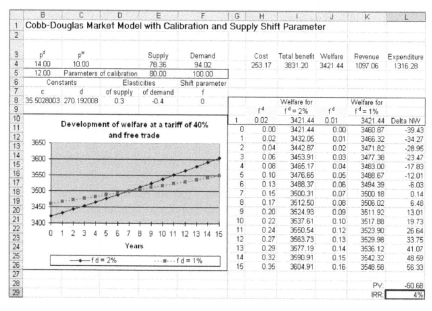

	B	C	D	E	F	G	H	I	J	K	L
1	Cobb-Douglas Market Model with Calibration and Supply Shift Parameter										
2											
3	p^d	p^w		Supply	Demand		Cost	Total benefit	Welfare	Revenue	Expenditure
4	14.00	10.00		78.36	94.02		253.17	3831.20	3421.44	1097.06	1316.28
5	12.00	Parameters of calibration		80.00	100.00						
6	Constants			Elasticities	Shift parameter						
7	c	d	of supply	of demand	f						
8	35.5028003	270.192008	0.3	-0.4	0			Welfare for		Welfare for	
9							f^d	f^d = 2%	f^d	f^d = 1%	
10						t	0.02	3421.44	0.01	3421.44	Delta NW
11						0	0.00	3421.44	0.00	3460.87	-39.43
12						1	0.02	3432.05	0.01	3466.32	-34.27
13						2	0.04	3442.87	0.02	3471.82	-28.95
14						3	0.06	3453.91	0.03	3477.38	-23.47
15						4	0.08	3465.17	0.04	3483.00	-17.83
16						5	0.10	3476.65	0.05	3488.67	-12.01
17						6	0.13	3488.37	0.06	3494.39	-6.03
18						7	0.15	3500.31	0.07	3500.18	0.14
19						8	0.17	3512.50	0.08	3506.02	6.48
20						9	0.20	3524.93	0.09	3511.92	13.01
21						10	0.22	3537.61	0.10	3517.88	19.73
22						11	0.24	3550.54	0.12	3523.90	26.64
23						12	0.27	3563.73	0.13	3529.98	33.75
24						13	0.29	3577.19	0.14	3536.12	41.07
25						14	0.32	3590.91	0.15	3542.32	48.59
26						15	0.35	3604.91	0.16	3548.58	56.33
27											
28										PV:	-60.68
29										IRR:	4%

Chart (rows 10–26, columns B–F): "Development of welfare at a tariff of 40% and free trade", vertical axis from 3400 to 3650, horizontal axis "Years" 0–15, series: ◆ f d = 2%, ■ f d = 1%.

Figure 10.7 Development of welfare at a tariff of 40 per cent and free trade (exercise10d.xls).

protection is not so positive: price protection results in only 4 per cent interest, which, at an interest rate of 10 per cent, is equal to a negative present value of infant industry protection.

Step 10.5 Let us finally solve Exercise 10e. For comparison, copy the values for ΔNW, PV and IRR (in other words, for the whole range L11:L29) to N11:N29. Next, implement the producer subsidy of 40 per cent with $p^s = 14$, $p^d = 10$ and $p^w = 10$. We can see that the producer subsidy is clearly superior to infant industry protection. The present value of the welfare effects is positive with 154.19 and the internal rate of return is 37 per cent. The 'static' welfare loss of this policy instrument will already be outweighed by the 'dynamic' welfare gain in the third year, compared to the seventh year in the case of infant industry protection (cf. Figure 10.8 and exercise10e.xls).

	G	H	I	J	K	L	M	N	O
6								Infant	
7								industry	Producer
8			Welfare for		Welfare for			protection	subsidy
9		f^d	f^d = 2%	f^d	f^d = 1%			at 14,14,10	at 14,10,10
10	t	0.02	3446.41	0.01	3446.41	Delta NW		Delta NW	Delta NW
11	0	0.00	3446.41	0.00	3460.87	-14.46		-39.43	-14.46
12	1	0.02	3457.02	0.01	3466.32	-9.30		-34.27	-9.30
13	2	0.04	3467.84	0.02	3471.82	-3.98		-28.95	-3.98
14	3	0.06	3478.88	0.03	3477.38	1.50		-23.47	1.50
15	4	0.08	3490.14	0.04	3483.00	7.14		-17.83	7.14
16	5	0.10	3501.62	0.05	3488.67	12.96		-12.01	12.96
17	6	0.13	3513.34	0.06	3494.39	18.94		-6.03	18.94
18	7	0.15	3525.28	0.07	3500.18	25.10		0.14	25.10
19	8	0.17	3537.47	0.08	3506.02	31.45		6.48	31.45
20	9	0.20	3549.90	0.09	3511.92	37.98		13.01	37.98
21	10	0.22	3562.58	0.10	3517.88	44.70		19.73	44.70
22	11	0.24	3575.51	0.12	3523.90	51.61		26.64	51.61
23	12	0.27	3588.70	0.13	3529.98	58.72		33.75	58.72
24	13	0.29	3602.16	0.14	3536.12	66.04		41.07	66.04
25	14	0.32	3615.88	0.15	3542.32	73.56		48.59	73.56
26	15	0.35	3629.88	0.16	3548.58	81.29		56.33	81.29
27									
28					PV:	154.19		-60.68	154.19
29					IRR:	37%		4%	37%

Development of welfare at a producer subsidy of 40% and free trade

Figure 10.8 Impact of a producer subsidy and the infant industry argument on the development of welfare (exercise10e.xls).

References

Chiang, A.C. and Wainwright, K. (2005) *Fundamental Methods of Mathematical Economics* (4th edn), Boston, MA: McGraw-Hill, pp. 256–9.

Corden, W.M. (1997) *Trade Policy and Economic Welfare* (2nd edn), New York, Oxford: Oxford University Press, pp. 139–61.

Just, R.E., Hueth, D.L. and Schmitz, A. (2004) *The Welfare Economics of Public Policy: A Practical Approach to Project and Policy Evaluation*, Cheltenham, Northampton, MA: Edward Elgar, pp. 572–86.

Koester, U. (2005) *Grundzüge der landwirtschaftlichen Marktlehre* (3rd edn), Munich: Vahlen, pp. 239–42 (WiSo-Kurzlehrbücher: Reihe Volkswirtschaft).

Nicholson, W. (2005) *Microeconomic Theory: Basic Principles and Extensions* (9th edn), Mason, OH: Thomson, pp. 500–12.

Pindyck, R.S. and Rubinfeld, D.L. (2005) *Microeconomics* (6th edn), Upper Saddle River, NJ: Pearson Prentice Hall, pp. 547–57.

Varian, H.R. (2003) *Intermediate Microeconomics: A Modern Approach* (6th edn), New York: W.W. Norton, pp. 191–201.

Winston, W.L. (2004) *Operations Research* (4th edn), Belmont, CA: Brooks/Cole, pp. 76–82.

11 Optimal structural policies

Objective

In Chapter 11 we will analyse the formulation and design of structural policies. We will discuss which and to what extent structural policies should be funded, and show what consequences budget constraints have in this context.

Theory

In the discussion of structural policies thus far, we have considered only one structural policy at a time and analysed the impact of this policy on political objectives, in particular welfare. If, however, several structural policies can be pursued at the same time, the question arises to what extent each of these policies should be financed to achieve the defined targets and objectives. The structure and principles of this optimisation problem will be discussed on the basis of Chapter 10. We will again focus our analysis on the net welfare effects of structural policies.

Let us first consider different structural policies for which the present value of net welfare effects has been calculated. Figure 11.1 shows the aggregated present value of altogether four structural policies and compares the aggregated present value with the budget expenditure for these policies in the period zero. The structural policies are depicted in order of their contribution to the objective resulting in a step function as shown. But which combination of the different policies would deliver an optimal structural policy? Apparently, structural policy 4 should not be taken up at all, since it would lower the aggregated present value. The other three structural policies should be implemented, since these would increase the aggregated present value. According to their contribution to the welfare objective we can assign the greatest importance to structural policy 1, followed by structural policies 2 and 3.

However, this statement is only correct if all three structural policies can be financed. If a budget constraint limits the financial scope for implementing the policies in period zero, an optimal structural policy may consist of a different combination of the three different policies, resulting in a different hierarchy of the considered three structural policies. If, for example, for the budget constraint *BE*

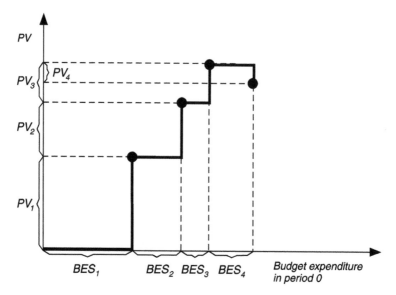

Figure 11.1 Aggregated present value of net welfare effects and budget expenditure for different structural policies in period zero.

implies that $BES_1 + BES_2 < BE < BES_1 + BES_2 + BES_3$, structural policy 3 would not be implemented, while for $BES_2 + BES_3 < BE < BES_1$ structural policy 1 would be abandoned and structural policies 2 and 3 implemented. This shows that in this example the relevance of the structural policies depends on the specific budget constraint. Moreover, it is important to note that for simplification the budget constraint has been limited to period zero. Finally, the relevance of structural policies may also depend on the implemented price policies, since these affect the extent of net welfare effects of structural policies.

The above example shows that the contribution of a structural policy to the political objective cannot be used as a stand-alone indicator to decide whether the structural policy should be implemented. In addition, developing a hierarchy (ranking) of the different contributions of structural policies to the political objectives is not particularly helpful. Without budget constraint a ranking is redundant, since all structural policies with a positive present value should be implemented; and with a budget constraint the recommendation of certain combinations of structural policies based on ranking may simply be wrong, since, following the greedy method, this approach must not lead to an optimal solution (cf. Keller *et al.* 2004, pp. 15–17, or Albright 2001, pp. 367–80).

From a mathematical point of view the discussed example is an integer, and more specifically a binary (0–1-)optimisation problem of the knapsack type, where structural policies have certain budget requirements and lead to a certain contribution to political objectives. In Figure 11.1, for example, it is assumed that only the specific amount of budget expenditure BES_1 for structural policy 1 leads to the present value of net welfare effects PV_1. A lower budget for structural policy

1 would make this policy ineffective, while a budget above BES_1 would not provide any additional (positive) impact on PV_1. Such an assumption might be appropriate for a concrete optimisation problem, but other conditions and assumptions are also plausible.

Let us now examine a continuous optimisation problem assuming that structural policies are arbitrarily divisible and a certain present value of net welfare effects PV_i (BES_i) can be defined for a structural policy i, so that for each argument BES_i a respective present value PV_i may be determined. Usually in this context we assume a strictly concave shape of the function, as defined in the law of diminishing returns. Figure 11.2 takes this into account; the figure modifies the example from Figure 11.1 accordingly, and depicts the respective functions.

As a result we get an optimisation problem which complies with the well-known condition of optimal input use of a firm. In our case the structural policies are to be financed to an extent which maximises the targeted political objective (the aggregated present value of net welfare effects), taking into account a budget constraint. If we assume that the budget can be fully utilised, we can solve this problem with the Lagrange method. If we consider only two structural policies, the Lagrange function may be defined as:

$$L = PV_1\,(BES_1) + PV_2\,(BES_2) + \lambda\,(BE - BES_1 - BES_2) \qquad (11.1)$$

with BE – budget expenditure (for the structural policies in period zero)
         λ – Lagrange multiplier.

The required condition for an optimum is:

$$\frac{dPV_1}{dBES_1} = \frac{dPV_2}{dBES_2} = \lambda. \qquad (11.2)$$

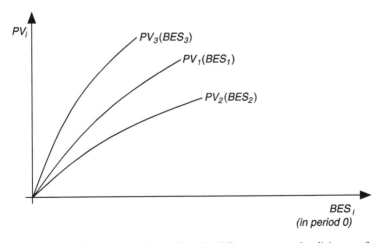

Figure 11.2 Present value of net welfare effects for different structural policies as a function of budget expenditure in period 0.

Hence, it applies for an optimal structural policy that the marginal present value of net welfare effects (in other words, the discounted 'marginal value product') of the first structural policy is equal to the marginal present value of the second structural policy or more generally: the marginal present value of all structural policies is the same.

In Figure 11.2 this condition is fulfilled if all functions have the same slope. This relationship is again depicted in Figure 11.3 showing the marginal present value functions. Without budget constraint the optimum would apparently be at BES_1' and BES_2'. In this case the shadow price of the budget constraint would be zero ($\lambda' = 0$). At λ'' the optimum condition results in BES_1'' and BES_2'', and at λ''' in BES_1''' and BES_2'''. For λ'' the hatched area illustrates the loss of present value, which would occur if budget expenditure for structural policy 1 would be increased at the expense of structural policy 2.

Of course, the functions shown in this example are based on simplified assumptions, and in reality it is important to estimate such functions in the best possible way. The rule for an optimal structural policy, derived above, then provides an indication for the assessment and improvement of the actual formulation of structural policies.

The allocation of budget expenditures and priority setting for different policies is apparently a complex optimisation problem. The example of the optimal formulation of structural policies outlines the principal approach, which, depending on the considered problem setting, needs to be further specified. Specific attention generally needs to be paid to the contribution of different policies to the political objective, in particular if more than one political objective needs to be taken into account. Moreover, budget constraints are usually more complex than here. A generalisation and a more in-depth discussion of budget allocation and priority setting will be conducted in Part IV.

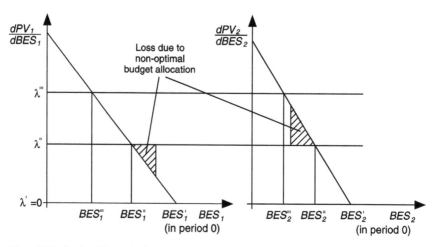

Figure 11.3 Optimal formulation of structural policies.

Exercise 11

Consider again the supply function for the period t:

$$q_i^s(p^s) = c\,(1 + f^d)^t\,(p^s)^{\varepsilon^s}$$

with $\quad \varepsilon^s = 0.3$

and the demand function

$$q^d(p^d) = d\,(p^d)^{\varepsilon^d}$$

with $\quad \varepsilon^d = -0.4$.

For the calibration we again take the values from Exercise 4: $p^s = 15$, $p^d = 12$, $q^s = 80$ and $q^d = 100$; the world market price is $p^w = 10$. Solve the following problems:

(a) The following structural policies are considered:

Policy	Average shift parameter (%)	Budget expenditure	
		Period 0	Period 1–15
A	1.0	200	
B	1.5	200	5
C	1.8	300	

Calculate the present value of net welfare effects of these structural policies for $i = 0.1$ and discuss which structural policies should be implemented at a budget constraint of 500 (400) in period 0.

(b) How does the importance of the discussed policies under (a) change at free trade?

(c) The following figures apply for structural policy A:

Average shift parameter (%)	Budget expenditure	
	Period 0	Period 1–15
1.3	100	
2.0	200	
2.5	300	
3.1	400	10
3.5	500	20

Display the present value of net welfare effects of the structural policy as a function of budget expenditure in period 0.

(d)   The following figures apply for structural policy B:

Average shift parameter (%)	Budget expenditure	
	Period 0	Period 1–15
1.0	100	
1.8	200	5
2.5	300	10
3.2	400	20
3.6	500	20

Display also the present value of net welfare effects of this structural policy as a function of budget expenditure in period 0 and compare the functions of both structural policies A and B.

(e)   To what extent would you fund structural policies A and B if budget expenditure were limited to 500 (300) in period 0?

Solution

Step 11.1 In the first step we need to expand the model exercise10c.xls. To do this, move the range J8:L29 by two columns to the right (cf. Step 2.1). In the then empty cells J11:J26 and K11:K26 enter the values for the budget expenditure for the structural policy and net welfare (as difference of the values in the columns I and J), respectively, for the different periods. Similarly, for the base situation without structural policy, move the range N8:N29 by two columns to the right and add budget expenditure and net welfare in the resulting gap. Finally, correct all cells for ΔNW as difference of the cells in column K and column O (cf. Figure 11.4 and exercise11a.xls).

Step 11.2 In the base situation without structural policy it applies: $f^d = 0$; check all entries in L10 and M9 if the shift parameter is zero. Then examine the different structural policies by entering the respective values for f^d in H10 (and I9) and for budget expenditure in J11:J26. You can then draw a table for the values of *PV* and *IRR* (cf. Figure 11.4 and exercise11a.xls).

According to the calculated present values, the structural policies B and C should be implemented in period 0, taking into account a budget constraint of 500; implementing structural policies B and C would lead to the highest aggregated present value of net welfare. However, at a budget constraint of only 400, the situation is different, and structural policies A and B should now be implemented. Funding only structural policy C, the policy option with the highest present value, would in this case lead to a lower result than funding the combination of policies A and B.

Step 11.3 In Exercise 11b we assume free trade. All prices in the range A4:C4 have the value of 10. Proceed as in Step 11.2 (cf. Figure 11.5 and exercise11b.xls).

	G	H	I	J	K	L	M	N	O	P
2							Foreign	Government	Producer	Consumer
3		Cost	Total benefit	Welfare	Revenue	Expenditure	exchange	budget	surplus	surplus
4		276.92	3908.72	3431.80	1200.00	1200.00	-200.00	-200.00	923.08	2708.72
5										
6										
7										
8			Welfare for				Welfare for			
9		f^d	$f^d = 1.8\%$			f^d	$f^d = 0\%$			
10	t	0.018	3431.80	BES	NW	0	3431.80	BES	NW	Delta NW
11	0	0.00	3431.80	300	3131.80	0	3431.80	0	3431.80	-300.00
12	1	0.02	3441.22	0	3441.22	0	3431.80		3431.80	9.42
13	2	0.04	3450.80	0	3450.80	0	3431.80		3431.80	19.00
14	3	0.05	3460.56	0	3460.56	0	3431.80		3431.80	28.76
15	4	0.07	3470.49	0	3470.49	0	3431.80		3431.80	38.69
16	5	0.09	3480.60	0	3480.60	0	3431.80		3431.80	48.80
17	6	0.11	3490.90	0	3490.90	0	3431.80		3431.80	59.10
18	7	0.13	3501.38	0	3501.38	0	3431.80		3431.80	69.58
19	8	0.15	3512.04	0	3512.04	0	3431.80		3431.80	80.24
20	9	0.17	3522.90	0	3522.90	0	3431.80		3431.80	91.10
21	10	0.20	3533.96	0	3533.96	0	3431.80		3431.80	102.16
22	11	0.22	3545.21	0	3545.21	0	3431.80		3431.80	113.41
23	12	0.24	3556.67	0	3556.67	0	3431.80		3431.80	124.87
24	13	0.26	3568.33	0	3568.33	0	3431.80		3431.80	136.53
25	14	0.28	3580.21	0	3580.21	0	3431.80		3431.80	148.41
26	15	0.31	3592.29	0	3592.29	0	3431.80		3431.80	160.49
27				Structural policy	A	B	C			
28				PV:	60.07	160.11	183.70		PV:	183.70
29				IRR:	13%	18%	16%		IRR:	16%

Figure 11.4 Present value of net welfare effects of three structural policies (exercise11a.xls).

	G	H	I	J	K	L	M	N	O	P
2							Foreign	Government	Producer	Consumer
3		Cost	Total benefit	Welfare	Revenue	Expenditure	exchange	budget	surplus	surplus
4		163.47	3991.62	3460.87	708.37	1075.65	-367.28	0.00	544.90	2915.97
5										
6										
7										
8			Welfare for				Welfare for			
9		f^d	$f^d = 1.8\%$			f^d	$f^d = 0\%$			
10	t	0.018	3460.87	BES	NW	0	3460.87	BES	NW	Delta NW
11	0	0.00	3460.87	300	3160.87	0	3460.87	0	3460.87	-300.00
12	1	0.02	3470.68	0	3470.68	0	3460.87		3460.87	9.81
13	2	0.04	3480.66	0	3480.66	0	3460.87		3460.87	19.79
14	3	0.05	3490.83	0	3490.83	0	3460.87		3460.87	29.96
15	4	0.07	3501.18	0	3501.18	0	3460.87		3460.87	40.31
16	5	0.09	3511.71	0	3511.71	0	3460.87		3460.87	50.84
17	6	0.11	3522.43	0	3522.43	0	3460.87		3460.87	61.56
18	7	0.13	3533.35	0	3533.35	0	3460.87		3460.87	72.48
19	8	0.15	3544.46	0	3544.46	0	3460.87		3460.87	83.59
20	9	0.17	3555.78	0	3555.78	0	3460.87		3460.87	94.90
21	10	0.20	3567.29	0	3567.29	0	3460.87		3460.87	106.42
22	11	0.22	3579.02	0	3579.02	0	3460.87		3460.87	118.14
23	12	0.24	3590.95	0	3590.95	0	3460.87		3460.87	130.08
24	13	0.26	3603.10	0	3603.10	0	3460.87		3460.87	142.23
25	14	0.28	3615.47	0	3615.47	0	3460.87		3460.87	154.60
26	15	0.31	3628.06	0	3628.06	0	3460.87		3460.87	167.19
27				Structural policy	A	B	C			
28				PV:	60.07	160.11	183.70		PV:	203.88
29				IRR:	13%	18%	16%		IRR:	17%
30										
31			Free trade	PV:	70.92	176.73	203.88			
32				IRR:	14%	18%	17%			

Figure 11.5 Present value of net welfare effects of three structural policies at free trade (exercise11b.xls).

In this case the budget constraint leads to the same combination of structural policies, but with higher values for the political objectives.

Step 11.4 In Exercises 11c and 11d you proceed as in Step 11.2. The base situation is defined by $p^s = 15$, $p^d = 12$, $p^w = 10$ and $f^d = 0$ (0 in cell L10). Draw a table for the present value of net welfare effects of the different structural policies and display the respective chart, as shown in Figure 11.6.

It becomes clear that both structural policies follow the law of diminishing returns. Structural policy A has initially a high increase in return,

	G	H	I	J	K	L	M	N	O	P
2										
3		Cost	Total benefit	Welfare	Revenue	Expenditure	Foreign exchange	Government budget	Producer surplus	Consumer surplus
4		276.92	3908.72	3431.80	1200.00	1200.00	-200.00	-200.00	923.08	2708.72
5										
6										
7										
8				Welfare for				Welfare for		
9		f^d	$f^d = 3.6\%$			f^d	$f^d = 0\%$			
10	t	0.036	3431.80	BES	NW	0	3431.80	BES	NW	Delta NW
11	0	0.00	3431.80	500	2931.80	0	3431.80	0	3431.80	-500.00
12	1	0.04	3450.63	20	3430.63	0	3431.80		3431.80	-1.17
13	2	0.07	3470.14	20	3450.14	0	3431.80		3431.80	18.34
14	3	0.11	3490.35	20	3470.35	0	3431.80		3431.80	38.55
15	4	0.15	3511.29	20	3491.29	0	3431.80		3431.80	59.49
16	5	0.19	3532.98	20	3512.98	0	3431.80		3431.80	81.18
17	6	0.24	3555.46	20	3535.46	0	3431.80		3431.80	103.65
18	7	0.28	3578.74	20	3558.74	0	3431.80		3431.80	126.94
19	8	0.33	3602.86	20	3582.86	0	3431.80		3431.80	151.06
20	9	0.37	3627.85	20	3607.85	0	3431.80		3431.80	176.05
21	10	0.42	3653.74	20	3633.74	0	3431.80		3431.80	201.93
22	11	0.48	3680.56	20	3660.56	0	3431.80		3431.80	228.76
23	12	0.53	3708.34	20	3688.34	0	3431.80		3431.80	256.54
24	13	0.58	3737.13	20	3717.13	0	3431.80		3431.80	285.33
25	14	0.64	3766.95	20	3746.95	0	3431.80		3431.80	315.15
26	15	0.70	3797.85	20	3777.85	0	3431.80		3431.80	346.05
27				Structural policy	A	B	Delta PV for A	Delta PV for B		
28			Present value at	100	242.24	160.07	242.24	160.07	PV:	391.13
29			different budget	200	341.91	245.67	99.66	85.60	IRR:	17%
30			constraints	300	391.61	315.55	49.71	69.88		
31			in period 0	400	403.43	359.59	11.82	44.04		
32				500	357.84	391.13	-45.59	31.54		

Comparison of the present value of net welfare effects of two structural policies

Figure 11.6 Comparison of the present value of net welfare effects of two structural policies (exercise11cde.xls).

which then decreases sharply at higher budget expenditure until it even becomes negative at a budget expenditure of 500. Structural policy B, on the other hand, has initially a lower increase in return, which does decline at a lower rate (compared to option A).

Step 11.5 If, according to Exercise 11e, our available budget in period 0 is constrained to 500, we obtain the maximum aggregated present value by funding structural policy A with 200 monetary units and structural policy B with 300 units. If, however, our budget is limited to only 300, we obtain the maximum aggregated present value by funding policy A with 200 units and policy B with 100 units (cf. Figure 11.6, bottom table). Hence one should look at changes in return for changing budget expenditures of each structural policy as a guideline for an optimal funding mix of these policies.

References

Albright, S.C. (2001) *VBA for Modelers: Developing Decision Support Systems with Microsoft® Excel*, Belmont, CA: Duxbury Press, pp. 367–80.

Chiang, A.C. and Wainwright, K. (2005) *Fundamental Methods of Mathematical Economics* (4th edn), Boston, MA: McGraw-Hill, pp. 347–55.

Edmonds, J. (1971) 'Matroids and the greedy algorithm', *Mathematical Programming*, 1, pp. 127–30.

Jensen, P.A. and Board, J.F. (2003) *Operations Research: Models and Methods*, Indianapolis, IN: John Wiley, pp. 266–70.

Keller, H., Pferschy, U. and Pisinger, D. (2004) *Knapsack Problems*, Berlin: Springer, pp. 15–17.

Mas-Colell, A., Whinston, M.D. and Green, J.A. (1995) *Microeconomic Theory*, New York, Oxford: Oxford University Press, pp. 956–9.

Nicholson, W. (2005) *Microeconomic Theory: Basic Principles and Extensions* (9th edn), Mason, OH: Thomson, pp. 38–44.

Winston, W.L. (1999) *Financial Models Using Simulation and Optimization*, Newfield, NY: Palisade Corporation, pp. 1–4, 107–12.

Part III
Multi-market models

12 Interdependencies of markets

Objective

In Chapter 12 we extend the analysis of price policies to multiple markets. We will show how a model for two markets may be formulated using Excel. We will then discuss the consequences of price policies in this context.

Theory

Previously, we focused our discussion on the implications of price policies on one market, assuming that there are no interdependencies between the considered market and other markets. We ignored the fact that price policies implemented in one market can lead to spill-over effects on supply, demand and prices in other markets, which can again cause feedback effects on the market where the price policy has initially been implemented. Similarly, we did not take into account the fact that price policies on other markets can affect quantities and prices on the considered market. Such a simplification is acceptable for some problem settings, but if interdependencies between markets are significant, or even the main subject of the analysis, the framework for the analysis needs to be extended, taking into account such effects between different markets.

Figure 12.1 outlines the problem setting, showing two commodity markets in two different situations. In the first market a protectionist price policy is implemented in an import situation, while the second market is in equilibrium at autarky without government intervention. If the price protection in the first market is now increased from p_1 to p'_1, the second market would be affected. For example, in this case the price increase in the first market would provide an incentive for producers to use fewer resources for product 2 which would lead to a leftward shift of the supply curve in this market. In addition, consumers would consume more of product 2 due to the higher price of product 1, which would lead to a rightward shift of the demand curve in the second market. In a new equilibrium in the second market the price would have increased to p'_2 and the quantity declined to q'_2.

However, as a result of the increased price in the second market, supply and demand shifts then also occur in the first market. Figure 12.1 shows that such a

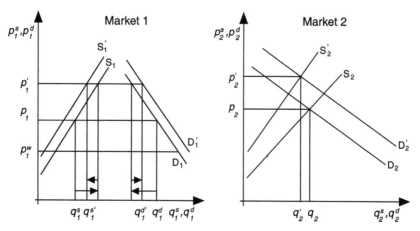

Figure 12.1 Interdependencies between markets.

feedback effect on the first market reduces the quantity effects of the initial price increase (p_1 to p_1'), as indicated by the arrows. Hence, in the case of interdependent markets, supply and demand shifts in other markets, leading to price changes, need also to be considered, since they may change the outcome of price policies in the considered market. However, we have to keep in mind that Figure 12.1 shows only a specific example of interdependent markets out of a wide range of possible different cases. Generally, in order to analyse specific problem settings in interdependent markets, the relevant shifts of supply and demand curves need to be identified and the specific price policy framework has to be taken into account.

A commonly used approach to capture interdependencies between markets is to define cross-price elasticities. The extended supply function $q_1^s = q_1^s (p_1^s, p_2^s)$ describes that the supply of the first product depends on the price of this product and the price of the second product. Accordingly, we may, in addition to the direct price elasticity of supply ε_{11}^s, define the cross-price elasticity ε_{12}^s as follows:

$$\varepsilon_{12}^s = \frac{\partial q_1^s}{\partial p_2^s} \cdot \frac{p_2^s}{q_1^s} \tag{12.1}$$

with ε_{12}^s – cross-price elasticity of supply (of the first product with respect to the price of the second product).

In (12.1) the cross-price elasticity of supply indicates by how many percentage points the quantity supplied of the first product changes if the supply price of the second product increases by 1 per cent. Depending on the sign of the cross-price elasticity we can distinguish between a substitutive (–) or complementary (+) relationship in supply. The extent of supply interdependencies is defined by the absolute value of the cross-price elasticity; at a cross-price elasticity of zero no interdependencies exist.

Similarly, cross-price elasticities may be derived for the supply of the second product as well as for the demand functions of both markets. The cross-price elasticity of demand ε_{21}^d indicates by how many percentage points the quantity demanded of the second product changes if the price of the first product increases by 1 per cent. For substitutive products the cross-price elasticity of demand is positive and for complementary products it is negative.

If we continue to assume iso-elastic supply and demand functions, we can formulate a two-market model as follows:

$$q_1^s(p_1^s, p_2^s) = c_1 \cdot (p_1^s)^{\varepsilon_{11}^s} \cdot (p_2^s)^{\varepsilon_{12}^s}; \qquad \varepsilon_{11}^s > 0 \tag{12.2}$$

$$q_2^s(p_1^s, p_2^s) = c_2 \cdot (p_1^s)^{\varepsilon_{21}^s} \cdot (p_2^s)^{\varepsilon_{22}^s}; \qquad \varepsilon_{22}^s > 0 \tag{12.3}$$

$$q_1^d(p_1^d, p_2^d) = d_1 \cdot (p_1^d)^{\varepsilon_{11}^d} \cdot (p_2^d)^{\varepsilon_{12}^d}; \qquad \varepsilon_{11}^d < 0 \tag{12.4}$$

$$q_2^d(p_1^d, p_2^d) = d_2 \cdot (p_1^d)^{\varepsilon_{21}^d} \cdot (p_2^d)^{\varepsilon_{22}^d}; \qquad \varepsilon_{22}^d < 0 \tag{12.5}$$

where the cross-price elasticities ε_{12}^s, ε_{21}^s, ε_{12}^d and ε_{21}^d may be positive, zero or negative.

On this basis we can now derive the relevant political variables for both markets, calculating, for example, foreign exchange, government budget and welfare. However, an adequate empirical foundation of the extended model requires information about the cross-price elasticities. Ideally, the cross-price elasticities would be obtained through econometric estimation, but in many cases more or less economically plausible values are chosen for the analysis. In addition, in the case of a multi-market model it applies that all supply and demand functions need to be calibrated, i.e. the relevant constants for the model equations have to be determined. Based on (12.2), for example, we can define the equation for the supply constant of the first product:

$$c_1 = \frac{q_1^s}{(p_1^s)^{\varepsilon_{11}^s} \cdot (p_2^s)^{\varepsilon_{12}^s}}. \tag{12.6}$$

This formula shows that with the extension of the model from one market to two markets the calculation of the constant changes, because the quantity supplied is now also explained via the price relation between the two markets. We could also say that the information obtained from a market model increases with a higher degree of endogenisation of markets. For the other supply constant and the demand constants we proceed in the same way. Note that now the cross-price elasticities also affect the calibration. Hence, if different values for the cross-price elasticity are chosen, the model has to be calibrated again.

On the basis of the formulated two-market model we can now analyse how price policies affect relevant political objectives in both markets. Comparing the results to a scenario with cross-price elasticities of zero will show the consequences of considering market interdependencies in the analysis, or, vice versa, the consequences of not considering such interdependencies.

For example, Figure 12.2 shows the consequences of an increased world market

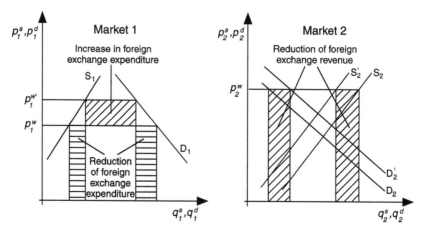

Figure 12.2 Consequences of an increased world market price of one product for foreign exchange revenue in interdependent markets.

price of one product for foreign exchange on two markets, assuming free trade in both markets. Since the price of the second product remains constant, supply and demand curves in the first market do not shift. As a result of the increased world market price, foreign exchange expenditure in this market rises by the diagonally hatched area, but at the same time the decline of imports reduces foreign exchange expenditure indicated by the horizontally hatched areas. In the second market, shifts of the supply and demand curves occur due to the increased price of the first product resulting in lower foreign exchange revenue indicated by the hatched area.

The result depends on the extent of the cross-price effects and on the price policies pursued in the considered markets. If a country pursues an autarky policy in the second market, the increase in the world market price in the first market would, of course, not affect foreign exchange in the second market, since, by definition, foreign exchange does not exist at autarky. But feedback effects from the second to the first market would then lead to shifts of supply and demand curves in the first market, which would further affect foreign exchange in this market.

Figure 12.3 shows another example of the importance of cross-price effects in the analysis of price policies. The graph first shows the impact of an increasing protectionist price policy on an import market without any cross-price effects and is similar to Figure 1.3 (compare with B_1). If we then consider cross-price effects, for example, with respect to a protected export market, the increase of the domestic price in the first (import) market would lead to additional budget expenditure in the export market. As a result, we obtain the budget function B_1 for the first market, which is, under the given price policy assumptions (i.e. constant p_2), the same as the budget function without cross-price effects; but, in addition, we obtain the budget function B_2 for the second market (in relation to p_1), and the aggregated budget function $B = B_1 + B_2$. The result shows how under these price policy assumptions market interdependencies affect the budget effects of an

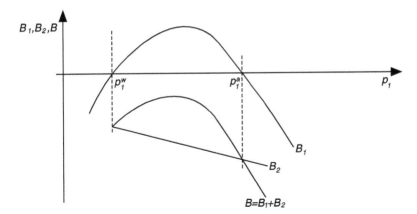

Figure 12.3 Budget functions in two markets with an increasing protectionist price policy in the first market and a given protectionist policy in the second market.

increasing protectionist price policy. Under different price policy settings, for example, a closed market and a producer subsidisation in the second market, budget functions could be derived in the same way to examine the implications of an increasing protectionist price policy in the first market for this political variable.

Exercise 12

Consider the supply functions

$$q_1^s(p_1^s, p_2^s) = c_1 (p_1^s)^{\varepsilon_{11}^s} (p_2^s)^{\varepsilon_{12}^s}$$

$$q_2^s(p_1^s, p_2^s) = c_2 (p_1^s)^{\varepsilon_{21}^s} (p_2^s)^{\varepsilon_{22}^s}$$

with $\quad \varepsilon_{11}^s = \varepsilon_{22}^s = 0.3 \quad$ and $\quad \varepsilon_{12}^s = \varepsilon_{21}^s = -0.1$

and the demand functions

$$q_1^d(p_1^d, p_2^d) = d_1 (p_1^d)^{\varepsilon_{11}^d} (p_2^d)^{\varepsilon_{12}^d}$$

$$q_2^d(p_1^d, p_2^d) = d_2 (p_1^d)^{\varepsilon_{21}^d} (p_2^d)^{\varepsilon_{22}^d}$$

with $\quad \varepsilon_{11}^d = \varepsilon_{22}^d = -0.4 \quad$ and $\quad \varepsilon_{12}^d = \varepsilon_{21}^d = 0.2.$

Develop a market model in Excel and solve the following problems:

(a) Assume free trade and the world market prices are $p_1^w = 10$ and $p_2^w = 15$. Under this policy the country is an importer of the first product with a quantity supplied of $q_1^s = 80$ and quantity demanded of $q_1^d = 100$. The country is an exporter of the second product with $q_2^s = 120$ and $q_2^d = 100$. Calibrate the supply and demand functions accordingly.

(b) Show how an increase of the world market price of the first product to $p_1^w = 15$ affects revenue, expenditure and foreign exchange on both markets. How would the result differ without any cross-price effects?

(c) The country now pursues autarky in the second market. Show how in this case an increase of the world market price of the first product to $p_1^w = 15$ affects revenue, expenditure and foreign exchange in both markets. How would the result differ without any cross-price effects?

(d) Show graphically how in comparison to free trade a gradual increase of the protection rate on the first market to 50 per cent affects budget expenditure both on the markets and in total. On the second market assume a protection-ist price policy with a protection rate of 20 per cent.

(e) Solve Exercise 12d under the assumptions that no trade on the second market takes place and that a producer subsidisation of 10 per cent is implemented.

Solution

Step 12.1 Start with the initial Cobb–Douglas model for one market with calibra-tion used in Exercise 4 (compare with Figure 4.3 and exercise4a.xls). Move the constants c and d and the elasticities to B11:E11 or the whole range B6:E8 to B9:E11. Move also the range A5:F5 with the parameters of calibration to A6:F6. Then copy and paste this range A6:F6 to A7:F7, the constants and elasticities in B11:E11 to B12:E12 and finally the complete row 4 to row 5. Now we have two identical independent markets (cf. Figure 12.4).

	A	B	C	D	E	F	G	H	I
1			Cobb-Douglas Model with two Identical Independent Markets						
2									
3	p^s	p^d	p^w		Supply	Demand		Cost	Total benefit
4	15	12	10		80	100		276.92308	3908.72417
5	15	12	10		80	100		276.92308	3908.72417
6	15	12	Parameters of calibration		80	100			
7	15	12	Parameters of calibration		80	100			
8									
9			Constants		Elasticities				
10		c	d	of supply	of demand				
11		35.5028003	270.192008	0.3	-0.4				
12		35.5028003	270.192008	0.3	-0.4				

	J	K	L	M	N	O	P
1							
2							
3	Welfare	Revenue	Expenditure	Foreign exchange	Government budget	Producer surplus	Consumer surplus
4	3431.8011	1200	1200	-200	-200	923.076923	2708.72417
5	3431.8011	1200	1200	-200	-200	923.076923	2708.72417

Figure 12.4 Cobb–Douglas model with two identical independent markets (exercise12.xls).

Step 12.2 Now enter the cross-price elasticities in the two markets (for supply −0.1, and for demand 0.2) and create an elasticity matrix with ε_{ij}^s and ε_{ij}^d. To do this, move E11 to G11, E12 to H12 and D12 to E12 and then enter the cross-price elasticities in E11 and D12 and H11 and G12, respectively. Be careful that the linkages of the functions with the own-price elasticities remain and make sure that the cross-price elasticities are correctly incorporated into all relevant functions. For example, in E4 we should obtain the following formula for the quantity supplied: = B11*A4^D11*A5^E11. The same approach applies for the other quantities. We then have to adjust the constants c_1, c_2, d_1 and d_2. Following (12.6) we get the formula = E6/A6^D11/A7^E11 in B11. Accordingly, we derive the formulas for the other constants from (12.3) to (12.5).

Step 12.3 For the functions of cost and benefit we integrate *ceteris paribus* with respect to the own market price. Hence we add at the end of each formula for cost and benefit (H4:I5) the factor $(p_j)^{\varepsilon_{ij}}$, i.e. for example, in H4 we add *A5^E11 (no additional brackets).

Some help for controlling the correctness of the model is given by the symmetry of the markets. To check the structure of the model we can use the 'Trace precedents' operation in Excel (click on 'Tools', 'Formula auditing' and then on 'Trace precedents').

We then implement free trade with world market prices of 10 and 15 and calibrate the model according to Exercise 12a. If everything is correct you get the values as shown in Figure 12.5 (cf. exercise12a.xls).

	A	B	C	D	E	F	G	H	I
1			Cobb-Douglas Model with Calibration for two Interdependent Markets						
2									
3	p^s	p^d	p^w		Supply	Demand		Cost	Total benefit
4	10	10	10		80	100		184.61538	3710.87967
5	15	15	15		120	100		415.38462	4148.34042
6	10	10	Calibration Market 1		80	100			
7	15	15	Calibration Market 2		120	100			
8									
9			Constants		Elasticities of supply			Elasticities of demand	
10		c	d	Market 1	Market 2		Market 1	Market 2	
11	Market 1	52.5652958	146.144255	0.3	-0.1		-0.4	0.2	
12	Market 2	67.0430662	186.395964	-0.1	0.3		0.2	-0.4	

	J	K	L	M	N	O	P
1							
2							
3	Welfare	Revenue	Expenditure	Foreign exchange	Government budget	Producer surplus	Consumer surplus
4	3326.2643	800	1000	-200	0	615.384615	2710.87967
5	4032.9558	1800	1500	300	0	1384.61538	2648.34042

Figure 12.5 Calibrated Cobb–Douglas market model with two interdependent markets (exercise12a.xls).

Step 12.4 To solve Exercise 12b we have to change the price in the first market and compute the impact on revenue, expenditure and foreign exchange (cf. Figure 12.6). We can see that the higher price in the first market leads to significant changes in the political variables in both markets.

To compare this result with the situation without cross-price effects we first have to enter 0 for all cross-price elasticities. The result is shown in Figure 12.7. For the first market it is the same result, since due to the constant price in the second market no feedback effects occur in the first market, either with or without cross-price effects. But without cross-price effects the price change in the first market does not have any impact on the second market.

Step 12.5 To simulate autarky in the second market, apply the Solver for both model variations (target cell: E5; changing cell: A5; and constraints: E5 = F5; in cell B5 we have the formula = A5), and Exercise 12c is solved (cf. Figures 12.8 and 12.9).

Figure 12.8 shows first that at autarky in the second market and under consideration of cross-price effects different base values for the variables apply. The world market price increase in the first market now leads to a

	A	B	C	D	E	F	G	H	I
1			Cobb-Douglas Model with Calibration for two Interdependent Markets						
2									
3	p^s	p^d	p^w		Supply	Demand		Cost	Total benefit
4	15.00	15.00	15.00		90.35	85.03		312.74	3527.26
5	15.00	15.00	15.00		115.23	108.45		398.88	4498.76
6	10	10	Calibration Market 1		80	100			
7	15	15	Calibration Market 2		120	100			
8									
9		Constants			Elasticities of supply			Elasticities of demand	
10		c	d		Market 1	Market 2		Market 1	Market 2
11	Market 1	52.5652958	146.144255		0.3	-0.1		-0.4	0.2
12	Market 2	67.0430662	186.395964		-0.1	0.3		0.2	-0.4

	J	K	L	M	N	O	P
1							
2							
3	Welfare	Revenue	Expenditure	Foreign exchange	Government budget	Producer surplus	Consumer surplus
4	3294.31	1355.22	1275.42	79.79	0.00	1042.47	2251.84
5	4201.65	1728.48	1626.71	101.77	0.00	1329.60	2872.05
6	Base situation						
7	Market 1	800	1000	-200			
8	Market 2	1800	1500	300			
9							
10	Differences						
11	Market 1	555.22	275.42	279.79			
12	Market 2	-71.52	126.71	-198.23			

Figure 12.6 Impact of a price increase in the first market considering cross-price effects (exercise 12b1.xls).

	A	B	C	D	E	F	G	H	I
1			Cobb-Douglas Model with Calibration for two Interdependent Markets						
2									
3	p^s	p^d	p^w		Supply	Demand		Cost	Total benefit
4	15.00	15.00	15.00		90.35	85.03		312.74	3527.26
5	15.00	15.00	15.00		120.00	100.00		415.38	4148.34
6	10	10	Calibration Market 1		80	100			
7	15	15	Calibration Market 2		120	100			
8									
9			Constants		Elasticities of supply			Elasticities of demand	
10		c	d		Market 1	Market 2		Market 1	Market 2
11	Market 1	40.0949787	251.188643		0.3	0		-0.4	0
12	Market 2	53.2542004	295.417694		0	0.3		0	-0.4

	J	K	L	M	N	O	P
1							
2							
3	Welfare	Revenue	Expenditure	Foreign exchange	Government budget	Producer surplus	Consumer surplus
4	3294.31	1355.22	1275.42	79.79	0.00	1042.47	2251.84
5	4032.96	1800.00	1500.00	300.00	0.00	1384.62	2648.34
6	Base situation						
7	Market 1	800	1000	-200			
8	Market 2	1800	1500	300			
9							
10	Differences						
11	Market 1	555.22	275.42	279.79			
12	Market 2	0.00	0.00	0.00			

Figure 12.7 Impact of a price increase in the first market without cross-price effects (exercise12b2.xls).

significant rise of revenue and expenditure in the second market, while the increase in foreign exchange in the first market is now smaller than at free trade in both markets, and in the second market, of course, the increase is equal to zero.

Without cross-price effects the world market price increase would lead to the same effects in the first market as at free trade in both markets. Since no market interdependencies exist, the impact of the price change in the first market is independent of the price policy pursued in the second market. Because such interdependencies or cross-price effects do not exist in this example, the second market will also not be affected by the price change in the first market.

Step 12.6 To solve Exercise 12d use model exercise12a.xls and set the protectionist price at 18 for the second market in the cells A5 and B5. Generate a parameter series for the domestic price of the first product in the range G14:G24. With 'Data, table' we can then easily generate the respective values for government budget expenditure (with the entry A4 in 'Column input cell' and the formula = A4 in cell B4), which can then be transformed into a chart with the 'Chart wizard' (cf. Figure 12.10).

	A	B	C	D	E	F	G	H	I
1			Cobb-Douglas Model with Calibration for two Interdependent Markets						
2									
3	p^s	p^d	p^w		Supply	Demand		Cost	Total benefit
4	15.00	15.00	15.00		91.13	83.57		315.47	3466.64
5	13.75	13.75	15.00		112.27	112.27		356.37	4553.72
6	10	10	Calibration Market 1		80	100			
7	15	15	Calibration Market 2		120	100			
8									
9		Constants			Elasticities of supply			Elasticities of demand	
10		c	d		Market 1	Market 2		Market 1	Market 2
11	Market 1	52.5652958	146.144255	0.3	-0.1			-0.4	0.2
12	Market 2	67.0430662	186.395964	-0.1	0.3			0.2	-0.4

	J	K	L	M	N	O	P
1							
2							
3	Welfare	Revenue	Expenditure	Foreign exchange	Government budget	Producer surplus	Consumer surplus
4	3264.68	1367.02	1253.50	113.51	0.00	1051.55	2213.13
5	4197.36	1544.26	1544.26	0.00	0.00	1187.89	3009.46
6	Base situation						
7	Market 1	821.11	949.24	-128.13			
8	Market 2	1282.99	1282.99	0.00			
9							
10	Differences						
11	Market 1	545.91	304.26	241.64			
12	Market 2	261.28	261.28	0.00			

Figure 12.8 Impact of a price increase in the first market considering cross-price effects and at autarky in the second market (exercise12c1.xls).

	A	B	C	D	E	F	G	H	I
1			Cobb-Douglas Model with Calibration for two Interdependent Markets						
2									
3	p^s	p^d	p^w		Supply	Demand		Cost	Total benefit
4	15.00	15.00	15.00		90.35	85.03		312.74	3527.26
5	11.56	11.56	15.00		110.98	110.98		296.07	4293.02
6	10	10	Calibration Market 1		80	100			
7	15	15	Calibration Market 2		120	100			
8									
9		Constants			Elasticities of supply			Elasticities of demand	
10		c	d		Market 1	Market 2		Market 1	Market 2
11	Market 1	40.0949787	251.188643	0.3	0			-0.4	0
12	Market 2	53.2542004	295.417694	0	0.3			0	-0.4

	J	K	L	M	N	O	P
1							
2							
3	Welfare	Revenue	Expenditure	Foreign exchange	Government budget	Producer surplus	Consumer surplus
4	3294.31	1355.22	1275.42	79.79	0.00	1042.47	2251.84
5	3996.94	1282.99	1282.99	0.00	0.00	986.91	3010.03
6	Base situation						
7	Market 1	800.00	1000.00	-200.00			
8	Market 2	1282.99	1282.99	0.00			
9							
10	Differences						
11	Market 1	555.22	275.42	279.79			
12	Market 2	0.00	0.00	0.00			

Figure 12.9 Impact of a price increase in the first market without cross-price effects and at autarky in the second market (exercise12c2.xls).

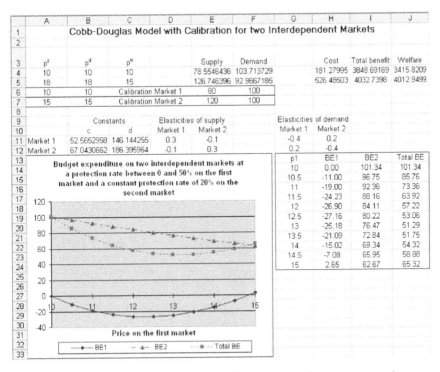

Figure 12.10 Budget expenditure in two interdependent markets at a protection rate between 0 and 50 per cent in the first market and a constant protection rate of 20 per cent in the second market (exercise12d.xls).

Figure 12.10 shows that the increase in the domestic price of the first product leads initially to decreasing but then increasing aggregated budget expenditure. The assumed protectionist price policy for the second product results in budget expenditure through export subsidies in this market. An increase in the domestic price of the first product would then to some extent reduce the budget expenditure in the second market. In the first market the increasing protectionist price policy would at first lead to tariff revenues and end up in additional export subsidies in this market.

Step 12.7 Let us now solve the last exercise in this chapter with our model. To do this, we separate the domestic prices of the second product from the world market price and introduce a producer subsidy of 10 per cent (i.e. we have the exogenous value 15 in cell B5 and the formula = 1.1*B5 in cell A5). Due to the interdependencies between the markets, we now obtain different autarky prices in the second market (since there is no trade in this market) for the different domestic prices of the first product. Hence, we need to compute a Solver solution (target cell: E5;

	A	B	C	D	E	F	G	H	I	J
1			Cobb-Douglas Model with Calibration for two Interdependent Markets							
2										
3	p^s	p^d	p^w		Supply	Demand		Cost	Total benefit	Welfare
4	10.00	10.00	10.00		81.67	94.15		188.46	3493.86	3180.54
5	12.21	11.10	15.00		112.81	112.81		317.80	4313.72	3995.93
6	10	10	Calibration Market 1		80	100				
7	15	15	Calibration Market 2		120	100				
8										
9			Constants		Elasticities of supply			Elasticities of demand		
10		c	d		Market 1	Market 2		Market 1	Market 2	
11	Market 1	52.5652958	146.144255		0.3	-0.1		-0.4	0.2	
12	Market 2	67.0430662	186.395964		-0.1	0.3		0.2	-0.4	

Chart (rows 13–33):

Budget expenditure on two interdependent markets at a protection rate between 0 and 50% on the first market and a producer subsidy of 10% on the second market, without trade

Price on the first market

Legend: ◆ BE1   ▲ BE2   ■ Total BE

p1	BE1	BE2	Total BE
10	0.00	125.19	125.19
10.5	-5.01	128.02	123.00
11	-7.68	130.77	123.09
11.5	-8.18	133.45	125.27
12	-6.65	136.07	129.43
12.5	-3.22	138.64	135.42
13	1.99	141.15	143.14
13.5	8.89	143.60	152.49
14	17.37	146.01	163.38
14.5	27.35	148.37	175.72
15	38.76	150.69	189.45

Figure 12.11 Budget expenditure in two interdependent markets at a protection rate between 0 and 50 per cent in the first market and a producer subsidy of 10 per cent in the second market, without trade (exercise12e.xls).

changing cell: B5; constraints: E5 = F5) for each of the values for p_1 (in cells A4 and B4). The respective values for budget expenditure are incorporated into the range H14:J24. If you have deleted the previous content of the 'Data, table' operation in the range H15:J24, you can use the chart from Step 12.6 for this step. The result is shown in Figure 12.11 and exercise12e.xls.

Again, the increase in the domestic price of the first product leads initially to decreasing but then increasing aggregated budget expenditure. However, in this case the positive budget effect on the first market is small and turns rather quickly into budget expenditure. In addition, the increase in the domestic price of the first product enhances the negative budget effect of the producer subsidy for the second market. Overall, under the assumed price policy setting the burden for the aggregated budget grows with an increasing protectionist price policy in the first market.

References

Chiang, A.C. and Wainwright, K. (2005) *Fundamental Methods of Mathematical Economics* (4th edn), Boston, MA: McGraw-Hill, pp. 40–5.

Jechlitschka, K. and Lotze, H. (1997) 'Theorie und Anwendung eines Mehr-Markt-Modells zur sektoralen Analyse von Agrarpolitiken', *Zeitschrift für Agrarinformatik*, 5 (2), pp. 26–31.

Pindyck, R.S. and Rubinfeld, D.L. (2005) *Microeconomics* (6th edn), Upper Saddle River, NJ: Pearson Prentice Hall, pp. 32–6, 579–83.

von Lampe, M. (1998) 'The World Agricultural Trade Simulation System WATSIM', Discussion Paper No. 5 presented at the University of Bonn.

Wahl, O., Weber, G. and Frohberg, K. (2000) 'Documentation of the Central and Eastern European Countries Agricultural Simulation Model', Discussion Paper No. 27 presented at the Institut für Agrarentwicklung in Mittel und Osteuropa, Halle (Saale).

Weber, G. (2001) 'Agricultural policy analysis in transition countries with CEEC-ASIM: who will lose, who will gain by the EU-accession?', in T. Heckelei, H.P. Witzke and W. Henrichsmeyer (eds) *Agricultural Sector Modelling and Policy Information Systems*, Kiel: Vauk, pp. 212–20.

13 Microeconomic foundations

Objective

In Chapter 13 we want to further extend and improve the two-market model. We will explain which microeconomic foundations need to be considered and how these may be integrated into a two-market model.

Theory

Already in Chapter 4 we have argued that the formulation of supply and demand functions needs to fulfil two conditions. The functions should reflect the real decision-making behaviour of producers and consumers and they should be based on empirical information. With respect to the first condition we address the microeconomic foundations of supply and demand functions.

The microeconomic foundations of the formulated single-market models are quite simple and obvious. Supply and demand functions are based on economic theory assuming profit maximisation of producers and utility maximisation of consumers. But note that these models apply the rather crude assumption that interdependencies between the considered market and the rest of the economy either do not exist or are only minor and may be ignored. On this basis we can define welfare indicators, which for consumers do not provide exact but acceptable approximate values for welfare changes. The appropriate choice of price elasticities ensures the empirical consistency of such models.

In multi-market models the microeconomic foundations are less obvious and more complex. Let us first examine the supply side and the response of a profit-maximising firm, producing two products, on price changes. If only the price of one product changes, supply of both products would be affected, as discussed earlier. But what impact may be expected if both prices change at the same percentage? From general equilibrium models we know the consideration that the supply of different products in an economy does not change if all prices change at the same percentage. This follows the assumption that firms are free of 'price illusion'. Similarly, one may assume that supply quantities do not change in the formulated two-market model if prices change at the same rate.

One has to be aware, however, that such a condition is rather restrictive for a two-market model. A multi-market model is not a general equilibrium model and the outlined condition, if applied to a two-market model, means that we reflect the decision-making behaviour of a firm only with respect to these two markets. We assume that the resources used for the two products are given and do not depend on the production of other commodities in the economy; hence there are no interdependencies between the considered two products and the rest of the economy. This may be plausible for a certain case, but in other cases it may not, underlining the specific character of partial equilibrium models to focus on specific markets. Hence, depending on the problem setting, it is crucial to consider the most relevant markets when formulating a multi-market model. The relevance of the discussed condition needs to be considered for each model development and application.

Let us now assume that the quantities $q_1^s = q_1^s \, (p_1^s, \, p_2^s)$ and $q_2^s = q_2^s \, (p_1^s, \, p_2^s)$ in the formulated two-market model do not change if p_1^s and p_2^s increase by the same percentage. Such a property defines homogeneous functions with a homogeneity of degree zero. Generally, a function $y \, (x)$ is homogeneous of the degree r, if:

$$\lambda^r y = y \, (\lambda x_1, \, \ldots, \, \lambda x_n). \tag{13.1}$$

We can show that the formulated Cobb–Douglas supply functions are homogeneous and that the homogeneity degree is equal to the sum of the price elasticities. From the above discussion we can thus derive that the following conditions apply for the elasticities of the functions:

$$\varepsilon_{11}^s + \varepsilon_{12}^s = 0 \tag{13.2}$$

and

$$\varepsilon_{21}^s + \varepsilon_{22}^s = 0. \tag{13.3}$$

Accordingly, these equations describe the homogeneity condition for supply functions.

There is another condition that applies for supply functions of a profit-maximising firm producing two products:

$$\frac{\partial q_1^s}{\partial p_2^s} = \frac{\partial q_2^s}{\partial p_1^s}. \tag{13.4}$$

This symmetry condition describes that the quantity response of one product to the price change of another product is the same as the quantity response of this other product to a price change of the first product. The symmetry condition in (13.4) may be rewritten as:

$$\varepsilon_{12}^s \, p_1^s \, q_1^s = \varepsilon_{21}^s \, p_2^s \, q_2^s . \tag{13.4}'$$

Following this symmetry condition cross-price elasticities of supply functions have to be in a specific relationship to fulfil the condition.

Furthermore, general equilibrium models refer to the curve properties of profit functions with respect to product prices, which also need to be considered in multi-market models. A profit function should be convex with respect to the product prices, since it is indeed plausible that a price increase of a product would lead overall to a non-decreasing profit increase. Furthermore, the supply functions may be derived as the first partial derivatives of a profit function, so that the second partial derivatives of the profit function, relevant for the properties of the profit function, are given through the first partial derivatives of the supply functions. Hence, the profit function in the discussed two-market case is convex if the following conditions apply for the supply functions:

$$\frac{\partial q_1^s}{\partial p_1^s}, \frac{\partial q_2^s}{\partial p_2^s} \geq 0 \tag{13.5}$$

and

$$\frac{\partial q_1^s}{\partial p_1^s} \frac{\partial q_2^s}{\partial p_2^s} \geq \frac{\partial q_1^s}{\partial p_2^s} \frac{\partial q_2^s}{\partial p_1^s}. \tag{13.6}$$

From (13.5) it immediately follows that the direct price elasticities of supply may not be negative. In addition, through rewriting (13.6) we obtain the following condition:

$$\varepsilon_{11}^s \varepsilon_{22}^s \geq \varepsilon_{12}^s \varepsilon_{21}^s. \tag{13.6'}$$

Hence the product of the direct price elasticities has to be bigger than, or equal to, the product of the cross-price elasticities, whereby the specific relationship between the cross-price elasticities, defined in (13.4)', needs to be considered.

The discussed microeconomic foundations of the supply functions have thus a direct impact on the definition of, and restrictions for, the price elasticities of supply. If these conditions are seen to be appropriate for a specific market model, they could be incorporated by computing the corresponding elasticities, based on given start values for these elasticities. These correct, or microeconomically adjusted, elasticities should be as close as possible to the start values, but consider the discussed conditions. The following optimisation approach can provide such a microeconomic adjustment of the elasticities for a two-market model:

$$\min_{\varepsilon_{ij}^s} \sum_{i=1}^{2} \sum_{j=1}^{2} \left(\varepsilon_{ij}^s - \varepsilon_{ij}^{s*} \right)^2 \tag{13.7}$$

with the constraints:

$$\varepsilon_{11}^s + \varepsilon_{12}^s \quad = 0$$

$$\varepsilon_{21}^s + \varepsilon_{22}^s \quad = 0$$

$$\varepsilon_{12}^s \, p_1^s \, q_1^s \; - \varepsilon_{21}^s \, p_2^s \, q_2^s \; = 0$$

$$\varepsilon_{11}^s, \varepsilon_{22}^s \; \geq 0$$

$$\varepsilon_{11}^s \, \varepsilon_{22}^s \; \geq \varepsilon_{12}^s \, \varepsilon_{21}^s$$

where * denotes the start values for the elasticities.

Similar to the supply side, homogeneity and symmetry conditions as well as the curve properties of the expenditure function need to be reflected in the microeconomic foundation of the demand side. In addition, an adding-up condition has to be considered.

The microeconomic foundations on the demand side are derived from the idea of utility-maximising households or consumers. Such households will make their decisions on what and how much they consume depending on product prices and income. Hence, the demand for products does not only depend on prices, but also on income. This implies that in a first step the demand functions in our two-market model need to be extended as follows:

$$q_1^d (p_1^d, p_2^d, y) = d_1 (p_1^d)^{\varepsilon_{11}^d} (p_2^d)^{\varepsilon_{12}^d} y^{\eta_1}; \qquad \varepsilon_{11}^d < 0 \qquad (13.8)$$

$$q_2^d (p_1^d, p_2^d, y) = d_2 (p_1^d)^{\varepsilon_{21}^d} (p_2^d)^{\varepsilon_{22}^d} y^{\eta_2}; \qquad \varepsilon_{22}^d < 0 \qquad (13.9)$$

with y – income

          η_i – income elasticity of demand of product $i = 1, 2$.

The income elasticity of demand of the first product indicates by how many percentage points the quantity demanded of this product changes if the income increases by 1 per cent. It applies:

$$\eta_1 = \frac{\partial q_1^d}{\partial y} \frac{y}{q_1^d}. \qquad (13.10)$$

η_i will be positive for many products, but negative income elasticities of demand are also possible.

The adding-up condition postulates that the expenditure of a household will usually be equal to the income of this household. While this seems plausible for the total consumption of a household, such an assumption does not necessarily apply for single products, since a household will generally not spend a given amount of its income on a specific product. In a multi-market context, however, we could apply an 'adding-up condition' assuming that households will spend a certain income for the products included in a model. By applying this assumption, we again consider the part of the economy included in the model as independent from the rest of the economy. Hence, also for the demand side it is crucial to model the most relevant markets for a specific problem setting and to reflect the relevance of an adding-up condition for the specific case.

If the adding-up condition is considered relevant, it seems plausible to interpret the income variable y in (13.8) and (13.9) as income for the considered products and consequently to determine y through the expenditure for these products. It thus applies $y = E$. The income elasticities of demand would then be the expenditure elasticities of demand for these products. For our two-market case it would apply:

$$p_1^d q_1^d (p_1^d, p_2^d, y) + p_2^d q_2^d (p_1^d, p_2^d, y) = y. \tag{13.11}$$

After differentiation and some rearrangements we get the so-called adding-up condition, defined as:

$$w_1 \eta_1 + w_2 \eta_2 = 1 \tag{13.12}$$

with $\qquad w_i = \dfrac{p_i^d q_i^d}{y}$

and $\qquad w_i$ – share of expenditure for product $i = 1, 2$ in total expenditure for the considered products.

Consequently, the sum of the income elasticities, weighted with the expenditure shares of the products considered, has to be 1.

The adding-up condition emphasises that by using a multi-market model we only consider, and capture in the model, a part of the economy; in fact, the condition describes the relationship between the expenditure elasticities within the considered part of the economy. Two further remarks may help to clarify the link between the markets considered in a model and the overall economy. If, for example, Y is defined as the available income for total consumption, we could rewrite (13.11) as:

$$p_1^d q_1^d (p_1^d, p_2^d, y(Y)) + p_2^d q_2^d (p_1^d, p_2^d, y(Y)) = y(Y). \tag{13.11'}$$

Equation (13.12) would then be:

$$\eta_{y,Y} (w_1 \eta_1 + w_2 \eta_2) = \eta_{y,Y}. \tag{13.12'}$$

Equation (13.12)′ shows the consequences of using the formulated adding-up condition in a multi-market model. Setting the model in the context of the overall economy would mean to 'scale' the income elasticities accordingly. The scaling factor $\eta_{y,Y}$ would be the income elasticity of demand with respect to the products considered in the model. Hence, the 'correct' income elasticity of demand of single products, for example, with respect to the first product, could be interpreted as the product of the expenditure elasticity of this product and the scaling factor, the income elasticity of demand of all considered products in the model:

$$\eta_{q_1^d,Y} = \eta_{q_1^d,y}\, \eta_{y,Y}. \tag{13.13}$$

A second comment in this context refers to the analysis of income changes. Using a multi-market model we need to pay attention to which variable we want to analyse: the change in income in the whole economy or the change in expenditure for the considered products. It applies:

$$\frac{dy}{y} = \eta_{y,Y}\frac{dY}{Y}. \tag{13.13}'$$

On the basis of the adding-up condition we can examine further relevant conditions on the demand side, similar to the supply side. For example, if a utility-maximising household is free of price illusion, it will not change its consumption pattern if all prices and the income of the household change by the same percentage. Applying this homogeneity condition to our two-market model, which could be suitable or too restrictive depending on the specific problem setting, would mean that demand does not change if the product prices and the amount of expenditure for the two products change by the same percentage. We can show that the demand functions, formulated in (13.8) and (13.9), are homogeneous and that the homogeneity degree is equal to the sum of the price elasticities and the respective income elasticity. The homogeneity condition requires a homogeneity degree of zero, so that for both demand functions the following conditions may be formulated:

$$\varepsilon_{11}^d + \varepsilon_{12}^d + \eta_1 = 0 \tag{13.14}$$

and

$$\varepsilon_{21}^d + \varepsilon_{22}^d + \eta_2 = 0. \tag{13.15}$$

With respect to the symmetry condition on the demand side, it applies that the quantity response of a product to a price change of another product is the same as the quantity response of the other product to a price change of the first product. Similar to the supply side, this relationship describes the substitution effect between products due to price changes. However, it has to be taken into account that the observed demand curves, the so-called Marshallian demand curves, reflect not only substitution effects but also income effects. To eliminate these income effects, quantity responses need to be considered on the basis of income-compensated demand curves, the so-called Hicksian demand curves.

The relationship is outlined in Figure 13.1. A price increase from p^d to $p^{d'}$ leads to a decline of demand from q^d to $q^{d''}$. As a consequence of the higher product price the household substitutes this product with other products, but the household also consumes less, since its real income has decreased. In order to eliminate this income effect, the household would have to be compensated for the loss of

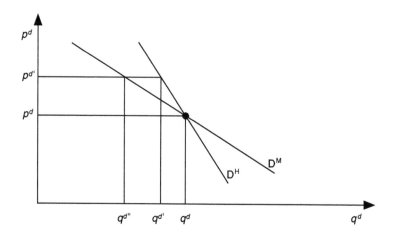

D^M – Marshallian demand curve
D^H – Hicksian demand curve

Figure 13.1 Substitution and income effects of price changes.

income to maintain its utility level after substitution in consumption. This hypo-thetical situation is described by the Hicksian demand function. The total quan-tity effect thus consists of the substitution effect from q^d to $q^{d'}$ and the income effect from $q^{d'}$ to $q^{d''}$.

The symmetry condition then requires that the cross-price derivatives of the Hicksian demand functions are symmetric. Hence, it applies:

$$\frac{\partial q_1^{d(H)}}{\partial p_2^d} = \frac{\partial q_2^{d(H)}}{\partial p_1^d} \tag{13.16}$$

whereby (H) indicates the Hicksian demand functions. The symmetry condition may be further operationalised using the Slutsky equation, which describes the relationship between the Marshallian and the Hicksian demand function, for example, with respect to the first product, as follows:

$$\frac{\partial q_1^d}{\partial p_2^d} = \frac{\partial q_1^{d(H)}}{\partial p_2^d} - \frac{\partial q_1^d}{\partial y} q_2^d. \tag{13.17}$$

After some rearrangements of (13.16) and considering the Slutsky equation, the following symmetry condition can be finally defined:

$$w_1 \left(\varepsilon_{12}^d + w_2 \eta_1 \right) = w_2 \left(\varepsilon_{21}^d + w_1 \eta_2 \right). \tag{13.16'}$$

As for the supply side, also on the demand side the symmetry condition requires a specific relationship for cross-price elasticities.

Similarities with the supply side also exist with respect to the curve properties of the respective relevant functions. On the demand side we have to consider the curve properties of the expenditure function of a utility-maximising household. The expenditure function, with respect to product prices, should be concave. The expenditure function indicates the lowest required expenditure to reach a certain utility level at given product prices. If a product price now increases, it seems plausible that the price increase leads to a non-increasing expenditure increase. Similar to the supply side, the Hicksian demand functions can now be derived as first partial derivatives of the expenditure function, so that the second partial derivatives of the expenditure function, which are relevant for the assessment of the curve properties, can be obtained by the first partial derivatives of the Hicksian demand functions. In our discussed two-market case the expenditure function is concave if it applies for the Hicksian demand functions:

$$\frac{\partial q_1^{d(H)}}{\partial p_1^d}, \ \frac{\partial q_2^{d(H)}}{\partial p_2^d} \leq 0 \tag{13.18}$$

and

$$\frac{\partial q_1^{d(H)}}{\partial p_1^d} \frac{\partial q_2^{d(H)}}{\partial p_2^d} \geq \frac{\partial q_1^{d(H)}}{\partial p_2^d} \frac{\partial q_2^{d(H)}}{\partial p_1^d}. \tag{13.19}$$

These curve properties can also be further operationalised through the Slutsky equation. From (13.18) it follows:

$$\varepsilon_{11}^d + w_1 \eta_1 \leq 0 \tag{13.18'}$$

and

$$\varepsilon_{22}^d + w_2 \eta_2 \leq 0. \tag{13.18''}$$

Accordingly we get from (13.19):

$$(\varepsilon_{11}^d + w_1 \eta_1)(\varepsilon_{22}^d + w_2 \eta_2) \geq (\varepsilon_{12}^d + w_2 \eta_1)(\varepsilon_{21}^d + w_1 \eta_2). \tag{13.19'}$$

While the above conditions underline the similarities with the supply side, the equations also point out the difference to the microeconomic foundation on the supply side, as income or expenditure elasticities need to be taken into account on the demand side.

Considering microeconomic conditions thus means to impose restrictions on the choice of price and income elasticities on the demand side, if this is considered appropriate in the specific case. The following optimisation approach can provide such a microeconomic adjustment of the elasticities for the discussed two-market model:

$$\min_{\varepsilon^d_{ij}, \eta_i} \left(\sum_{i=1}^{2} \sum_{j=1}^{2} (\varepsilon^d_{ij} - \varepsilon^{d*}_{ij})^2 + \sum_{i=1}^{2} (\eta_i - \eta^*_i)^2 \right) \tag{13.20}$$

with the constraints:

$$w_1 \eta_1 + w_2 \eta_2 = 1$$

$$\varepsilon^d_{11} + \varepsilon^d_{12} + \eta_1 = 0$$

$$\varepsilon^d_{21} + \varepsilon^d_{22} + \eta_2 = 0$$

$$w_1 (\varepsilon^d_{12} + w_2 \eta_1) = w_2 (\varepsilon^d_{21} + w_1 \eta_2)$$

$$\varepsilon^d_{11} + w_1 \eta_1 \leq 0$$

$$\varepsilon^d_{22} + w_2 \eta_2 \leq 0$$

$$(\varepsilon^d_{11} + w_1 \eta_1)(\varepsilon^d_{22} + w_2 \eta_2) \geq (\varepsilon^d_{12} + w_2 \eta_1)(\varepsilon^d_{21} + w_1 \eta_2)$$

where * again denotes the start value for the elasticities.

As a result of the optimisation, the 'correct' and adjusted elasticities would then be incorporated into the model and used for the model calibration and subsequent policy analysis.

It is important to keep in mind that the discussed microeconomic adjustment of multi-market models should not automatically be conducted and, in particular, should not always be done in the same way. For each problem setting and specific model it needs to be assessed if, and in what form, a microeconomic adjustment of the elasticities is required. Overall, the outlined microeconomic adjustment is a useful approach to improve the quality of a formulated multi-market model, analysing a number of markets in the context of an overall economy in a theoretically sound way.

In addition to the microeconomic foundations of our multi-market model we also have to reconsider the formulation of welfare indicators. We have derived these indicators, such as total benefit, cost, foreign exchange, consumer surplus, producer surplus and government budget, from the observed supply and demand functions. Such an approach is widely used and may be applied without problems for the welfare indicators foreign exchange and government budget as well as for cost and producer surplus which are derived from supply functions, assuming the model reflects the microeconomic foundations as discussed. However, the situation is different if we look at indicators derived from demand functions. Total benefit and consumer surplus, even with a microeconomic foundation of the model, only provide approximations of the respective welfare levels, because Marshallian demand functions include both substitution and income effects.

Such an approximation is acceptable so long as we restrict the analysis to a small part of the economy such as a commodity market where we can abstract from income effects in our model calculations. However, in larger models, which include more markets and hence a bigger part of the economy, the application of welfare indicators based on Marshallian demand functions becomes questionable.

Against this background it has been argued that welfare indicators based on income-compensated Hicksian demand functions are more suited for welfare assessment. Figure 13.2 shows how the change in welfare for consumers may be described on the basis of Hicksian demand functions. First, the graph depicts the decrease in consumer surplus due to a price increase by the bold-framed area. The compensating variation (CV) describes the decline of welfare for consumers on the basis of the utility level in the base situation, indicated by the vertically hatched area. The equivalent variation (EV), on the other hand, describes the decline of welfare for consumers on the basis of the utility level in the new situation, here indicated by the horizontally hatched area. It has been shown that both the compensating variation and the equivalent variation are better suited to indicate welfare changes for consumers than a change in consumer surplus.

The problem is, however, that Hicksian demand functions cannot be observed and welfare indicators are thus difficult to calculate on such a basis. For that reason we continue to use Marshallian demand functions for welfare assessment in our multi-market models. As a consequence of this caveat, we have to accept certain inaccuracies in welfare indicators, which are calculated on this basis: i.e. total benefit, consumer surplus and welfare. In addition, we do not conduct optimisation exercises with respect to these variables, but restrict ourselves to comparisons of different scenarios.

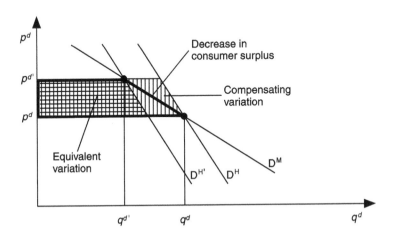

D^M – Marshallian demand curve

D^H – Hicksian demand curve

Figure 13.2 Consumer surplus, compensating variation and equivalent variation at a price change.

Exercise 13

Consider the supply functions

$$q_1^s(p_1^s, p_2^s) = c_1(p_1^s)^{\varepsilon_{11}^s}(p_2^s)^{\varepsilon_{12}^s}$$

$$q_2^s(p_1^s, p_2^s) = c_2(p_1^s)^{\varepsilon_{21}^s}(p_2^s)^{\varepsilon_{22}^s}$$

with $\varepsilon_{11}^s = \varepsilon_{22}^s = 0.3$ and $\varepsilon_{12}^s = \varepsilon_{21}^s = -0.1$

and the demand functions

$$q_1^d(p_1^d, p_2^d, y) = d_1(p_1^d)^{\varepsilon_{11}^d}(p_2^d)^{\varepsilon_{12}^d}y^{\eta_1}$$

$$q_2^d(p_1^d, p_2^d, y) = d_2(p_1^d)^{\varepsilon_{21}^d}(p_2^d)^{\varepsilon_{22}^d}y^{\eta_2}$$

with $\varepsilon_{11}^d = \varepsilon_{22}^d = -0.4,\quad \varepsilon_{12}^d = \varepsilon_{21}^d = 0.2$ and $\eta_1 = \eta_2 = 1.$

Formulate a market model in Excel and solve the following problems:

(a) Correct the above elasticities considering the homogeneity condition, the symmetry condition and the curve properties for supply and demand functions and the adding-up condition on the demand side. Solve the following exercises on the basis of this microeconomic adjustment using the corrected elasticities.

(b) As in Exercise 12, assume free trade; the world market prices are $p_1^w = 10$ and $p_2^w = 15$. Under this policy the country is an importer of the first product; the quantity supplied is $q_1^s = 80$ and the quantity demanded is $q_1^d = 100$. The country is an exporter of the second product with $q_2^s = 120$ and $q_2^d = 100$. Calibrate the model accordingly.

(c) Examine how an increase in the world market prices of both products of 10 per cent would affect supply, demand and expenditure. How would the result differ, if at the same time income (defined as expenditure for the considered products) were to rise by 10 per cent?

(d) At what level would domestic prices have to be set by the government to maximise producer surplus, without causing additional budget expenditure?

(e) Show graphically how in comparison to free trade a gradual increase in the protection rates in both markets to 50 per cent affects producer surplus, consumer surplus, government budget and welfare in both markets.

Solution

Step 13.1 To correct the elasticity values in Exercise 13a, add the factor y^{η_i} to the demand and total benefit function of both markets in model exercise 12a.xls. Enter the value 2500 for y in cell H7 defining expenditure in the base situation as well as in cell G7 as an additional parameter of calibration for *y*. We then have to adjust the constants d_1 and d_2 respectively. For d_1 we get the formula = F6/B6^G11/B7^H11/G7^I11 in C11. The income elasticities of demand for both products are placed in I11 and I12. Thus we have calibrated the model again (cf. Figure 13.3 and exercise13a.xls).

Then, add below the given start values of the elasticities a range for the variable (adjusted) elasticity values and enter 1 in each of these cells. Below, you can calculate the differences of the start values and variable elasticities and then write the formula for the sum of the squares of these differences (using the Excel function SUMSQ) in cell F30, which later needs to be minimised according to the functions in (13.7) and (13.20). You can implement the left-hand sides of the constraints in (13.7) and (13.20) as shown in Figure 13.3 and enter the constraints into the Solver (compare with exercise13a.xls).

Then run the Solver and it will produce the desired solution. The result shows that some of the adjusted elasticities deviate quite substantially from the given start values. Figure 13.4 also shows that all microeconomic conditions are fulfilled.

Step 13.2 Enter the calculated elasticity values in the cells D11:E12 and G11:I12 and the model is automatically calibrated for the adjusted elasticity

Figure 13.3 Calculation of microeconomically adjusted elasticity values (exercise13a.xls).

	A	B	C	D	E	F	G	H	I
1			Market model with microeconomically adjusted elasticities						
2									
3	p^s	p^d	p^w		Supply	Demand		Cost	Total benefit
4	10.00	10.00	10.00		80.00	100.00		155.48	3001.15
5	15.00	15.00	15.00		120.00	100.00		174.30	3458.99
6	10.00	10.00	Calibration Market 1		80.00	100.00	Income	Income	
7	15.00	15.00	Calibration Market 2		120.00	100.00	2500.00	2500	
8									
9		Constants		Elasticities of supply			Elasticities of demand		Income
10		c	d	Market 1	Market 2		Market 1	Market 2	elasticities
11	Market 1	88.2205445	0.60931774	0.24	-0.24	Initial values	-0.74	-0.20	0.94
12	Market 2	114.895061	0.45320568	-0.11	0.11		-0.17	-0.87	1.04
13									
14				0.24	-0.24	Variables	-0.74	-0.20	0.94
15				-0.11	0.11		-0.17	-0.87	1.04
16				0	0	Differences	0	0	0
17				0	0		0	0	0
18						Conditions			
19						Adding-up	1	=1	
20									
21				0	=0	Homogeneity	0	=0	
22				0	=0		0	=0	
23									
24				0	=0	Symmetry	9.765E-09	=0	
25									
26				0.24123711	>=0	Curve	-0.363077	<=0	
27				0.10721649	>=0	properties	-0.242051	<=0	
28				0.0258646	0.025864598		0.0878832	>=	0.08788325
29						Sum of the squares of the differences			
30						0			

Figure 13.4 Market model with microeconomically adjusted elasticity values (exercise 13b.xls).

values (cf. Figure 13.4 and exercise 13b.xls). Exercise 13b is thus also solved.

Step 13.3 Exercise 13c can now be solved quickly. Enter the value 11 in cell C4, the value 16.5 in cell C5 and finally the value 2750 for the income in cell H7. At a price increase for both products of 10 per cent supply quantities do not change, while demand decreases due to the income effect. If we increase the income by 10 per cent too, demand remains unchanged at the original level (cf. Figure 13.5).

Step 13.4 Exercise 13d may be solved with the Solver using model exercise 13b.xls. First, reset the Solver with the 'Reset all' button. Enter the formula for the sum of producer surplus of both markets in cell O6 and choose this cell as target cell to be maximised. Then enter the sum of budget revenue in cell N6 and define the constraint N6 > = 0. Define A4:A5 as changing cells for the uniform domestic prices. The Solver produces the solution $p_1 \approx 12.38$ and $p_2 \approx 15.13$ (cf. Figure 13.6).

The result again shows the importance of market interdependencies. Without consideration of cross-price effects this optimisation problem should have produced the autarky price as the market price of both products. However, the market interdependencies lead to an optimal solution under the given price policy, which deviates from autarky.

	A	B	C	D	E	F	G	H	I
1			Market model with microeconomically adjusted elasticities						
2									
3	p^s	p^d	p^w		Supply	Demand		Cost	Total benefit
4	11.00	11.00	11.00		80.00	100.00		171.03	3143.53
5	16.50	16.50	16.50		120.00	100.00		191.73	3621.41
6	10.00	10.00	Calibration Market 1		80.00	100.00	Income	Income	
7	15.00	15.00	Calibration Market 2		120.00	100.00	2500.00	2750	
8									
9		Constants		Elasticities of supply			Elasticities of demand		Income
10		c	d	Market 1	Market 2		Market 1	Market 2	elasticities
11	Market 1	88.2205445	0.60931774	0.24	-0.24	Initial values	-0.74	-0.20	0.94
12	Market 2	114.895061	0.45320568	-0.11	0.11		-0.17	-0.87	1.04

	J	K	L	M	N	O	P
2							
3	Welfare	Revenue	Expenditure	Foreign exchange	Government budget	Producer surplus	Consumer surplus
4	2752.50	880.00	1100.00	-220.00	0.00	708.97	2043.53
5	3759.68	1980.00	1650.00	330.00	0.00	1788.27	1971.41
6		Total expenditure E: 2750					

Figure 13.5 Implications of a world market price increase and income increase of 10 per cent (exercise13c.xls).

	A	B	C	D	E	F	G	H	I
1			Market model with microeconomically adjusted elasticities						
2									
3	p^s	p^d	p^w		Supply	Demand		Cost	Total benefit
4	12.38	12.38	10.00		84.06	85.24		202.34	2833.82
5	15.13	15.13	15.00		117.39	95.62		171.98	3321.61
6	10.00	10.00	Calibration Market 1		80.00	100.00	Income	Income	
7	15.00	15.00	Calibration Market 2		120.00	100.00	2500.00	2500	
8									
9		Constants		Elasticities of supply			Elasticities of demand		Income
10		c	d	Market 1	Market 2		Market 1	Market 2	elasticities
11	Market 1	88.2205445	0.60931774	0.24	-0.24		-0.74	-0.20	0.94
12	Market 2	114.895061	0.45320568	-0.11	0.11		-0.17	-0.87	1.04

	J	K	L	M	N	O	P
2							
3	Welfare	Revenue	Expenditure	Foreign exchange	Government budget	Producer surplus	Consumer surplus
4	2619.68	1041.11	1055.72	-11.80	2.81	838.76	1778.10
5	3476.06	1775.99	1446.74	326.44	-2.81	1604.02	1874.86
6			E: 2502.46554	Sum:	0.00	2442.78	

Figure 13.6 Maximisation of producer surplus without additional budget expenditure (exercise13d.xls).

Step 13.5 Finally, solve Exercise 13e. First, implement free trade again. Then integrate the protection rate, and also the subsidy rates, in the model (similar to Step 3.5 or 4.6). We can now generate the values of the relevant functions of both markets for the different protection rates by using the 'Data table' operations and show the result in a graph (cf. Figure 13.7 and exercise13e.xls).

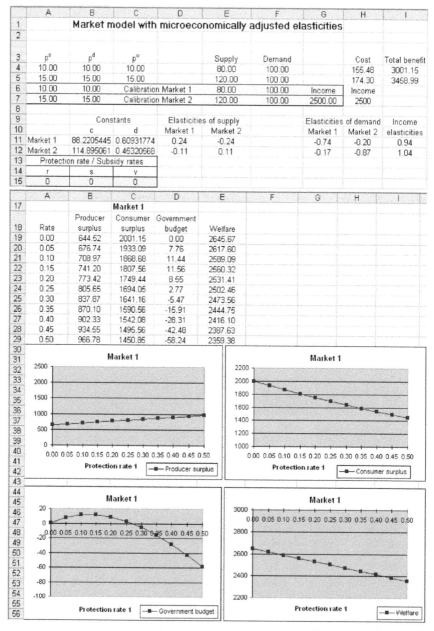

Figure 13.7 Implications of an increase in the protection rate on both markets from 0 to 50 per cent (exercise13e.xls).

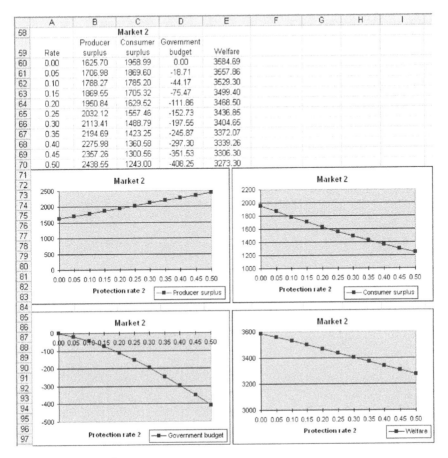

	A	B	C	D	E
58			Market 2		
59	Rate	Producer surplus	Consumer surplus	Government budget	Welfare
60	0.00	1625.70	1958.99	0.00	3584.69
61	0.05	1706.98	1869.60	-18.71	3557.86
62	0.10	1788.27	1785.20	-44.17	3529.30
63	0.15	1869.55	1705.32	-75.47	3499.40
64	0.20	1950.84	1629.52	-111.86	3468.50
65	0.25	2032.12	1557.46	-152.73	3436.85
66	0.30	2113.41	1488.79	-197.55	3404.65
67	0.35	2194.69	1423.25	-245.87	3372.07
68	0.40	2275.98	1360.58	-297.30	3339.26
69	0.45	2357.26	1300.56	-351.53	3306.30
70	0.50	2438.55	1243.00	-408.25	3273.30

Figure 13.7 continued.

The figure shows that the principal shape of the functions is the same as with the single-market models, but the cross-price effects now lead to different values.

References

Chiang, A.C. and Wainwright, K. (2005) *Fundamental Methods of Mathematical Economics* (4th edn), Boston, MA: McGraw-Hill, pp. 291–346, 383–90.

Mas-Colell, A., Whinston, M.D. and Green, J.A. (1995) *Microeconomic Theory*, New York, Oxford: Oxford University Press, pp. 67–75, 80–91, 135–43.

Nicholson, W. (2005) *Microeconomic Theory: Basic Principles and Extensions* (9th edn), Mason, OH: Thomson, pp. 131–48.

Varian, H.R. (2003) *Intermediate Microeconomics: A Modern Approach* (6th edn), New York: W.W. Norton, pp. 137–56, 254–8.

Wahl, O., Weber, G. and Frohberg, K. (2000) 'Documentation of the Central and Eastern European Countries Agricultural Simulation Model', Discussion Paper No. 27 presented at the Institut für Agrarentwicklung in Mittel und Osteuropa, Halle (Saale).

Winston, W.L. (2004) *Operations Research* (4th edn), Belmont, CA: Brooks/Cole, pp. 630–5.

14 Formulation of a four-market model

Objective

In Chapter 14 we will formulate a multi-market model for four markets and then apply the model to the analysis of price policies. We will show how the microeconomic foundations of market models, discussed on the basis of two markets, may be extended to more markets.

Theory

To develop a four-market model, supply and demand quantities need to be formulated as functions of all four prices. In addition, the income variable needs to be considered on the demand side. For the supply side we can write:

$$q_i^s(p_1^s, p_2^s, p_3^s, p_4^s) = c_i \, (p_1^s)^{e_{i1}^s} \, (p_2^s)^{e_{i2}^s} \, (p_3^s)^{e_{i3}^s} \, (p_4^s)^{e_{i4}^s} \tag{14.1}$$

with $\quad i = 1, \ldots, 4.$

Analogously, we get for the demand side:

$$q_i^d(p_1^d, p_2^d, p_3^d, p_4^d, y) = d_i \, (p_1^d)^{e_{i1}^d} \, (p_2^d)^{e_{i2}^d} \, (p_3^d)^{e_{i3}^d} \, (p_4^d)^{e_{i4}^d} \, y^{n_i} \tag{14.2}$$

with $\quad i = 1, \ldots, 4.$

In order to use and calibrate the model empirically, the quantities supplied and demanded, supply and demand prices, world market prices, and price and income elasticities need to be defined for all four products. In addition, the microeconomic foundation of the model requires that certain restrictions for the elasticities are fulfilled, as explained in Chapter 13. Let us consider the following elasticity matrix for the supply side:

$$\boldsymbol{\varepsilon^s} = \begin{bmatrix} \varepsilon_{11}^s & \varepsilon_{12}^s & \varepsilon_{13}^s & \varepsilon_{14}^s \\ \varepsilon_{21}^s & \varepsilon_{22}^s & \varepsilon_{23}^s & \varepsilon_{24}^s \\ \varepsilon_{31}^s & \varepsilon_{32}^s & \varepsilon_{33}^s & \varepsilon_{34}^s \\ \varepsilon_{41}^s & \varepsilon_{42}^s & \varepsilon_{43}^s & \varepsilon_{44}^s \end{bmatrix} \tag{14.3}$$

with $\boldsymbol{\varepsilon^s}$ – price elasticity matrix on the supply side.

According to the homogeneity condition the sum of each row of this matrix has to be zero. To consider the symmetry condition and the curve property (convexity), the matrix of the derivatives of the supply functions with respect to the prices needs to be determined in a first step:

$$\mathbf{H^s} = \begin{bmatrix} \dfrac{\partial q_1^s}{\partial p_1^s} & \dfrac{\partial q_1^s}{\partial p_2^s} & \dfrac{\partial q_1^s}{\partial p_3^s} & \dfrac{\partial q_1^s}{\partial p_4^s} \\[2mm] \dfrac{\partial q_2^s}{\partial p_1^s} & \dfrac{\partial q_2^s}{\partial p_2^s} & \dfrac{\partial q_2^s}{\partial p_3^s} & \dfrac{\partial q_2^s}{\partial p_4^s} \\[2mm] \dfrac{\partial q_3^s}{\partial p_1^s} & \dfrac{\partial q_3^s}{\partial p_2^s} & \dfrac{\partial q_3^s}{\partial p_3^s} & \dfrac{\partial q_3^s}{\partial p_4^s} \\[2mm] \dfrac{\partial q_4^s}{\partial p_1^s} & \dfrac{\partial q_4^s}{\partial p_2^s} & \dfrac{\partial q_4^s}{\partial p_3^s} & \dfrac{\partial q_4^s}{\partial p_4^s} \end{bmatrix} \tag{14.4}$$

with $\mathbf{H^s}$ – matrix of the derivatives of the supply functions with respect to the prices.

$\mathbf{H^s}$ can be calculated from $\boldsymbol{\varepsilon^s}$; since it applies for every element of $\mathbf{H^s}$:

$$\frac{\partial q_i^s}{\partial p_j^s} = \varepsilon_{ij}^s \frac{q_i^s}{p_j^s} \tag{14.5}$$

with $i, j = 1, \ldots, 4.$

It follows:

$$\mathbf{H^s} = \begin{bmatrix} q_1^s & 0 & 0 & 0 \\ 0 & q_2^s & 0 & 0 \\ 0 & 0 & q_3^s & 0 \\ 0 & 0 & 0 & q_4^s \end{bmatrix} \cdot \boldsymbol{\varepsilon^s} \cdot \begin{bmatrix} \dfrac{1}{p_1^s} & 0 & 0 & 0 \\[2mm] 0 & \dfrac{1}{p_2^s} & 0 & 0 \\[2mm] 0 & 0 & \dfrac{1}{p_3^s} & 0 \\[2mm] 0 & 0 & 0 & \dfrac{1}{p_4^s} \end{bmatrix} \cdot \tag{14.6}$$

Following the symmetry condition $\mathbf{H^s}$ must be symmetric and the matrix must be positive semi-definite with respect to the curve properties. These properties are fulfilled if the matrix $\mathbf{H^s}$ is equal to its transpose $\mathbf{H^{sT}}$ (symmetry condition) and the determinants of all principal submatrices are not negative (curve properties).

On the demand side we can initially assume the following elasticity matrix:

$$
[\boldsymbol{\varepsilon^d}, \boldsymbol{\eta}] = \begin{bmatrix}
\varepsilon^d_{11} & \varepsilon^d_{12} & \varepsilon^d_{13} & \varepsilon^d_{14} & \eta_1 \\
\varepsilon^d_{21} & \varepsilon^d_{22} & \varepsilon^d_{23} & \varepsilon^d_{24} & \eta_2 \\
\varepsilon^d_{31} & \varepsilon^d_{32} & \varepsilon^d_{33} & \varepsilon^d_{34} & \eta_3 \\
\varepsilon^d_{41} & \varepsilon^d_{42} & \varepsilon^d_{43} & \varepsilon^d_{44} & \eta_4
\end{bmatrix}
\tag{14.7}
$$

with $[\boldsymbol{\varepsilon^d}, \boldsymbol{\eta}]$ – matrix of price and income elasticities on the demand side.

According to the adding-up condition the income variable in the demand functions would be defined by the sum of the expenditure for the four products, and for the 'income column' in the above matrix it would apply that the sum of the income elasticities of the four products, weighted by respective shares in expenditure, must be 1:

$$
\sum_{i=1}^{4} w_i \eta_i = 1.
\tag{14.8}
$$

To fulfil the homogeneity condition the sums of the matrix rows of $[\boldsymbol{\varepsilon^d}, \boldsymbol{\eta}]$ should each add up to zero. Similar to the supply side and again taking into account the symmetry condition and the curve properties, the matrix of the derivatives of the demand functions with respect to the prices has to be determined, now based on Hicksian demand functions:

$$
\mathbf{H^d} = \begin{bmatrix}
\dfrac{\partial q_1^{d(H)}}{\partial p_1^d} & \dfrac{\partial q_1^{d(H)}}{\partial p_2^d} & \dfrac{\partial q_1^{d(H)}}{\partial p_3^d} & \dfrac{\partial q_1^{d(H)}}{\partial p_4^d} \\[4mm]
\dfrac{\partial q_2^{d(H)}}{\partial p_1^d} & \dfrac{\partial q_2^{d(H)}}{\partial p_2^d} & \dfrac{\partial q_2^{d(H)}}{\partial p_3^d} & \dfrac{\partial q_2^{d(H)}}{\partial p_4^d} \\[4mm]
\dfrac{\partial q_3^{d(H)}}{\partial p_1^d} & \dfrac{\partial q_3^{d(H)}}{\partial p_2^d} & \dfrac{\partial q_3^{d(H)}}{\partial p_3^d} & \dfrac{\partial q_3^{d(H)}}{\partial p_4^d} \\[4mm]
\dfrac{\partial q_4^{d(H)}}{\partial p_1^d} & \dfrac{\partial q_4^{d(H)}}{\partial p_2^d} & \dfrac{\partial q_4^{d(H)}}{\partial p_3^d} & \dfrac{\partial q_4^{d(H)}}{\partial p_4^d}
\end{bmatrix}
\tag{14.9}
$$

with $\mathbf{H^d}$ – matrix of the derivatives of the Hicksian demand functions with respect to the prices.

$\mathbf{H^d}$ can be calculated from $[\boldsymbol{\varepsilon^d}, \boldsymbol{\eta}]$ by using the Slutsky equation; since for every element of $\mathbf{H^d}$ it applies:

$$\frac{\partial q_i^{d(H)}}{\partial p_j^d} = \frac{q_i^d}{p_j^d}(\varepsilon_{ij}^d + \eta_i \, w_j) \tag{14.10}$$

with $i, j = 1, \ldots, 4$.

It follows:

$$
\mathbf{H^d} = \begin{bmatrix} q_1^d & 0 & 0 & 0 \\ 0 & q_2^d & 0 & 0 \\ 0 & 0 & q_3^d & 0 \\ 0 & 0 & 0 & q_4^d \end{bmatrix} \cdot \left[\boldsymbol{\varepsilon^d} + \begin{bmatrix} \eta_1 \\ \eta_2 \\ \eta_3 \\ \eta_4 \end{bmatrix} \cdot [w_1, w_2, w_3, w_4] \right] \cdot
$$

$$
\begin{bmatrix} \dfrac{1}{p_1^d} & 0 & 0 & 0 \\[2mm] 0 & \dfrac{1}{p_2^d} & 0 & 0 \\[2mm] 0 & 0 & \dfrac{1}{p_3^d} & 0 \\[2mm] 0 & 0 & 0 & \dfrac{1}{p_4^d} \end{bmatrix} \cdot \tag{14.11}
$$

Following the symmetry condition $\mathbf{H^d}$ must be symmetric and with respect to the curve properties the matrix must be negative semi-definite. Analogous to the supply side, the symmetry condition is fulfilled if the matrix $\mathbf{H^d}$ is equal to its transpose $\mathbf{H^{dT}}$. With respect to the curve properties the determinants of all principal submatrices must be alternating non-positive and non-negative.

Following the microeconomic foundation of the elasticities the model can be calibrated and applied for the analysis of price policies. However, it is important to keep in mind that it has to be evaluated for each individual case, if, and in what form, a microeconomic adjustment were to be carried out.

Exercise 14

Consider the supply functions

$$q_i^s(p_1^s, p_2^s, p_3^s, p_4^s) = c_i \, (p_1^s)^{\varepsilon_{i1}^s} (p_2^s)^{\varepsilon_{i2}^s} (p_3^s)^{\varepsilon_{i3}^s} (p_4^s)^{\varepsilon_{i4}^s}$$

for $i = 1, \ldots, 4$

with $\varepsilon_{ii}^s = 0.3$ and $\varepsilon_{ij}^s = -0.1 \; (i \neq j)$

and the demand functions

$$q_i^d(p_1^d, p_2^d, p_3^d, p_4^d, y) = d_i\,(p_1^d)^{\varepsilon_{i1}^d}\,(p_2^d)^{\varepsilon_{i2}^d}\,(p_3^d)^{\varepsilon_{i3}^d}\,(p_4^d)^{\varepsilon_{i4}^d}\,y^{\eta_i}$$

for $i = 1, \ldots, 4$

with $\varepsilon_{ii}^d = -0.4,\ \varepsilon_{ij}^d = 0.2\ (i \neq j)$ and $\eta_i = 1$.

The following information on the four markets is available:

Market	Quantity supplied	Quantity demanded	Supply price	Demand price	World market price
1	80	100	10	10	10
2	120	100	15	15	15
3	100	120	14	14	12
4	70	70	18	18	15

In the first two markets the country pursues a free trade policy, in the third market a protectionist price policy and in the fourth market an autarky policy are implemented.

Formulate a market model in Excel and solve the following problems:

(a) Correct the above elasticities considering the homogeneity condition, the symmetry condition and relevant curve properties on the supply and demand sides and the adding-up condition on the demand side. Solve the following exercises on the basis of this 'microeconomic adjustment' using the corrected elasticities.
(b) Calibrate the model accordingly.
(c) Show how an increase in the world market price of the first product to $p_1^w = 15$ affects supply and demand.
(d) How does the implementation of free trade on all markets change government budget, foreign exchange, producer surplus and consumer surplus?
(e) Show graphically how in comparison to free trade a gradual increase of the protection rates of all products to 50 per cent affects producer surplus, consumer surplus and government budget on all markets.

Solution

Step 14.1 Previously, in Steps 12.1 to 12.3 we extended a single-market model to a two-market model, analysing the interdependencies between two markets and creating the file exercise12a.xls. We will now further extend the model from two to four interdependent markets. Thus, start with the model exercise12a.xls, set all prices to the value 10 (including the calibration values) and choose for each q_i^s the value 80 and for each q_i^d the value 100. Starting the modelling in this way will help to monitor our work using the symmetry of the defined markets. Move the range

A6:H12 to A8:H14 and then again move the range A11:H14 to A13:H16. Then copy the complete rows 4 and 5 and enter these in rows 6 and 7. Analogously, copy the complete rows 8 and 9 and paste them into rows 10 and 11. In order to create some space, move the range G13:H16 with the demand elasticities to the right into the range I13;J16. Fill the 4×4 matrices of the supply and demand elasticities with the given values in the ranges D15:G18 and I15:L18 (cf. Figure 14.1).

Enter the income elasticities with a value of 1 in the range M15:M18. For income we initially choose the arbitrarily fixed value of 100 and enter this in cell H9. We enter the same value 100 as calibration value for income in cell G9. Review the model framework and, analogously to Step 12.2 and Step 12.3, generate all formulas for q_i^s and q_i^d in E4:F7, following (14.1) and (14.2), as well as the cost and total benefit

	H6	▼		*fx* =A6*E6-B17*A4^D17*A5^E17*A6^(F17+1)/(F17+1)*A7^G17			
	A	B	C	D	E	F	G	H
1			Cobb-Douglas Market Model with 4 Interdependent Markets					
2								
3	p^s	p^d	p^w		Supply	Demand		Cost
4	10.00	10.00	10.00		80.00	100.00		184.62
5	10.00	10.00	10.00		80.00	100.00		184.62
6	10.00	10.00	10.00		80.00	100.00		184.62
7	10.00	10.00	10.00		80.00	100.00		184.62
8	10.00	10.00	Calibration Market 1		80.00	100.00	Income	Income
9	10.00	10.00	Calibration Market 2		80.00	100.00	100.00	100
10	10.00	10.00	Calibration Market 3		80.00	100.00		
11	10.00	10.00	Calibration Market 4		80.00	100.00		
12								
13			Constants		Elasticities of supply			
14		c	d	Market 1	Market 2	Market 3	Market 4	
15	Market 1	80	0.63095734	0.3	-0.1	-0.1	-0.1	
16	Market 2	80	0.63095734	-0.1	0.3	-0.1	-0.1	
17	Market 3	80	0.63095734	-0.1	-0.1	0.3	-0.1	
18	Market 4	80	0.63095734	-0.1	-0.1	-0.1	0.3	

	I	J	K	L	M	N	O	P
1								
2								
3	Total benefit	Welfare	Revenue	Expenditure	Foreign exchange	Government budget	Producer surplus	Consumer surplus
4	3710.88	3326.26	800.00	1000.00	-200.00	0.00	615.38	2710.88
5	3710.88	3326.26	800.00	1000.00	-200.00	0.00	615.38	2710.88
6	3710.88	3326.26	800.00	1000.00	-200.00	0.00	615.38	2710.88
7	3710.88	3326.26	800.00	1000.00	-200.00	0.00	615.38	2710.88
12								
13	Elasticities of demand				Income			
14	Market 1	Market 2	Market 3	Market 4	elasticities			
15	-0.4	0.2	0.2	0.2	1			
16	0.2	-0.4	0.2	0.2	1			
17	0.2	0.2	-0.4	0.2	1			
18	0.2	0.2	0.2	-0.4	1			

Figure 14.1 Cobb-Douglas market model with four interdependent markets (exercise14.xls).

functions in H4:I7. The Excel formulas are, for example, for cell

E4: $= B15*A4^D15*A5^E15*A6^F15*A7^G15$, for cell
F5: $= C16*B4^I16*B5^J16*B6^K16*B7^L16*H9^M16$, for cell
H6: $= A6*E6 - B17*A4^D17*A5^E17*A6^(F17 + 1)/$
$(F17 + 1)*A7^G17$ and for cell
I7: $= B7*F7 + C18*B4^I18*B5^J18*$
$B6^K18*(50^(L18 + 1) - B7^(L18 + 1))/(L18 + 1)*H9^M18.$

Furthermore, the formulas for c_i and d_i in the range B15:C18 need to be adjusted, following (14.1) and (14.2) and similar to Step 12.2, and the model is correctly calibrated. For example, in cell B15 we obtain the formula $= E8/(A8^D15*A9^E15*A10^F15*A11^G15)$ and in C18 the formula $= F11/(B8^I18*B9^J18*B10^K18*B11^L18*G9^M18)$. Admittedly, the model formulation is somewhat time-consuming, but the uniform price of 10 and the application of the 'Formula auditing' ('Trace precedents') help to simplify the task (cf. Figure 14.1 and exercise14.xls).

Step 14.2 You can now enter the data for price and quantities in the four markets into the model to solve our exercise. Bear in mind that you have to enter the value 5440 for the income in the cells G9 and H9, which is the sum of the expenditure for the four products (cf. Figure 14.2 and exercise14a1.xls).

Step 14.3 To solve Exercise 14a we will correct the elasticities, proceeding in this step as in Step 13.1. To model the necessary extension and generalisation for four markets we use the matrix formulas available in Excel. Note that a matrix formula can be entered through simultaneously pushing the Ctrl, Shift and Enter keys, whereby Excel then sets the matrix formulas in curly brackets ({ }).

Add again below the start values of the elasticities the range for the variable elasticities and enter below that the range for the differences. By using the SUMSQ Excel function we again compute the sum of the squares of these differences, which will then be minimised in the target cell of the Solver (cf. Figure 14.3 and exercise14a2.xls).

Let us now continue with the formulation of the matrices $\mathbf{H^s}$ and $\mathbf{H^d}$, which we need for the microeconomic adjustment. First, we calculate in N8:N11 the expenditure shares w_1, w_2, w_3 and w_4 with respect to the four products and enter the values in the range J8:J11. Furthermore, we need for the formulation of $\mathbf{H^s}$ and $\mathbf{H^d}$ some additional matrices following (14.6) and (14.11). We need the diagonal matrices

$$\begin{bmatrix} q_1^s & 0 & 0 & 0 \\ 0 & q_2^s & 0 & 0 \\ 0 & 0 & q_3^s & 0 \\ 0 & 0 & 0 & q_4^s \end{bmatrix}, \begin{bmatrix} q_1^d & 0 & 0 & 0 \\ 0 & q_2^d & 0 & 0 \\ 0 & 0 & q_3^d & 0 \\ 0 & 0 & 0 & q_4^d \end{bmatrix}$$

	A	B	C	D	E	F	G	H
1	Calibrated Cobb-Douglas Model with 4 Interdependent Markets							
2								
3	p^s	p^d	p^w		Supply	Demand		Cost
4	10.00	10.00	10.00		80.00	100.00		184.62
5	15.00	15.00	15.00		120.00	100.00		415.38
6	14.00	14.00	12.00		100.00	120.00		323.08
7	18.00	18.00	15.00		70.00	70.00		290.77
8	10.00	10.00	Calibration Market 1		80.00	100.00	Income	Income
9	15.00	15.00	Calibration Market 2		120.00	100.00	5440.00	5440.00
10	14.00	14.00	Calibration Market 3		100.00	120.00		
11	18.00	18.00	Calibration Market 4		70.00	70.00		
12								
13			Constants		Elasticities of supply			
14		c	d	Market 1	Market 2	Market 3	Market 4	
15	Market 1	91.3774779	0.00889002	0.3	-0.1	-0.1	-0.1	
16	Market 2	116.545074	0.01133855	-0.1	0.3	-0.1	-0.1	
17	Market 3	99.8384812	0.01305452	-0.1	-0.1	0.3	-0.1	
18	Market 4	63.2030764	0.0088545	-0.1	-0.1	-0.1	0.3	

	I	J	K	L	M	N	O	P
2								
3	Total benefit	Welfare	Revenue	Expenditure	Foreign exchange	Government budget	Producer surplus	Consumer surplus
4	3710.88	3326.26	800.00	1000.00	-200.00	0.00	615.38	2710.88
5	4148.34	4032.96	1800.00	1500.00	300.00	0.00	1384.62	2648.34
6	4889.84	4326.77	1400.00	1680.00	-240.00	40.00	1076.92	3209.84
7	3036.48	2745.71	1260.00	1260.00	0.00	0.00	969.23	1776.48
8			Total Expenditure E: 5440					
12								
13	Elasticities of demand				Income			
14	Market 1	Market 2	Market 3	Market 4	elasticities			
15	-0.4	0.2	0.2	0.2	1			
16	0.2	-0.4	0.2	0.2	1			
17	0.2	0.2	-0.4	0.2	1			
18	0.2	0.2	0.2	-0.4	1			

Figure 14.2 Calibrated market model with four interdependent markets (exercise14a1.xls).

and

$$
\begin{bmatrix}
\dfrac{1}{p_1^s} & 0 & 0 & 0 \\[2ex]
0 & \dfrac{1}{p_2^s} & 0 & 0 \\[2ex]
0 & 0 & \dfrac{1}{p_3^s} & 0 \\[2ex]
0 & 0 & 0 & \dfrac{1}{p_4^s}
\end{bmatrix},
\begin{bmatrix}
\dfrac{1}{p_1^d} & 0 & 0 & 0 \\[2ex]
0 & \dfrac{1}{p_2^d} & 0 & 0 \\[2ex]
0 & 0 & \dfrac{1}{p_3^d} & 0 \\[2ex]
0 & 0 & 0 & \dfrac{1}{p_4^d}
\end{bmatrix}
$$

which we depict as formulas through the relevant relationships in the range Q19:X26 (cf. Figure 14.3 and exercise14a2.xls).

Cobb-Douglas Model with Microeconomic Adjustment of the Elasticities
for 4 Interdependent Markets

	p^s	p^d	p^w	Supply	Demand		Cost	Total benefit	Welfare	Revenue	Expenditure	Foreign exchange	Government budget
	10,00	10,00	10,00	80,00	100,00		184,62	3710,88	3326,26	800,00	1000,00	-200,00	0,00
	15,00	15,00	15,00	120,00	100,00		415,38	4148,34	4032,96	1800,00	1500,00	300,00	0,00
	14,00	14,00	12,00	100,00	120,00		323,08	4889,84	4326,77	1400,00	1680,00	-240,00	40,00
	18,00	18,00	15,00	70,00	70,00		290,77	3036,48	2745,71	1260,00	1260,00	0,00	0,00
10,00	Calibration Market 1		80,00	100,00	Income	Income		fixed	w_1 0,1838235			variable	w_1 0,18382353
15,00	Calibration Market 2		120,00	100,00	5440,00	5440,00			w_2 0,2757363	E: 5440,00			w_2 0,27573529
14,00	Calibration Market 3		100,00	120,00					w_3 0,3088235				w_3 0,30882353
18,00	Calibration Market 4		70,00	70,00					w_4 0,2316176				w_4 0,23161765

Constants

	c	d
Market 1	91,377478	0,00689002
Market 2	116,54507	0,01133855
Market 3	99,838481	0,01305452
Market 4	63,203076	0,0088545

Elasticities of supply — Initial values

	Market 1	Market 2	Market 3	Market 4
Market 1	0,30	-0,10	-0,10	-0,10
Market 2	-0,10	0,30	-0,10	-0,10
Market 3	-0,10	-0,10	0,30	-0,10
Market 4	-0,10	-0,10	-0,10	0,30

Elasticities of demand — Initial values

	Market 1	Market 2	Market 3	Market 4	Income elasticities
Market 1	-0,40	0,20	0,20	0,20	1,00
Market 2	0,20	-0,40	0,20	0,20	1,00
Market 3	0,20	0,20	-0,40	0,20	1,00
Market 4	0,20	0,20	0,20	-0,40	1,00

Variables (supply | demand)

	Market 1	Market 2	Market 3	Market 4		Market 1	Market 2	Market 3	Market 4	Income elasticities
	0,30	-0,10	-0,10	-0,10		-0,40	0,20	0,20	0,20	1,00
	-0,10	0,30	-0,10	-0,10		0,20	-0,40	0,20	0,20	1,00
	-0,10	-0,10	0,30	0,30		0,20	0,20	-0,40	0,20	1,00
	-0,10	-0,10	-0,10	0,30		0,20	0,20	0,20	-0,40	1,00

Differences

	Market 1	Market 2	Market 3	Market 4		Market 1	Market 2	Market 3	Market 4	
	0,00	0,00	0,00	0,00		0,00	0,00	0,00	0,00	0,00
	0,00	0,00	0,00	0,00		0,00	0,00	0,00	0,00	0,00
	0,00	0,00	0,00	0,00		0,00	0,00	0,00	0,00	0,00
	0,00	0,00	0,00	0,00	SUMSQ	0,00				

	2,40	-0,53	-0,57	-0,44	H^s	-2,16	3,17	3,63	2,40	0,00
	-1,20	2,40	-0,86	-0,67		3,84	-0,83	3,63	2,40	
	-1,00	-0,67	2,14	-0,56	and	4,61	3,81	-0,78	2,88	
	-0,70	-0,47	-0,50	1,17	H^d	2,69	2,22	2,54	-0,65	

Figure 14.3 Calculation of microeconomically adjusted elasticity values of four interdependent markets (exercise 14a2.xls).

Continued overleaf

	Q	R	S	T	U	V	W	X
17	Additional matrices							
18								
19	80.00	0	0	0	100.00	0	0	0
20	0	120.00	0	0	0	100.00	0	0
21	0	0	100.00	0	0	0	120.00	0
22	0	0	0	70.00	0	0	0	70.00
23	0.10	0	0	0	0.10	0	0	0
24	0	0.07	0	0	0	0.07	0	0
25	0	0	0.07	0	0	0	0.07	0
26	0	0	0	0.06	0	0	0	0.06
27					0.18	0.28	0.31	0.23
28					0.18	0.28	0.31	0.23
29					0.18	0.28	0.31	0.23
30					0.18	0.28	0.31	0.23
31					-0.22	0.48	0.51	0.43
32					0.38	-0.12	0.51	0.43
33					0.38	0.48	-0.09	0.43
34					0.38	0.48	0.51	-0.17

	D	E	F	G	H	I	J	K	L	M
32					**Conditions**					
33					Adding-up	1	=1			
34										
35	0	=0			Homogeneity	1.2	=0			
36	0	=0				1.2	=0			
37	0	=0				1.2	=0			
38	0	=0				1.2	=0			
39										
40	2.40	-1.20	-1.00	-0.70	Symmetry	-2.16	3.84	4.61	2.69	
41	-0.53	2.40	-0.67	-0.47	$H^s = H^{s\,T}$	3.17	-0.83	3.81	2.22	
42	-0.57	-0.86	2.14	-0.50	and	3.63	3.63	-0.78	2.54	
43	-0.44	-0.67	-0.56	1.17	$H^d = H^{d\,T}$	2.40	2.40	2.88	-0.65	
44										
45	2.4	>=0			Curve	-2.161765	<=0			
46	5.12	>=0			properties	-10.38235	>=0			
47	7.3142857	>=0			(Leading principal minors)	158.06723	<=0			
48	-1.62E-15	>=0				-576	>=0			

Figure 14.3 continued.

We then formulate the dyadic product

$$\begin{bmatrix} \eta_1 \\ \eta_2 \\ \eta_3 \\ \eta_4 \end{bmatrix} \cdot [w_1, w_2, w_3, w_4]$$

with the matrix formula = MMULT(M19:M22;MTRANS(J8:J11)) in the range U27:X30, by using the key combination described above (after selecting the whole range U27:X30). We do this with respect to the variable income elasticities and fixed expenditure shares.

We generate the sum of this matrix and the matrix of the variable demand elasticities with the matrix formula = I19:L22 + U27:X30 in the range U31:X34. We can now calculate both matrices $\mathbf{H^d}$ and $\mathbf{H^s}$ in the ranges I28:L31 and D28:G31, respectively, using matrix multiplication and the matrix formulas = MMULT(MMULT(U19:X22;U31:X34); U23:X26) and = MMULT(MMULT(Q19:T22;D19:G22);Q23:T26) (cf. Figure 14.3 and exercise14a2.xls).

Let us now proceed with the constraints, starting with the homogeneity condition on the supply side. We write the formula = SUM(D19:G19) in cell D35 and copy it into the cells D36:D38. We thus obtain as a constraint for the Solver the condition D35:D38 = 0. To formulate the symmetry condition on the supply side we generate the transpose of the matrix $\mathbf{H^s}$ in the range D40:G43 by using the matrix formula = MTRANS(D28:G31). As constraint for the Solver we then obtain the condition $\mathbf{H^{sT}} = \mathbf{H^s}$, i.e. D40:G43 = D28:G31. To ensure the correct curve properties, all determinants of the principal submatrices of the matrix $\mathbf{H^s}$ must be non-negative. We restrict ourselves to the leading principal minors, which we generate with the respective matrix function MDET in the range D45:D48 (cf. Figure 14.3 and exercise 14a2.xls).

On the demand side we proceed accordingly, defining for the curve property that the relevant leading principal minors are alternating non-positive and non-negative (I45 ≤ 0, I46 ≥ 0, I47 ≤ 0, I48 ≥ 0). Besides the homogeneity condition (I35:I38 = 0) and symmetry condition (I40:L43 = I28:L31) we have to define the adding-up condition I33 = 1 entering the rather simple formula = SUMPRODUCT(J8:J11;M19:M22) in cell I33 (cf. Figure 14.3 and exercise14a2.xls).

We can now use the Solver to simultaneously adjust all elasticity values, as shown in Figure 14.4. Alternatively, we can also adjust the supply or demand and income elasticities separately. Whatever way we choose to adjust the elasticities, it can happen that the Solver does not find a feasible solution. But this does not mean that there is no feasible solution. Instead, the result of the optimisation is likely to depend on the chosen start values of the changing cells, which is what also happened in our case.

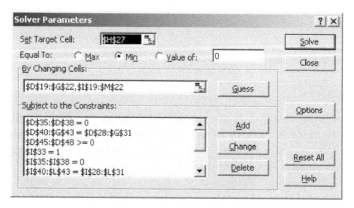

Figure 14.4 Solver parameters in the 'microeconomic adjustment' of all elasticity values.

	D	E	F	G	H	I	J	K	L	M
13	Elasticities of supply					Elasticities of demand				Income
14	Market 1	Market 2	Market 3	Market 4		Market 1	Market 2	Market 3	Market 4	elasticities
15	0.30	-0.10	-0.10	-0.10	Initial values	-0.40	0.20	0.20	0.20	1.00
16	-0.10	0.30	-0.10	-0.10		0.20	-0.40	0.20	0.20	1.00
17	-0.10	-0.10	0.30	-0.10		0.20	0.20	-0.40	0.20	1.00
18	-0.10	-0.10	-0.10	0.30		0.20	0.20	0.20	-0.40	1.00
19	0.30	0.00	0.00	0.00	Variables	-1.00	0.00	0.00	0.00	1.00
20	0.00	0.30	0.00	0.00		0.00	-1.00	0.00	0.00	1.00
21	0.00	0.00	0.30	0.00		0.00	0.00	-1.00	0.00	1.00
22	0.00	0.00	0.00	0.30		0.00	0.00	0.00	-1.00	1.00
23					Differences					
24	0.00	0.10	0.10	0.10		-0.60	-0.20	-0.20	-0.20	0.00
25	0.10	0.00	0.10	0.10		-0.20	-0.60	-0.20	-0.20	0.00
26	0.10	0.10	0.00	0.10	SUMSQ	-0.20	-0.20	-0.60	-0.20	0.00
27	0.10	0.10	0.10	0.00	2.04	-0.20	-0.20	-0.20	-0.60	0.00
28	2.40	0.00	0.00	0.00		-8.16	1.84	2.21	1.29	
29	0.00	2.40	0.00	0.00	H^s	1.84	-4.83	2.21	1.29	
30	0.00	0.00	2.14	0.00	and	2.21	2.21	-5.92	1.54	
31	0.00	0.00	0.00	1.17	H^d	1.29	1.29	1.54	-2.99	
32					Conditions					
33					Adding-up	1	=1			
34										
35	0.3 =0				Homogeneity	0	=0			
36	0.3 =0					0	=0			
37	0.3 =0					0	=0			
38	0.3 =0					0	=0			
39										
40	2.40	0.00	0.00	0.00	Symmetry	-8.16	1.84	2.21	1.29	
41	0.00	2.40	0.00	0.00	$H^s=H^{s\ T}$	1.84	-4.83	2.21	1.29	
42	0.00	0.00	2.14	0.00	and	2.21	2.21	-5.92	1.54	
43	0.00	0.00	0.00	1.17	$H^d=H^{d\ T}$	1.29	1.29	1.54	-2.99	
44										
45	2.4 >=0				Curve	-8.161765 <=0				
46	5.76 >=0				properties	36.029412 >=0				
47	12.342857 >=0				(Leading principal minors)	-132.3529 <=0				
48	14.4 >=0					0 >=0				

Figure 14.5 Choosing start values for the Solver (exercise14a3.xls).

If we first use the start values from the model in exercise14a2.xls, the Solver cannot find a solution. However, if we start with the values from Figure 14.5 and exercise14a3.xls the Solver finds an acceptable solution, as shown in Figure 14.6. The example shows that it may be

	D	E	F	G	H	I	J	K	L	M
13	Elasticities of supply					Elasticities of demand				Income
14	Market 1	Market 2	Market 3	Market 4		Market 1	Market 2	Market 3	Market 4	elasticities
15	0.30	-0.10	-0.10	-0.10	Initial values	-0.40	0.20	0.20	0.20	1.00
16	-0.10	0.30	-0.10	-0.10		0.20	-0.40	0.20	0.20	1.00
17	-0.10	-0.10	0.30	-0.10		0.20	0.20	-0.40	0.20	1.00
18	-0.10	-0.10	-0.10	0.30		0.20	0.20	0.20	-0.40	1.00
19	0.32	-0.12	-0.10	-0.10	Variables	-0.66	-0.09	-0.10	-0.08	0.93
20	-0.05	0.25	-0.11	-0.09		-0.08	-0.71	-0.13	-0.10	1.02
21	-0.06	-0.14	0.29	-0.10		-0.08	-0.12	-0.74	-0.10	1.05
22	-0.06	-0.13	-0.11	0.30		-0.07	-0.10	-0.11	-0.69	0.97
23					Differences					
24	0.02	-0.02	0.00	0.00		-0.26	-0.29	-0.30	-0.28	-0.07
25	0.05	-0.05	-0.01	0.01		-0.28	-0.31	-0.33	-0.30	0.02
26	0.04	-0.04	-0.01	0.00	SUMSQ	-0.28	-0.32	-0.34	-0.30	0.05
27	0.04	-0.03	-0.01	0.00	1.45	-0.27	-0.30	-0.31	-0.29	-0.03
28	2.58	-0.63	-0.60	-0.44		-4.93	1.11	1.34	0.77	
29	-0.63	2.03	-0.92	-0.62	H^s	1.11	-2.90	1.32	0.77	
30	-0.60	-0.92	2.09	-0.53	and	1.34	1.32	-3.57	0.93	
31	-0.44	-0.62	-0.53	1.18	H^d	0.77	0.77	0.93	-1.79	
32					Conditions					
33					Adding-up	1	=1			
34										
35	0	=0			Homogeneity	0	=0			
36	0	=0				0	=0			
37	0	=0				-1.78E-15	=0			
38	0	=0				0	=0			
39										
40	2.58	-0.63	-0.60	-0.44	Symmetry	-4.93	1.11	1.34	0.77	
41	-0.63	2.03	-0.92	-0.62	$H^s=H^{s\,T}$	1.11	-2.90	1.32	0.77	
42	-0.60	-0.92	2.09	-0.53	and	1.34	1.32	-3.57	0.93	
43	-0.44	-0.62	-0.53	1.18	$H^d=H^{d\,T}$	0.77	0.77	0.93	-1.79	
44										
45	2.5801948	>=0			Curve	-4.927333	<=0			
46	4.8304071	>=0			properties	13.052159	>=0			
47	6.5289486	>=0			(Leading principal minors)	-28.85421	<=0			
48	3.624E-15	>=0				2.563E-13	>=0			

Figure 14.6 Calculated elasticity values with the Solver (exercise14a4.xls).

necessary to try different start values (or seed values) until a solution is found.

If we obtain zero values in the leading principal minors, it is not guaranteed that H^s and H^d are positive (negative) semi-definite. In such cases we have to check the eigenvalues or carry out a triangulation of the Hessian matrix H (see e.g. Jensen and Bard 2003; Klein 2002). On the accompanying online content in the directory Exercise-15 you will find an Excel model (triangulation.xls) for the triangulation of square matrices, which allows you to check the positive (negative) semi-definite properties.

If the generated result is in fact an optimal solution with respect to our objective function, minimising the deviation from the initial elasticities, remains unclear. Generally, due to the derivative-based methods applied by the Solver (e.g. the reduced-gradient method or quasi-Newton method), we recommend the use of several sets of seed values for the changing cells, in particular for rather complex models. Another (sometimes) useful procedure may be to run the Solver in several steps or several times and to accept a solution as seed values for the next Solver run. This also applies for non-linear problems (with respect to local optima) as well as for problems with non-smooth functions or a non-connected feasible region. In addition, Solver solutions can sometimes depend on the defined Solver options, for example, with respect to convergence and precision (click on 'Options' under 'Solver parameters').

Step 14.4 We now enter the calculated elasticity values in the ranges D15:G18 and I15:M18, and the model is automatically calibrated for the adjusted elasticities (cf. Figure 14.7).

Step 14.5 To solve Exercise 14c, enter the value 15 in cell C4 and link (due to the

	A	B	C	D	E	F	G	H
1	**Calibrated Market Model with 4 Interdepedendent Markets**							
2	**and „Microeconomically Adjusted" Elasticity Values**							
3	p^s	p^d	p'''		Supply	Demand		Cost
4	10.00	10.00	10.00		80.00	100.00		195.10
5	15.00	15.00	15.00		120.00	100.00		364.07
6	14.00	14.00	12.00		100.00	120.00		317.43
7	18.00	18.00	15.00		70.00	70.00		293.20
8	10.00	10.00	Calibration Market 1		80.00	100.00	Income	Income
9	15.00	15.00	Calibration Market 2		120.00	100.00	5440.00	5440.00
10	14.00	14.00	Calibration Market 3		100.00	120.00		
11	18.00	18.00	Calibration Market 4		70.00	70.00		
12								
13			Constants		Elasticities of supply			
14		c	d	Market 1	Market 2	Market 3	Market 4	
15	Market 1	92.171455	0.31978653	0.32	-0.12	-0.10	-0.10	Initial values
16	Market 2	118.59673	0.24589809	-0.05	0.25	-0.11	-0.09	
17	Market 3	101.36191	0.23598837	-0.06	-0.14	0.29	-0.10	
18	Market 4	64.093901	0.24485094	-0.06	-0.13	-0.11	0.30	

	I	J	K	L	M	N	O	P
3	Total benefit	Welfare	Revenue	Expenditure	Foreign exchange	Government budget	Producer surplus	Consumer surplus
4	3135.35	2740.25	800.00	1000.00	-200.00	0.00	604.90	2135.35
5	3654.55	3590.49	1800.00	1500.00	300.00	0.00	1435.93	2164.55
6	4215.52	3658.10	1400.00	1680.00	-240.00	40.00	1082.57	2535.52
7	2776.78	2483.58	1260.00	1260.00	0.00	0.00	966.80	1516.78
8	fixed	w_1 0.1838235		E: 5440.00	variable	w_1 0.18382353		
9		w_2 0.2757353				w_2 0.27573529		
10		w_3 0.3088235				w_3 0.30882353		
11		w_4 0.2316176				w_4 0.23161765		
12								
13	Elasticities of demand				Income			
14	Market 1	Market 2	Market 3	Market 4	elasticities			
15	-0.66	-0.09	-0.10	-0.08	0.93			
16	-0.08	-0.71	-0.13	-0.10	1.02			
17	-0.08	-0.12	-0.74	-0.10	1.05			
18	-0.07	-0.10	-0.11	-0.69	0.97			

Figure 14.7 Calibrated market model with four interdepedented markets and 'microeconomically adjusted' elasticity values (exercise 14b.xls).

assumed free trade situation) the domestic prices in A4 and B4 with the cell C4. Since on the fourth market an autarky policy has been implemented, link A7 and B7 accordingly and determine the new equilibrium with the Solver (target cell: e.g. E4; changing cell: A7; constraints: E7 = F7). We get an expected response from demand and supply on the first market, but also the other markets are affected: both supply and demand decrease slightly on all three markets (cf. Figure 14.8).

Step 14.6 Apply the link of the domestic prices with the world market price in the first market (Step 14.5) in all other markets (through copy A4:B4 and paste in A5:B7) and observe the changes on the markets (cf. Figure 14.9). With the transition to free trade there would no longer be any budget revenue in the third market and foreign exchange expenditure would increase significantly. As expected, producer surplus would decrease and consumer surplus increase.

Step 14.7 To solve Exercise 14e, integrate a uniform protection rate for all products in the model exercise14d.xls. Choose cell A22 and enter for the

A4		=	=C4					
	A	B	C	D	E	F	G	H
1	Calibrated Market Model with 4 Interdepedendent Markets							
2	and „Microeconomically Adjusted" Elasticity Values							
3	p^s	p^d	p^w		Supply	Demand		Cost
4	15.00	15.00	15.00		91.20	76.42		333.62
5	15.00	15.00	15.00		117.48	97.01		356.44
6	14.00	14.00	12.00		97.64	116.19		309.92
7	17.95	17.95	15.00		68.18	68.18		284.77

Figure 14.8 Impact of an increase in the world market price of the first product to $p_1^w = 15$ (exercise14c.xls).

	A	B	C	D	E	F	G	H
1	Calibrated Market Model with 4 Interdepedendent Markets							
2	and „Microeconomically Adjusted" Elasticity Values							
3	p^s	p^d	p^w		Supply	Demand		Cost
4	10.00	10.00	10.00	.	82.78	102.99		201.88
5	15.00	15.00	15.00		124.10	103.81		376.50
6	12.00	12.00	12.00		97.27	137.03		264.65
7	15.00	15.00	15.00		67.33	80.76		235.02

	I	J	K	L	M	N	O	P
3	Total benefit	Welfare	Revenue	Expenditure	Foreign exchange	Government budget	Producer surplus	Consumer surplus
4	3228.99	2825.05	827.80	1029.87	-202.07	0.00	625.92	2199.12
5	3793.84	3721.62	1861.44	1557.17	304.28	0.00	1484.95	2236.67
6	4486.49	3744.64	1167.21	1644.42	-477.20	0.00	902.57	2842.08
7	2982.53	2546.10	1009.98	1211.39	-201.41	0.00	774.96	1771.14

Figure 14.9 Impact of a transition to free trade on all markets (exercise14d.xls).

protection rate the start value 0 in this cell. We should then obtain the formula = (1 + A22)*C4 for the supply price of the first product in cell A4. In cell B4 we enter the formula = A4, i.e. the demand price is equal to the supply price. In the same way, proceed for the prices of the other products. You can then analyse the impact of an increasing protection rate on producer surplus, consumer surplus and government budget of all products by using the 'Data table' Excel operation and finally display the values in a graph (cf. Figure 14.10 and exercise14e.xls).

	A	B	C	D	E	F	G	H
49				Market 1			Market 2	
50	Protection rate		PS 1	CS 1	B 1	PS 2	CS 2	B 2
51	r		625.92	2199.12	0.00	1484.95	2236.67	0.00
52		0	625.92	2199.12	0.00	1484.95	2236.67	0.00
53		0.05	657.22	2120.69	7.82	1559.19	2128.70	-18.98
54		0.1	688.51	2046.69	11.47	1633.44	2027.27	-44.80
55		0.15	719.81	1976.69	11.47	1707.69	1931.72	-76.55
56		0.2	751.11	1910.31	8.28	1781.94	1841.47	-113.50
57		0.25	782.40	1847.22	2.25	1856.18	1756.03	-155.02
58		0.3	813.70	1787.14	-6.30	1930.43	1674.95	-200.56
59		0.35	845.00	1729.81	-17.09	2004.68	1597.87	-249.69
60		0.4	876.29	1675.00	-29.90	2078.93	1524.45	-302.01
61		0.45	907.59	1622.54	-44.53	2153.17	1454.39	-357.20
62		0.5	938.88	1572.22	-60.79	2227.42	1387.44	-414.96
63								

Figure 14.10 Producer surplus, consumer surplus and government budget of four products at increasing protection rates (exercise14e.xls). *Continued opposite*

	I	J	K	L	M	N
49	Market 3			Market 4		
50	PS 3	CS 3	B 3	PS 4	CS 4	B 4
51	902.57	2842.08	0.00	774.96	1771.14	0.00
52	902.57	2842.08	0.00	774.96	1771.14	0.00
53	947.70	2720.33	19.77	813.71	1687.73	7.26
54	992.82	2606.09	32.11	852.46	1609.22	9.39
55	1037.95	2498.60	38.02	891.20	1535.12	7.07
56	1083.08	2397.19	38.32	929.95	1464.99	0.83
57	1128.21	2301.28	33.70	968.70	1398.48	-8.85
58	1173.34	2210.38	24.73	1007.45	1335.26	-21.58
59	1218.47	2124.04	11.92	1046.20	1275.05	-37.04
60	1263.59	2041.88	-4.32	1084.94	1217.60	-54.93
61	1308.72	1963.57	-23.62	1123.69	1162.70	-75.00
62	1353.85	1888.79	-45.67	1162.44	1110.15	-97.04

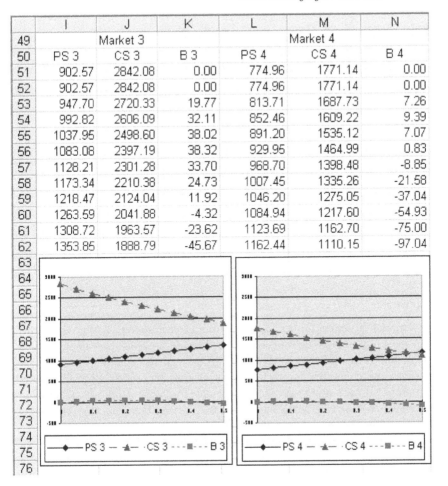

Figure 14.10 continued.

References

Chiang, A.C. and Wainwright, K. (2005) *Fundamental Methods of Mathematical Economics* (4th edn), Boston, MA: McGraw-Hill, pp. 301–7.

Jensen, P.A. and Bard, J.F. (2003) *Operations Research: Models and Methods*, Indianapolis, IN: John Wiley, pp. 328–35.

Klein, M.W. (2002) *Mathematical Methods for Economics* (2nd edn), Boston, MA: Addison Wesley, pp. 287–315.

Padberg, M. (1995) *Linear Optimization and Extensions*, Berlin: Springer, pp. 25–9, 205–7.

Stoer, J. and Witzgall, C. (1970) *Convexity and Optimization in Finite Dimensions I*, Berlin: Springer.

Walkenbach, J. (2004) *Microsoft® Office Excel 2003 Bible*, Indianapolis, IN: John Wiley.

Winston, W.L. (2004) *Operations Research* (4th edn), Belmont, CA: Brooks/Cole, pp. 11–48, 617–19.

15 Model framework for a 12-market model

Objective

In Chapter 15 we will introduce a model framework which may be used for the analysis of up to 12 different markets.

Theory

The model structure for a 12-market model corresponds to the theoretical principles of multi-market models discussed in the previous three chapters. The supply and demand functions of the Cobb–Douglas type describe the quantities supplied and demanded for each product as a function of all 12 producer and consumer prices as well as the income variable on the demand side. The welfare assessment is based on Marshallian demand curves. The data basis consists of quantities supplied and demanded, producer and demand prices, world market prices as well as price and income elasticities for each the 12 products and markets.

The standard Solver of Excel has the capacity to run a microeconomic adjustment of the elasticity values considering the homogeneity condition, the symmetry condition and curve properties on the supply and demand side, plus the adding-up condition on the demand side for up to eight markets. Similar to Chapter 14, this adjustment is modelled in the sheet 'Adjustment' in exercise15.xls. For a microeconomic adjustment of the elasticities on 12 markets we need to install a more powerful Solver, for example, the Premium-Solver developed by Frontline Systems Inc. The model structure may immediately be used for policy analysis and may also be further extended and revised, if required, depending on specific problem setting.

Exercise 15

You have the following information about eight markets:

Market	Quantity supplied	Quantity demanded	Supply price	Demand price	World market price
1	80	100	10	10	10
2	120	100	15	15	15
3	100	120	14	14	12
4	90	70	20	20	18
5	140	130	18	18	16
6	100	120	18	18	20
7	110	110	20	20	24
8	70	70	18	18	15

For the first two products the country pursues free trade, while for the third to fifth products a protectionist price policy has been implemented. In the sixth market a tax or 'negative protection' has been implemented and in the last two markets the country pursues an autarky policy.

The following start values for the matrix of price elasticities on the supply side apply:

$$\varepsilon^s = \begin{bmatrix} 0.5 & 0 & -0.1 & -0.1 & 0 & -0.2 & 0 & -0.1 \\ 0 & 0.3 & 0 & 0 & 0 & -0.2 & 0 & 0 \\ -0.1 & 0 & 0.2 & 0 & -0.1 & 0 & 0 & 0.1 \\ -0.1 & 0 & 0 & 0.4 & 0 & 0 & -0.1 & 0.1 \\ 0 & 0 & -0.1 & 0 & 0.3 & 0 & 0 & 0 \\ -0.2 & 0.2 & 0 & 0 & 0 & 0.3 & 0 & 0 \\ 0 & 0 & 0 & -0.1 & 0 & 0 & 0.3 & 0 \\ -0.1 & 0 & 0.1 & 0.1 & 0 & 0 & 0 & 0.1 \end{bmatrix}$$

The following start values for the matrix of price and income elasticities on the demand side apply:

$$[\varepsilon^d, \eta] = \begin{bmatrix} -0.4 & 0 & 0.05 & 0 & 0.1 & 0 & 0 & 0.1 & 1 \\ 0 & -0.4 & 0 & 0 & 0.1 & 0.2 & 0 & 0 & 1 \\ 0.05 & 0 & -0.6 & 0.1 & 0 & 0 & 0.1 & 0 & 1 \\ 0 & 0 & 0.1 & -0.5 & 0 & 0 & 0 & 0.05 & 1 \\ 0.1 & 0.1 & 0 & 0 & -0.2 & 0.2 & 0 & 0 & 1 \\ 0 & 0.2 & 0 & 0 & 0.2 & -0.3 & 0 & 0.1 & 1 \\ 0 & 0 & 0.1 & 0 & 0 & 0 & -0.4 & 0 & 1 \\ 0.1 & 0 & 0 & 0.05 & 0 & 0.1 & 0 & -0.4 & 1 \end{bmatrix}$$

Use the model structure for 12 markets in exercise15.xls and solve the following problems:

(a) Adjust the given elasticity values considering the homogeneity condition, the symmetry condition and curve properties on the supply and demand sides as well as the adding-up condition on the demand side. Then calibrate your model and solve the following problems on the basis of the conducted 'microeconomic adjustment'.

(b) At what level do the prices have to be set to maximise budget revenue?

(c) Assume again the base situation. How would a gradual increase of the protection rates of the first two products to 50 per cent affect the welfare of both markets, assuming that all other product prices remain constant?

(d) How, in comparison to the base situation, would a transition to free trade in all markets affect the quantities supplied and demanded?

(e) Assume the base situation and determine an optimal price policy to maximise (total) producer surplus with a maximum budget expenditure of 1000.

Solution

Step 15.1 First, have a look at the structure of the 12-market model in exercise-15.xls. The model consists of four linked sheets: 'Input&Calibration', 'Adjustment', 'Scenario' and 'Differences'.

The sheet 'Input&Calibration' serves as a kind of template for the insertion of the start values and provides the automatic calibration of the model. Only the white cells and ranges can be edited and filled with data. For markets which are not required data remain unchanged (i.e. the value 1 for prices and quantities and 0 for elasticities). Adjust the totals formula in cell S18 according to the considered markets. After all input data have been inserted, copy the value from S18 into cell U18. If necessary, you can also vary the integration limits for the calculation of the benefit and cost integrals in the cells AX3 and AZ3 (see also Chapter 4).

In the range BB6:BM17, enter the values for the elasticity of demand of a product with respect to the supply of the other considered products, if this relationship is seen as relevant for the specific problem setting. In this way we can take into account that the quantities supplied can go directly into the demand functions as input, for example, in the case of cereals used as feed in livestock production systems. If such a consideration is not relevant for the problem examined, leave the zero values unchanged.

Next, enter the values of the relevant expenditure shares of the considered products from the range BO6:BO17 into the range BP6:BP17, or, respectively, enter the value zero for markets which are not used in the model.

If you refrain from a microeconomic adjustment of the elasticities, you can change different variables of the developed model in the sheet 'Scenario'. This usually applies only for the values in the yellow highlighted ranges, i.e. prices, eventually required shift factors of supply and demand, total income, and elasticities. This sheet may also be used for Solver applications of more complex policy scenarios.

Finally, differences between the scenario model and the calibrated (or reference) model can be depicted in the sheet 'Differences', both as absolute and percentage changes.

Step 15.2 If you want to carry out a microeconomic adjustment of the elasticity values (after you have entered all start values in the sheet 'Input-&Calibration'), as required in Exercise 15a and as carried out in Chapter 13 (Step 13.1) and Chapter 14 (Step 14.3), you can do this using the Solver in the sheet 'Adjustment'. In the upper part of this sheet you will find a copy of the model developed in the 'Input&Calibration' sheet. Similar to Step 14.3 and the model in exercise14a2.xls, you will find the modelling of the 'microeconomic adjustment' in the lower part of the 'Adjustment' sheet (ranges W18:AV95, BB30:BM53 and BQ30:CB77), including the necessary target cell, changing cells and constraints for the Solver (but here for a 12-market model).

The adjustment of the elasticities should now be carried out separately for the demand and supply side. When you open the Solver, you will already find the relevant setting of the Solver for the demand side, but for all 12 markets. The setting thus needs to be adjusted with respect to the number of the considered markets. A separate adjustment of the elasticity values is required due to the limited capacity of the Standard-Solver. The capacity of the Standard-Solver usually only allows an adjustment of the elasticities of a maximum of eight markets (cf. the Theory section in this chapter, p. 180). In addition, we can also check with the model triangulation.xls if the H-matrices are semi-definite.

Assuming type compatibility, you can activate the adequate start setting of the Solver for the supply side by clicking on 'Options', 'Load model . . .' and then selecting the 'Model area' W56:W61. If necessary the setting can be revised. The Solver parameter for the demand side may be found in the range AV56:AV73. The feasibility of the obtained Solver solution, in accordance with the precision setting, can be easily visually checked with the display in the sheet 'Adjustment'. However, the Solver reactions explained in Chapter 14 may, of course, also occur in this case.

To adopt the 'microeconomically adjusted' elasticity values in your model, which you have successfully calculated in the sheet 'Adjustment', copy the values of the respective cells in the range W18:AH29 and AJ18:AV29 of the 'Input&Calibration' sheet into the respective cells in the range W6:AH17 and AJ6:AV17 of the same sheet and thus substitute the start values of the elasticities. You do not need to worry about a new calibration of the model as it is done automatically, and you can continue with the analysis using the sheets 'Scenario' and 'Differences', as described in Step 15.1.

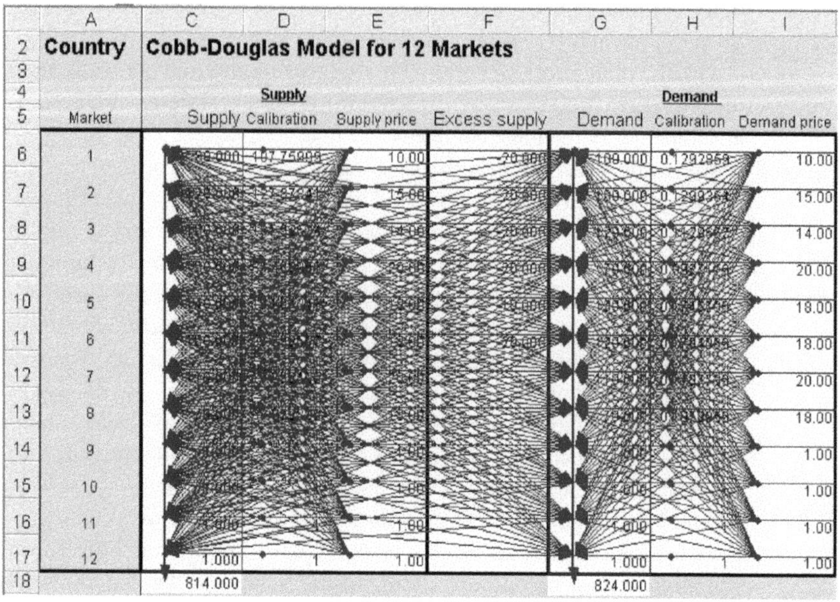

Figure 15.1 Complex structure of a 12-market model.

Figure 15.1 provides an insight into the complexity of the linkages within a 12-market model showing the 'Trace precedents' for the sum of the quantities supplied and demanded.

Step 15.3 You will find a model filled in and adjusted with the data given in Exercise 15 in exercise15a1.xls (cf. Figure 15.2). Correct the elasticity values according to Exercise 15a and you will see the solution in Figure 15.3 and exercise15a2.xls.

Step 15.4 After the adoption of the adjusted elasticity values in the model you can solve Exercise 15b with the Solver in the sheet 'Scenario'. Target cell is the cell X18 with the sum of the single budget values. Changing cells are the producer prices in E6:E13, whereby you have to link the consumer prices in I6:I13 with the producer prices through the formulas = E6 to = E13. The result is shown in Figure 15.4 and exercise15b.xls.

Step 15.5 To solve Exercise 15c, set the start values of the prices again, but maintain the linkages of the domestic prices. As in Step 14.7 you then enter the protection rate for the first two products, generate the data series for the welfare of these two markets at different protection rates by using the 'Data, table' operation and graphically display the data series (cf. Figure 15.5 and exercise15c.xls).

Step 15.6 When you choose prices in the sheet 'Scenario' according to a free trade situation as required in Exercise 15d, you can immediately see the

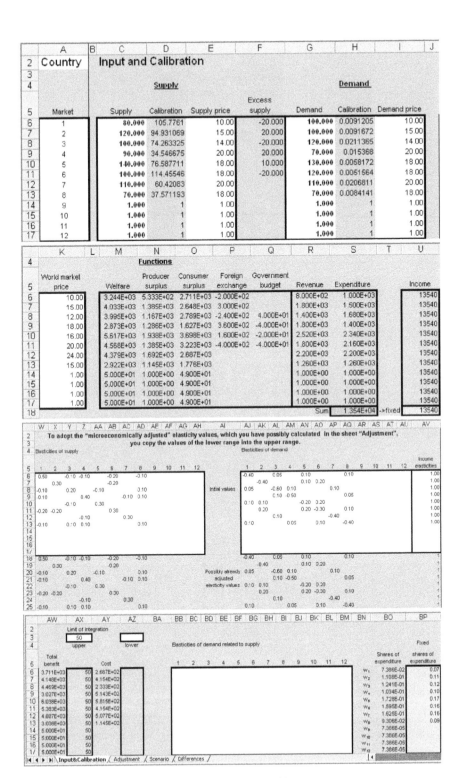

Figure 15.2 A model with eight markets (exercise 15a1.xls).

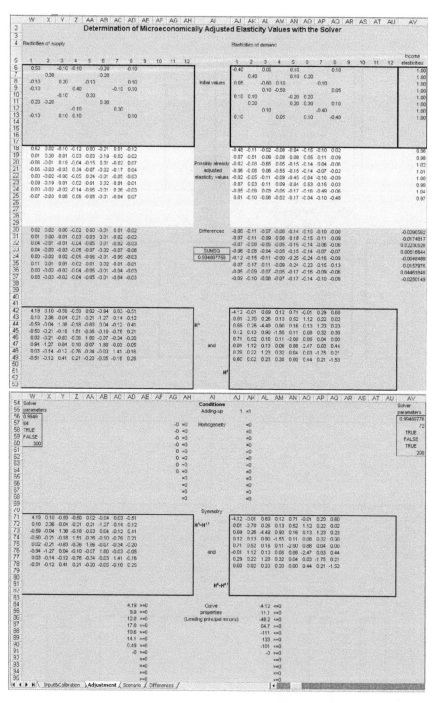

Figure 15.3 Calculation of 'microeconomically adjusted' elasticity values (exercise15a2.xls).

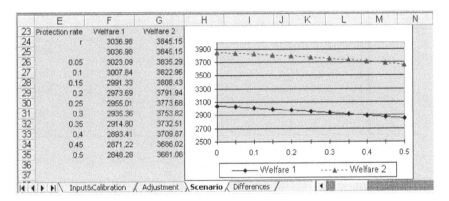

	A	B	C	D	E	F	G	H	I
2	Country		Multi-Market Model for 12 Markets						
3									
4					Supply			Demand	
5	Market		Supply	Calibration	Supply price	Excess supply	Demand	Calibration	Demand price
6	1		85.764	107.75999	11.52	-7.515	93.279	0.1292859	11.52
7	2		114.695	127.87841	13.66	8.193	106.501	0.1299364	13.66
8	3		101.418	101.92534	14.16	-17.358	118.776	0.1129667	14.16
9	4		83.105	84.480969	16.42	5.753	77.352	0.0927119	16.42
10	5		137.468	138.07348	16.12	0.068	137.400	0.1746796	16.12
11	6		105.975	91.790507	20.88	-4.723	110.698	0.1704069	20.88
12	7		116.032	107.99495	21.42	8.681	107.351	0.1107739	21.42
13	8		68.547	68.029836	17.18	-4.455	73.003	0.1078959	17.18
14	9		1.000	1	1.00		1.000	1	1.00
15	10		1.000	1	1.00		1.000	1	1.00
16	11		1.000	1	1.00		1.000	1	1.00
17	12		1.000	1	1.00		1.000	1	1.00

Input&Calibration / Adjustment \Scenario / Differences /

Figure 15.4 Prices at maximising total budget revenue with eight markets (exercise 15b.xls).

	E	F	G
23	Protection rate	Welfare 1	Welfare 2
24	r	3036.98	3845.15
25		3036.98	3845.15
26	0.05	3023.09	3835.29
27	0.1	3007.84	3822.96
28	0.15	2991.33	3808.43
29	0.2	2973.69	3791.94
30	0.25	2955.01	3773.68
31	0.3	2935.36	3753.82
32	0.35	2914.80	3732.51
33	0.4	2893.41	3709.87
34	0.45	2871.22	3686.02
35	0.5	2848.28	3661.06

Input&Calibration / Adjustment \Scenario / Differences /

Figure 15.5 Impact of an increasing protection rate on welfare values of the first two products (exercise 15c.xls).

impact of this policy in the sheet 'Differences' (cf. Figure 15.6 and exercise 15d.xls).

Step 15.7 In contrast to Exercise 15b, the producer surplus will be maximised in Exercise 15e considering a constraint on total budget expenditure. As in Step 15.4, use the Solver in the sheet 'Scenario'. Choose as target cell U18 (with the formula = SUM(U6:U13)) and the constraint is X18 > = −1000. If the Solver finds an error, which it generated itself through a negative price, you can run the Solver again with new suitable prices (e.g. the world market prices). The optimal price policy is shown in Figure 15.7 and exercise 15e.xls, where you can also find the differences compared to the base situation in the sheet 'Differences'.

	A	B	C	D	E	F	G	H	I	J
2	Country		**Multi-Market Model for 12 Markets**							
3										
4				**Supply**				**Demand**		
5	Market		Supply	Calibration	Supply price	Excess supply	Demand	Calibration	Demand price	
6	1		82.313	107.75999	10.00	-15.518	97.831	0.1292859	10.00	
7	2		118.457	127.87841	15.00	15.393	103.064	0.1299364	15.00	
8	3		97.479	101.92534	12.00	-37.351	134.830	0.1129667	12.00	
9	4		84.485	84.480969	18.00	11.507	72.978	0.0927119	18.00	
10	5		137.941	138.07348	16.00	-0.475	138.416	0.1746796	16.00	
11	6		103.788	91.790507	20.00	-10.495	114.283	0.1704069	20.00	
12	7		118.490	107.99495	24.00	16.220	102.270	0.1107739	24.00	
13	8		67.647	68.029836	15.00	-9.633	77.280	0.1076959	15.00	
14	9		1.000	1	1.00		1.000	1	1.00	
15	10		1.000	1	1.00		1.000	1	1.00	
16	11		1.000	1	1.00		1.000	1	1.00	
17	12		1.000	1	1.00		1.000	1	1.00	
18										
19										
20										
21										
22	**Reference model**									
23				**Supply**				**Demand**		
24	Market		Supply	Calibration	Supply price	Excess supply	Demand	Calibration	Demand price	
25	1		80.000	107.75999	10.00	-20.000	100.000	0.1292859	10.00	
26	2		120.000	127.87841	15.00	20.000	100.000	0.1299364	15.00	
27	3		100.000	101.92534	14.00	-20.000	120.000	0.1129667	14.00	
28	4		90.000	84.480969	20.00	20.000	70.000	0.0927119	20.00	
29	5		140.000	138.07348	18.00	10.000	130.000	0.1746796	18.00	
30	6		100.000	91.790507	18.00	-20.000	120.000	0.1704069	18.00	
31	7		110.000	107.99495	20.00		110.000	0.1107739	20.00	
32	8		70.000	68.029836	18.00		70.000	0.1076959	18.00	
33	9		1.000	1	1.00		1.000	1	1.00	
34	10		1.000	1	1.00		1.000	1	1.00	
35	11		1.000	1	1.00		1.000	1	1.00	
36	12		1.000	1	1.00		1.000	1	1.00	

Figure 15.6 Impact of a free trade policy with eight interdependent markets (exercise-15d.xls).

	A	B	C	D	E	F	G	H	I	J
41	**Differences**									
42	**Absolute changes**									
43	Market		Supply	Calibration	Supply price	Excess supply	Demand	Calibration	Demand price	
44	1		2.313			4.482	-2.169			
45	2		-1.543			-4.607	3.064			
46	3		-2.521		-2.00	-17.351	14.830		-2.00	
47	4		-5.515		-2.00	-8.493	2.978		-2.00	
48	5		-2.059		-2.00	-10.475	8.416		-2.00	
49	6		3.788		2.00	9.505	-5.717		2.00	
50	7		8.490		4.00	16.220	-7.730		4.00	
51	8		-2.353		-3.00	-9.633	7.280		-3.00	
52	9									
53	10									
54	11									
55	12									
56										
57										
58										
59										
60	**Percentage changes**									
61	%									
62	Market		Supply	Calibration	Supply price	Excess supply	Demand	Calibration	Demand price	
63	1		2.892			-22.412	-2.169			
64	2		-1.286			-23.036	3.064			
65	3		-2.521		-14.286	86.756	12.358		-14.286	
66	4		-6.128		-10.000	-42.464	4.254		-10.000	
67	5		-1.470		-11.111	-104.748	6.474		-11.111	
68	6		3.788		11.111	-47.524	-4.764		11.111	
69	7		7.718		20.000	#DIV/0!	-7.028		20.000	
70	8		-3.362		-16.667	#DIV/0!	10.400		-16.667	
71	9					#DIV/0!				
72	10					#DIV/0!				
73	11					#DIV/0!				
74	12					#DIV/0!				

◄ ◄ ► ►◄ \ Input&Calibration / Adjustment / Scenario \ **Differences** / ◄

Figure 15.6 continued.

	A	B	C	D	E	F	G	H	I
2	**Country**		**Multi-Market Model for 12 Markets**						
3									
4				**Supply**				**Demand**	
5	Market		Supply	Calibration	Supply price	Excess supply	Demand	Calibration	Demand price
6	1		82.342	107.75999	14.43	8.203	74.139	0.1292859	14.43
7	2		113.618	127.87841	17.46	32.004	81.615	0.1299364	17.46
8	3		103.756	101.92534	18.74	14.996	88.760	0.1129667	18.74
9	4		82.235	84.480969	20.36	21.374	60.860	0.0927119	20.36
10	5		136.475	138.07348	20.84	32.607	103.868	0.1746796	20.84
11	6		106.840	91.790507	27.34	22.187	84.653	0.1704069	27.34
12	7		117.238	107.99495	28.83	37.565	79.673	0.1107739	28.83
13	8		69.505	68.029836	27.50	18.494	51.011	0.1078959	27.50
14	9		1.000	1	1.00		1.000	1	1.00
15	10		1.000	1	1.00		1.000	1	1.00
16	11		1.000	1	1.00		1.000	1	1.00
17	12		1.000	1	1.00		1.000	1	1.00

	R	S	T	U	V	W	X	Y	Z
4			**Functions**						
5	World market price		Welfare	Producer surplus	Consumer surplus	Foreign exchange	Government budget	Revenue	Expenditure
6	10.00		2.609E+03	7.796E+02	1.866E+03	8.203E+01	-3.635E+01	1.188E+03	1.070E+03
7	15.00		3.411E+03	1.532E+03	1.958E+03	4.801E+02	-7.882E+01	1.984E+03	1.425E+03
8	12.00		3.476E+03	1.629E+03	1.948E+03	1.799E+02	-1.010E+02	1.944E+03	1.663E+03
9	18.00		2.577E+03	1.254E+03	1.374E+03	3.847E+02	-5.043E+01	1.674E+03	1.239E+03
10	16.00		4.573E+03	2.296E+03	2.435E+03	5.217E+02	-1.578E+02	2.844E+03	2.165E+03
11	20.00		3.658E+03	2.205E+03	1.616E+03	4.437E+02	-1.629E+02	2.921E+03	2.314E+03
12	24.00		3.970E+03	2.690E+03	1.461E+03	9.016E+02	-1.816E+02	3.380E+03	2.297E+03
13	15.00		2.546E+03	1.794E+03	9.825E+02	2.774E+02	-2.312E+02	1.911E+03	1.403E+03
14	1.00		5.000E+01	1.000E+00	4.900E+01			1.000E+00	1.000E+00
15	1.00		5.000E+01	1.000E+00	4.900E+01			1.000E+00	1.000E+00
16	1.00		5.000E+01	1.000E+00	4.900E+01			1.000E+00	1.000E+00
17	1.00		5.000E+01	1.000E+00	4.900E+01			1.000E+00	1.000E+00
18				1.418E+04			-1.000E+03		

|◀ ◀ ▶ ▶|\ Input&Calibration / Adjustment \Scenario / Differences /

	A	B	C	D	E	F	G	H	I	J
41	**Differences**									
42	**Absolute changes**									
43	Market		Supply	Calibration	Supply price	Excess supply	Demand	Calibration	Demand price	
44	1		2.342		4.43	28.203	-25.861		4.43	
45	2		-6.382		2.46	12.004	-18.385		2.46	
46	3		3.756		4.74	34.996	-31.240		4.74	
47	4		-7.765		0.36	1.374	-9.140		0.36	
48	5		-3.525		2.84	22.607	-26.132		2.84	
49	6		6.840		9.34	42.187	-35.347		9.34	
50	7		7.238		8.83	37.565	-30.327		8.83	
51	8		-0.495		9.50	18.494	-18.989		9.50	
52	9									
53	10									
54	11									
55	12									

|◀ ◀ ▶ ▶|\ Input&Calibration / Adjustment / Scenario \Differences /

Figure 15.7 Optimal price policy for maximising total producer surplus considering a budget constraint with eight markets (exercise15e.xls).

References

Frontline Systems Inc (1996) *Solver User's Guide*, Nevada: Incline Village.

Fylstra, D., Lasdon, L., Watson, J. and Waren, A. (1998) 'Design and use of the Microsoft® Excel solver', *Interfaces*, 28, pp. 29–55.

Jechlitschka, K. and Lotze, H. (1997) 'Theorie und Anwendung eines Mehr-Markt-Modells zur sektoralen Analyse von Agrarpolitiken', *Zeitschrift für Agrarinformatik*, 5 (2), pp. 26–31.

Kirschke, D., Odening, M., Doluschitz, R., Fock, T., Hagedorn, K., Rost, D. and von Witzke, H. (1998) *Weiterentwicklung der EU-Agrarpolitik – Aussichten für die neuen Bundesländer*, Kiel: Vauk, pp. 6–15.

Part IV

Budget policy and priority setting

16 Optimisation approach

Objective

In Chapter 16 we will formulate an Excel model for budgeting and priority setting using linear programming. With this optimisation approach we will evaluate which policies should be financed to what extent to meet defined policy objectives in the best possible way.

Theory

In our previous discussion we have concentrated on the analysis of impacts of specific policies. If several policy measures can be implemented, which seems to be plausible for many policy-making problems, it needs to be evaluated how these measures may be compared and which measures should be implemented to what extent. If the measures imply budget expenditure, a classical budgeting problem occurs, posing the questions of how a given budget should be allocated to different policy measures to fulfil the defined objectives in the best possible way and how priorities may be set among the measures considered. The result of the optimisation problem which is the optimal budget expenditure for the considered policy measures then describes the priorities to be set to achieve the objectives.

If we define an objective function attributing a specific objective value to the budget expenditure of the policy measures considered, we have, from a mathematical point of view, a continuous optimisation problem. We have already discussed the formulation of optimal structural policies in Chapter 11, where the aggregated present values of net welfare effects of the considered structural policies were to be maximised. This problem setting will now be generalised.

Assume the objective function:

$$Z = \sum_{i=1}^{n} Z_i (BE_i) \tag{16.1}$$

with Z – objective variable

$i = 1, \ldots, n$ – index for the policy measures considered.

Let us assume that the functions Z_i fulfil the law of diminishing marginal returns, and hence are strictly concave. The value of the objective variable Z is the sum of the objective contributions of the different policy measures. The following budget constraint applies:

$$\sum_{i=1}^{n} BE_i \leq BE \tag{16.2}$$

with BE – (maximum) budget expenditure.

If we substitute (16.2) by the equality constraint

$$\sum_{i=1}^{n} BE_i = BE \tag{16.2}'$$

we can formulate the following Lagrangian function:

$$L = \sum_{i=1}^{n} Z_i (BE_i) + \lambda \left(BE - \sum_{i=1}^{n} BE_i \right) \tag{16.3}$$

The necessary condition for an optimum is:

$$\frac{dZ_1}{dBE_1} = \ldots = \frac{dZ_i}{dBE_i} = \ldots = \frac{dZ_n}{dBE_n} . \tag{16.4}$$

Hence, the different policy measures have to be financed to the extent that the marginal contributions to the objective are the same for all measures. Analogous to Figure 11.3, Figure 16.1 depicts the optimum condition for two arbitrary policy measures 1 and 2. The solution values BE_1^* and BE_2^* thus describe the priorities for financing these policy measures, and λ^* denotes the shadow price of the budget constraint; this is the value by which the objective value Z would increase if the budget constraint is relaxed by one unit.

The result is plausible, but only a first step in the analysis of budgeting and priority-setting problems. In particular, two problems require further attention and further specification of the optimisation approach. First, the objective function needs to be revised. It seems unrealistic to empirically determine objective functions as theoretically outlined above so that we have to accept simplified but still sensible assumptions. It also seems clear that in reality we not only consider

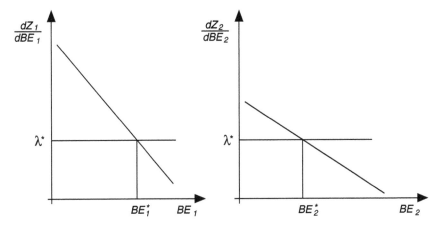

Figure 16.1 Optimal budget policy.

one objective, but we also have to take into account multiple objectives. Hence, the optimisation approach needs to be extended.

The second problem relates to the constraints which have to be taken into account in the optimisation approach. The budget constraint is obvious, but will not be the only one for policy-making problems. Hence, additional constraints need to be considered. With respect to the budget, minimum or maximum budget allocations can be plausible further constraints for specific policy measures. In addition, legal and institutional frameworks need to be considered as well as capital and labour availability. Thus, a variety and a diverse nature of constraints have to be considered for specific problem settings, making budget allocation and priority setting a complex decision-making problem.

Against this background, linear optimisation provides a powerful method for budgeting and priority setting. Figure 16.2 outlines this approach. The perspective is to find the maximum value of a linear objective function, taking into account a number of linear constraints in terms of equations and inequalities. As a result we obtain the optimal budget for the different policy measures considered; the solution thus outlines how the budget should be allocated and how priorities should be set.

Figure 16.2 shows an example of two objectives Z_1 and Z_2, where the coefficient z_{11} denotes the constant marginal and average contribution of one monetary unit of the policy measure 1 to the objective Z_1 and the coefficient z_{2i} denotes the respective contribution of the policy measure i to the objective Z_2. For the objective function Z_1 we can write accordingly:

$$Z_1 = \sum_{i=1}^{n} z_{1i} \, BE_i \, . \tag{16.5}$$

Policy measures

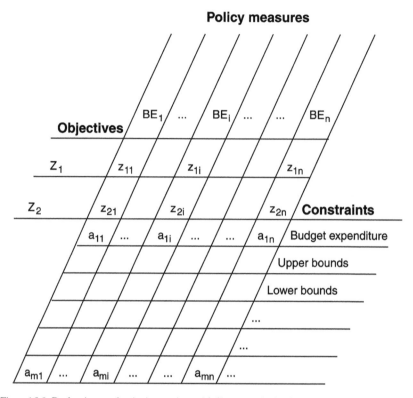

Figure 16.2 Budgeting and priority setting with linear optimisation.

We can formulate Z_2 in the same way. If we introduce weights for the two objectives, the aggregated objective function is:

$$Z = a_1 Z_1 + a_2 Z_2 \tag{16.6}$$

with a_1, a_2 – weights.

It is often assumed for the weights that $0 \leq a_1 \leq 1$ and $a_2 = 1 - a_1$.

With respect to the constraints, the coefficients indicate the relevant framework for the optimisation problem. For example, it applies for the budget constraint (16.2): $a_{11} = \ldots = a_{1i} = \ldots = a_{1n} = 1$. For other constraints the coefficients need to be determined for a specific case. For example, if we assume that for institutional reasons the financial allocation for policy measure 1 should be at least twice as high as for policy measure 2, it applies for this constraint:

$$BE_1 \geq 2BE_2 \tag{16.7}$$

or

$$- BE_1 + 2BE_2 \leq 0 \qquad (16.7)'$$

or

$$- 0.5\, BE_1 + BE_2 \leq 0. \qquad (16.7)''$$

Consequently, it would apply for $a_{j1} = -0.5$, $a_{j2} = 1$, and the constant value on the right-hand side of the inequality would be $b_j = 0$ (whereby j denotes the number of the constraint).

Finally, the outlined optimisation approach may be formulated as follows:

$$\max_{BE_1, \ldots, BE_n} Z = a \sum_{i=1}^{n} z_{1i}\, BE_i + (1 - a) \sum_{i=1}^{n} z_{2i}\, BE_i \qquad (16.8)$$

with the constraints

$$\sum_{i=1}^{n} a_{ri}\, BE_i \begin{Bmatrix} \leq \\ = \\ \geq \end{Bmatrix} b_r \quad \text{for } r = 1, \ldots, m$$

and

$$BE_i \geq 0 \quad \text{for } i = 1, \ldots, n,$$

where the index $r = 1, \ldots, m$ describes the constraints, which can occur as equation or inequality.

Figure 16.3 visualises the optimisation approach for two policy measures. The constraints define the hatched area of feasible solutions. In addition to the budget constraint R_1, a lower bound R_2 for BE_1 and an upper bound R_3 for BE_2 are assumed. Furthermore, the constraint R_4 applies, which, for example, may be seen as an institutional constraint. The value of the objective function Z increases the further the Z curve is shifted to the right. Following the definition of the objective function

$$Z = z_1\, BE_1 + z_2\, BE_2 \qquad (16.9)$$

we can write

$$BE_2 = \frac{Z}{z_2} - \frac{z_1}{z_2}\, BE_1. \qquad (16.9)'$$

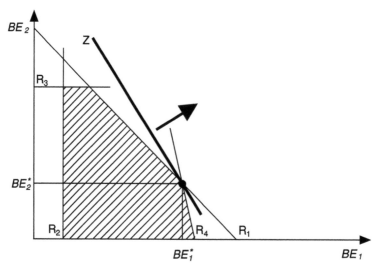

Figure 16.3 Set of feasible solutions for a linear optimisation problem.

As the optimal solution we get BE_1^* and BE_2^*. If the budget is allocated in that way, and hence the priorities are set accordingly, the maximum objective value is obtained under the given constraints.

Figure 16.3 shows that the result changes if the objective function and constraints change. Changing the objective coefficients or the weights in the objective function will lead to a rotation of the curve in Figure 16.3. This will eventually lead to a new solution if the rotation is big enough. It could also be the case that the slope of the objective function is the same as the slope of a constraint. In this case there are obviously multiple solutions to the optimisation problem with the same objective value. A change in a constraint would affect the value of an optimal solution in a similar way.

The chances and limitations of linear programming as an optimisation approach are discussed comprehensively in the literature, so that we do not need to explain this method in more detail. We need, however, to discuss some additional aspects with respect to applying the method for budget allocation and priority-setting problems. It seems rather trivial, but nevertheless needs to be pointed out that the discussed optimisation approach requires the definition of relevant policy measures, the objective function and relevant constraints for specific policy-making exercises. Thus, the matrix shown in Figure 16.2 needs to be formulated and filled in, which may not be an easy task for complex policy questions before the modelling per se can be carried out.

When conducting the task of filling in the matrix it could be helpful to do this step by step and to apply a certain 'zooming' approach. For example, in a first step, relevant objectives and constraints could be identified and coefficients generated based on expert opinion. For the coefficients of the objective function a simple scale of, say, 1 to 9 has proved to be appropriate. The coefficients 1, 2, 3 would then indicate a small contribution to the objective, while the coefficients 4, 5, 6 would define a medium and the coefficients 7, 8, 9 a high contribution to the objective. If more information is available (e.g. through research), a more detailed and differentiated approach could be chosen to improve the empirical basis of the optimisation approach. For example, the rather crude assessment of welfare effects of structural policies by experts could be substituted by the calculation of present values of net welfare effects in the framework of a market model, as explained in Chapter 11. Generally, such a 'zooming' approach would lead to a gradual improvement of policy decision-making support, instead of totally refraining from using a formalised optimisation approach due to insufficient information. In any case, what are the alternatives to solving complex budget allocation and priority-setting problems?

The optimisation approach discussed is a standard method which may be used for many relevant policy-making problems, but the approach may also be adjusted and extended for more specific problems. In Chapter 11 we discussed a discrete Boolean optimisation problem answering the question which structural policy should be implemented in a certain context and which policy should not. This problem setting could be generalised as a 0–1 optimisation problem on the basis of the discussed optimisation approach with additional objectives and constraints. You will find a similar approach in Albright (2001, pp. 367–80).

Exercise 16

A government allocates the budget to different rural development policy measures as follows:

(I)	Farm investment	70
(M)	Marketing support	100
(E)	Agri-environment	110
(R)	Rural infrastructure	50
(L)	Labour subsidies	70
	Total:	400

Using this policy the government aims to increase income in rural areas and to improve the environment. Experts have estimated the following contributions of the different policy measures to the two objectives:

	I	M	E	R	L
Income	8	5	2	8	6
Environment	2	5	8	4	9

The government wants to evaluate whether the priorities are set appropriately. In the evaluation the following constraints have to be taken into account: (1) budget expenditure for each of the different policy measures may not change by more than 50 per cent in either direction; (2) budget expenditure for farm investment and marketing support may not sum up to more than 50 per cent of the total budget; (3) budget expenditure for agri-environment needs to be at least three times as high as the amount spent for labour subsidies; and (4) both objectives, income and environment, should have the same weight.

Develop an Excel model for budgeting and priority setting with respect to rural development. Solve the following problems:

(a) Determine the priorities for the considered policy measures and draw up a table and a graph showing how an optimal budget allocation would differ from the current budget allocation.
(b) How would limiting the available budget to 350 affect the optimal allocation?
(c) How would changing the weights of the income and environment objectives to 2 : 1 affect the result?
(d) The government believes that the experts have underestimated the contribution of farm investment and marketing support to the environment objective. The government is convinced that these coefficients should be 8 for both measures. How would this judgement affect the optimal allocation (under the outlined conditions)?
(e) Assume that the budget allocation for farm investment and marketing support cannot be changed for political reasons. What is the consequence for priority setting in the rural development policy?

Solution

Step 16.1 Generate an Excel sheet as shown in Figure 16.4.

	A	B	C	D	E	F	G	H	I	J	K
1			I	M	E	R	L	Budgeting and Priority Setting			
2		x'	70.0	100.0	110.0	60.0	70.0				
3	Upper bounds		105	150	165	75	105	Usage		RHS	
4	Lower bounds		35	50	55	25	35	Ax		b	
5	Constraint1		0.5	0.5	-0.5	-0.5	-0.5	-30	<=	0	I+M <= 50% of BE
6	Constraint2		0	0	-1	0	3	100	<=	0	E >= 3*L
7	Constraint3		1	1	1	1	1	400	=	400	Budget expenditure(BE)
8											
9	Objective 1:							Weights			
10	Income coefficients		8	5	2	8	6	Income			
11	Income		2100					1			
12	Objective 2:										
13	Environment coefficients		2	5	8	4	9	Environment			
14	Environment		2350					1			
15											
16											
17	Weighted coefficients		10	10	10	12	15				
18	Weighted objective		4450								

Figure 16.4 Model for budgeting and priority setting.

Step 16.2 Select the ranges A2:F7, A10:F10, A13:F13, A17:F17, A11:B11, A14:B14 and A18:B18 (keep the Ctrl key pressed) and choose 'Insert', 'Name', 'Create' with the option 'Left column'. Using names improves the user-friendliness of models. For further improvements in the table, click on 'Window', 'Split' and 'Freeze panes' and fix the names or labels in the first row and column.

Step 16.3 In cell B11 we quantify the income objective as a linear function through the formula = SUMPRODUCT(B10:F10;B2:F2). If you carry out the selection using the mouse, the names will be automatically entered in the formula. In the same way you can generate formulas for the environment objective and the weighted objective in cells B14 and B18. We get the weighted contribution in B17 through the formula = \$H\$11*B10 + \$H\$14*B13. You can copy this formula to C17:F17 ('Paste special . . .', 'Formulas').

Step 16.4 The range B5:F7 contains the coefficient matrix for the three required constraints. Review and try to understand the modelling of this step. In cells H5 to H7, enter the SUMPRODUCT of the coefficients of the constraints and the vector x'.

Step 16.5 To finalise our model we now need the Solver. As target cell we choose the weighted objective function in B18 and as changing cells we choose the available funds (vector x) which have to be allocated to the policy measures. As you can see, the Solver also uses the chosen names. This is also the case for the constraints: Lower bounds <= x and Upper bounds >= x. Add the constraint H5:H6 <= J5:J6 and the budget constraint as the equation H7 = J7. You can see the parameter settings for the Solver in Figure 16.5. Since our model is linear, we can choose under 'Options' 'Assume linear model'; the non-negative assumptions would be redundant.

The Solver solution generates for the optimal budget allocation the budget expenditures of 35, 70, 165, 75 and 55. If you run the Solver

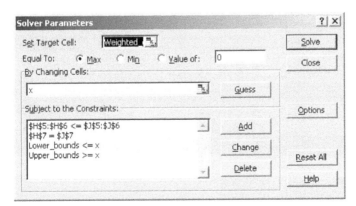

Figure 16.5 Solver setting of a model for budgeting and priority setting (exercise 16.xls).

with different start values, you will find out that several (alternative) optimal solutions exist for the considered optimisation problem (e.g. the values 55, 50, 165, 75, 55). With the same weights for both objectives in the aggregated objective function every point in the line segment (35, 70, 165, 75, 55) + α (20, −20, 0, 0, 0) with $\alpha \in$ [0, 1] is in fact an optimal solution with the value for the objective function of 4425 in cell B18. For the considered optimisation problem we thus have an 'edge' of optimal solutions. Three coefficients in the weighted objective function have the same value. Since in this case the Solver solution depends on the start values, you should try several start values to review and evaluate the relevance of the solution.

For specific optimisation problems the case discussed above of several optimal solutions may not often, or even never, occur, but you should keep in mind that linear optimisation can potentially lead to several alternative optimal solutions.

Let us now assume the first generated solution which is shown in Figure 16.6 and exercise16a.xls. To create a table and a graph with this optimal solution in comparison to the base situation is an easy exercise. Figure 16.6 shows that agri-environment and rural infrastructure should get a significantly higher budget allocation as compared to the base situation, while farm investment, marketing support and labour subsidies should get a smaller share of the budget.

Step 16.6 To solve Exercise 16b, set the right-hand side (RHS) of the budget equation (constraint 3) in cell J7 to 350 and then solve the model again (cf. Figure 16.7). This exercise shows that with a budget

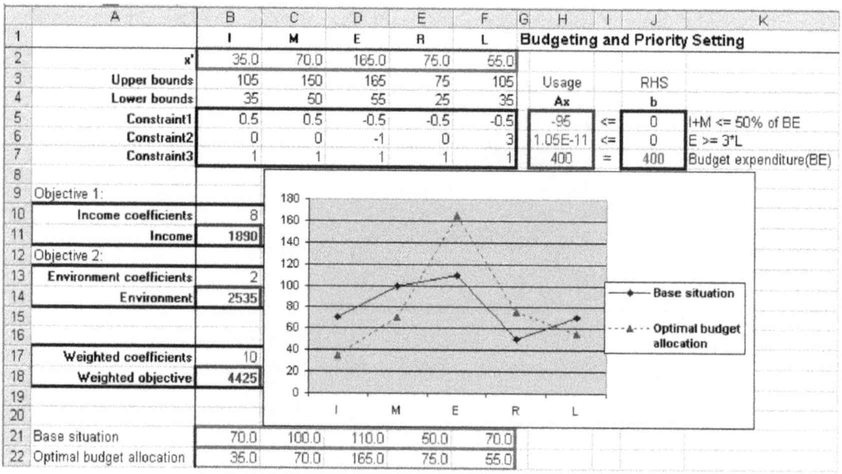

Figure 16.6 An optimal budget allocation (exercise16a.xls).

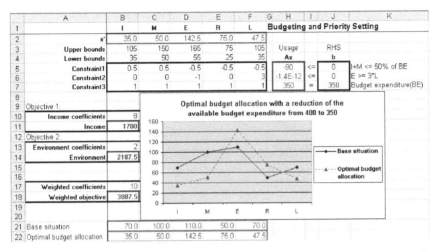

	A	B	C	D	E	F	G	H	I	J	K
1		I	M	E	R	L		**Budgeting and Priority Setting**			
2	x'	35.0	50.0	142.5	75.0	47.5					
3	Upper bounds	105	150	165	75	105		Usage		RHS	
4	Lower bounds	35	50	55	25	35		Ax		b	
5	Constraint1	0.5	0.5	-0.5	-0.5	-0.5		-90	<=	0	I+M <= 50% of BE
6	Constraint2	0	0	-1	0	3		-1.4E-12	<=	0	E >= 3*L
7	Constraint3	1	1	1	1	1		350	=	350	Budget expenditure(BE)
8											
9	Objective 1:										
10	Income coefficients	8									
11	Income	1700									
12	Objective 2:										
13	Environment coefficients	2									
14	Environment	2187.5									
15											
16											
17	Weighted coefficients	10									
18	Weighted objective	3887.5									
19											
20											
21	Base situation	70.0	100.0	110.0	50.0	70.0					
22	Optimal budget allocation	35.0	50.0	142.5	75.0	47.5					

Figure 16.7 An optimal budget allocation with a reduction of the available budget expenditure from 400 to 350 (exercise 16b.xls).

constraint of 350 the measures M, E and L should be reduced, while the measures I and R should remain unchanged. We see that a linear cut of all measures would be a rather naive policy response to an overall budget cut.

Step 16.7 Assume again a budget constraint of 400. Enter according to Exercise 16c in cell H11 the value 2, which changes the weighted objective function in the model accordingly. The model can then be solved again using the Solver (cf. Figure 16.8). The result shows that under this objective function a significant reallocation of funds between the measures would be required compared to the original weights, in particular a reduction of the allocation to agri-environment and an increase in farm investment.

Step 16.8 To solve Exercise 16d we only need to enter the value 8 in cells B13 and C13 and calculate the variants of Exercises 16a, 16b and 16c (cf. Figures 16.9 to 16.11). The figures show how the new objective coefficients would affect the optimal budget policy and allocation. In particular, farm investment would always need to be financed at the upper bound.

Step 16.9 In Exercise 16e we use the Solver again. Before that, set the lower and upper bound for farm investment to 70 in cells B3 and B4 respectively and the bounds for marketing support to 100 in cells C3 and C4 (cf. Figure 16.12). The figure shows that in this case the agri-environment measure could not be extended so much as without this constraint.

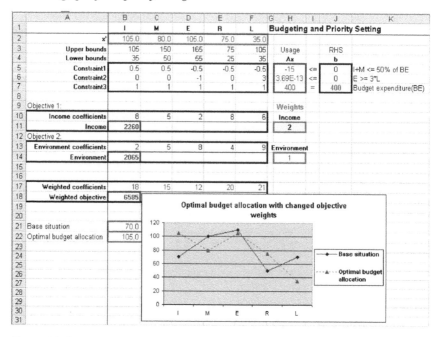

Figure 16.8 Optimal budget allocation with changed objective weightings (exercise 16c.xls).

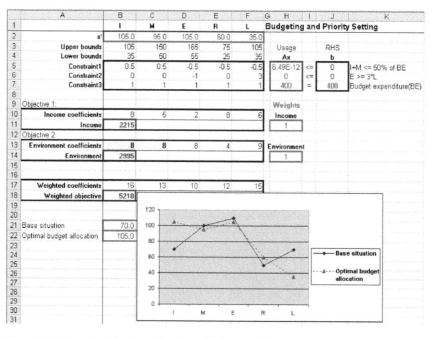

Figure 16.9 An optimal budget allocation with increased contributions to the environment objective (exercise 16d1.xls).

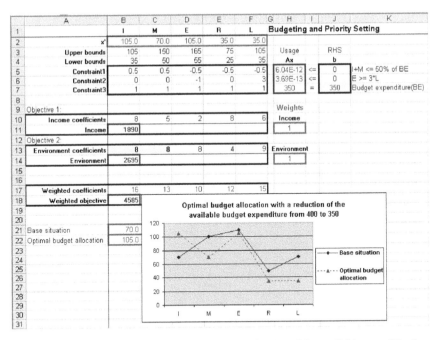

	I	M	E	R	L	Budgeting and Priority Setting			
x'	105.0	70.0	105.0	35.0	35.0				
Upper bounds	105	150	165	75	105	Usage		RHS	
Lower bounds	35	50	55	25	35	Ax		b	
Constraint1	0.5	0.5	-0.5	-0.5	-0.5	6.04E-12	<=	0	I+M <= 50% of BE
Constraint2	0	0	-1	0	3	3.69E-13	<=	0	E >= 3*L
Constraint3	1	1	1	1	1	350	=	350	Budget expenditure(BE)
Objective 1:						Weights			
Income coefficients	8	5	2	8	6	Income			
Income	1890					1			
Objective 2:									
Environment coefficients	8	8	8	4	9	Environment			
Environment	2695					1			
Weighted coefficients	16	13	10	12	15				
Weighted objective	4585								
Base situation	70.0								
Optimal budget allocation	105.0								

Optimal budget allocation with a reduction of the available budget expenditure from 400 to 350

Base situation

Optimal budget allocation

Figure 16.10 An optimal budget allocation with a reduction of the available overall budget from 400 to 350 and increased contributions to the environment objective (exercise16d2.xls).

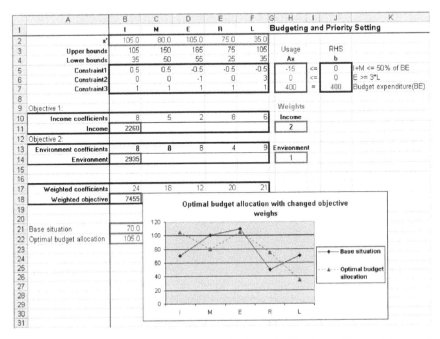

	I	M	E	R	L	Budgeting and Priority Setting			
x'	105.0	80.0	105.0	75.0	35.0				
Upper bounds	105	150	165	75	105	Usage		RHS	
Lower bounds	35	50	55	25	35	Ax		b	
Constraint1	0.5	0.5	-0.5	-0.5	-0.5	-15	<=	0	I+M <= 50% of BE
Constraint2	0	0	-1	0	3	0	<=	0	E >= 3*L
Constraint3	1	1	1	1	1	400	=	400	Budget expenditure(BE)
Objective 1:						Weights			
Income coefficients	8	5	2	8	6	Income			
Income	2260					2			
Objective 2:									
Environment coefficients	8	8	8	4	9	Environment			
Environment	2935					1			
Weighted coefficients	24	18	12	20	21				
Weighted objective	7455								
Base situation	70.0								
Optimal budget allocation	105.0								

Optimal budget allocation with changed objective weighs

Base situation

Optimal budget allocation

Figure 16.11 An optimal budget allocation with changed objective weights and increased contributions to the environment objective (exercise16d3.xls).

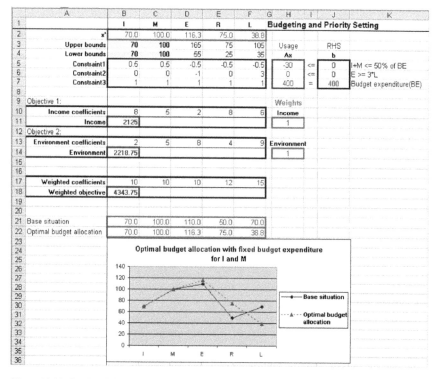

Figure 16.12 Optimal budget allocation with fixed budget expenditure for investment in holdings and marketing (exercise 16e.xls).

References

Albright, S.C. (2001) *VBA for Modelers: Developing Decision Support Systems with Microsoft® Excel*, Belmont, CA: Duxbury Press, pp. 367–80.

Chiang, A.C. (1984) *Fundamental Methods of Mathematical Economics* (3rd edn), Singapore: McGraw-Hill, pp. 651–75.

Jensen, P.A. and Board, J.F. (2003) *Operations Research: Models and Methods*, Indianapolis, IN: John Wiley, pp. 17–110.

Nožička, F., Guddat, J. and Hollatz, H. (1972) *Theorie der linearen Optimierung*, Berlin: Akademie Verlag, pp. 5–27, 90–199.

Winston, W.L. (2004) *Operations Research* (4th edn), Belmont, CA: Brooks/Cole, pp. 49–226.

17 Multiple objectives

Objectives

In Chapter 17 we want to examine the importance of the objective function for the introduced optimisation approach. We will show how multiple objectives can be considered and the consequences for budget allocation and priority setting.

Theory

In Chapter 16 we discussed how different objectives may be summarised to an aggregated linear objective function by using weights. This is indeed the easiest method to consider multiple objectives in the outlined optimisation approach. Following (16.5) and (16.6) we obtain for two objectives and two policy measures:

$$Z = a_1 (z_{11} \, BE_1 + z_{12} \, BE_2) + a_2 (z_{21} \, BE_1 + z_{22} \, BE_2) \tag{17.1}$$

and

$$Z = (a_1 z_{11} + a_2 z_{21}) \, BE_1 + (a_1 z_{12} + a_2 z_{22}) \, BE_2. \tag{17.1}'$$

Obviously, the aggregated objective function is a linear function of the budget expenditure for the considered policy measures and the slope is determined by the objective coefficients of the different policy measures and the weights of the objectives. Changing these variables would potentially lead to a new solution. Following Figure 16.3, we would get a rotation of the objective function in the case of two policy measures, and Figure 17.1 shows that for two different objective curves Z' and Z'' different optimal solutions are found.

The outlined approach may be extended to more objectives, but this requires more information. For policy-making problems we emphasise the need to focus on the most important objectives to reduce complexity. The optimisation approach is powerful and will also yield results for highly complex policy problems, but decision-makers may experience difficulties in providing the necessary information and interpreting the results and drawing conclusions.

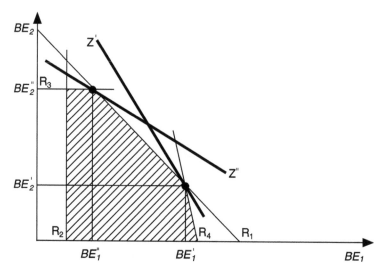

Figure 17.1 Solution values of linear optimisation with different objective functions.

A variety of approaches to consider multiple objectives have been suggested. For example, it would be possible to focus on maximising one or only a few objectives of a multiple objective program and to consider further objectives as constraints. With two objectives, then, Z_1 could be the objective function to be maximised and for Z_2 a constraint $Z_2 \geq Z_2^*$ would apply. One could show through a gradual change in the constraint (i.e. the lower bound Z_2^*) what consequences such changes in the constraint would have for the realisation of objective Z_1. Following this approach the trade-off between the two objectives could be traced. This approach is also called the constraint method.

The trade-off between two objectives may also be derived through a parametrisation of the weights and this method is called the weighting method. According to (16.8) the following objective function can be formulated:

$$Z = a \sum_{i=1}^{n} z_{1i} BE_i + (1 - a) \sum_{i=1}^{n} z_{2i} BE_i. \tag{17.2}$$

The idea is to gradually change a from $0 \leq a \leq 1$ and to show the consequences for the solution values.

Figure 17.2 shows the result of using this approach, considering an example with three policy measures. If only one objective, Z_1, is considered, the solution values are BE_1', BE_2' and BE_3' on the left axis of the figure. A gradual increase in the weight of objective Z_2, and an accordingly lower weight of objective Z_1, would initially not change the solution values, but will then lead to different values. Obviously, the first policy measure loses with an increasing weight of objective Z_2, while the second measure gains. For the third policy measure the objective weights

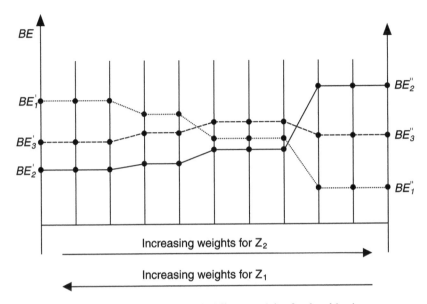

Figure 17.2 Optimal budget allocation with different weights for the objectives.

have only a very limited impact. If only objective Z_2 is considered the solution values are BE_1'', BE_2'' and BE_3'' on the right-hand side.

Figure 17.2 shows four different solutions altogether. If we generate the respective objective values Z_1 and Z_2 for these solutions, these values describe the different possibilities for realising the two objectives. In Figure 17.3 these solution values define the trade-off curve between the considered two objectives. It is evident that

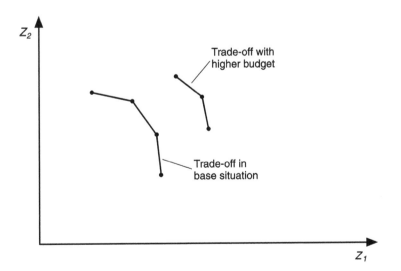

Figure 17.3 Trade-off curve with linear optimisation.

with changing objective coefficients and/or constraints, the trade-off curve will change. Figure 17.3 shows the consequence of a relaxation of the budget constraint, i.e. a higher budget is available to finance the considered policy measures. Apparently, this leads to an outward shift of the trade-off curve. The figure shows three solution points, which now define the possibilities for policy-making.

The outlined approaches may be used to analyse the consequences of multiple objectives in specific problem settings. It is emphasised that the number of objectives should be limited to keep a policy-making problem manageable. If a limitation to two objectives is not appropriate for a specific problem setting, trade-offs between two objectives may be examined by including other objectives as constraints. This would then raise the interesting question: How would changes in the 'objective constraints' affect the trade-off between the considered two objectives?

Thus, linear optimisation offers different useful tools to consider multiple objectives for budget allocation and priority setting. Technically, the handling of multi-dimensional objective functions is not problematic; the real problem is if the required information for complex models is available and if the obtained results can be interpreted in a useful way to provide answers for policy-making problems. Hence, a certain 'zooming' approach to modelling is necessary to formulate the appropriate model for a specific policy-making exercise.

Exercise 17

Let us again assume that a government wants to review the priorities of its rural development policy. Solve the following problems using the model developed in Exercise 16:

(a) How should priorities be set to maximise the income objective and, at the same time, to achieve at least 90 per cent (80 per cent) of the maximum value of the environment objective?
(b) How would a gradual increase in the weight of the environment objective in relation to the income objective affect the priorities? Display the result in a table and in a chart.
(c) Generate the trade-off curve for achieving the income and environment objectives.
(d) How do the possibilities change to achieve the income and environment objectives if the budget is cut by 25 per cent or increased by the same percentage?
(e) Solve Exercises 17b to 17d using a macro. Compute your model for a budget of 220 and interpret the results.

Solution

Step 17.1 Assume the model from Exercise 16a. To solve Exercise 17a you have first to determine the maximum value of the environment objective under the given constraints. To do this, choose as the weight for the income objective the value zero in cell H11 and solve the model for the environment objective only with the Solver. You will obtain a maximum value for the environment objective of 2585 (in cells B14 and B18), which you can copy, for example, to cell K14 (as value).

Step 17.2 We now add the additional constraint of the environment objective. Fill in the left-hand side of this new constraint (the respective values of the environment objective) in cell H15 by entering the formula = B14. As a reminder of the type of constraint, enter the character string '>=' in the cell to the right. We then fill in the right-hand side of the constraint by adding the formula = J14*K14 in cell J15, whereby the percentage share (initially 90 per cent) is in cell J14.

The next task is to change the weights of the objectives: 1 for the income objective and 0 for the environment objective (since the environment objective is considered through the additional constraint). We now include the new constraint H15 >= J15 in the Solver (click on 'Add') and solve the model. The solution is shown in Figure 17.4.

The result shows that by following this approach farm investment should attract more funding compared to the optimal solution with an aggregated objective function and equal weights for income and environment. On the other hand, marketing support, environment measures and labour subsidies would receive less funding. Apparently,

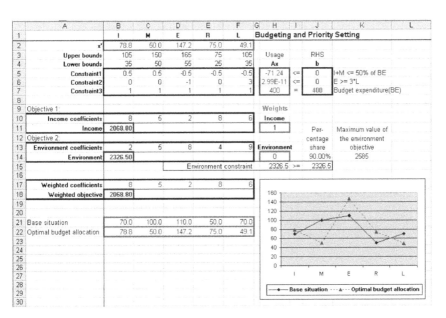

Figure 17.4 Priority setting with maximisation of the income objective and realisation of the environment objective of at least 90 per cent of the maximum objective value (exercise17a1.xls).

the new policy scenario in particular favours farm investment. As compared to the solution with equal weights the income objective value is now higher and the environment objective value is lower. For the 80 per cent variant of this exercise you have only to change the value in cell J14 and to run the Solver again. As shown in Figure 17.5, the further reduction in the environment constraint would, in particular, favour farm investment. In fact, farm investment would now be financed at its upper bound. In this policy scenario the income value would further increase to 2258.15. A further relaxation of the environment constraint to, for example, 50 per cent would not change this result significantly. Try to solve this variant using your model.

Step 17.3   Assume again the model from Exercise 16a. Delete the chart and the cells A21:F22; then enter a series of 0, 0.1, 0.2, ..., 1 in the range A20:A30. Write the formula = 1 − H14 in cell H11 and the formula = A20 in cell H14. If we vary the last formula from = A20 to = A30, we obtain a parametrisation of the weights from the income to the environment objective. Copy the values of the respective Solver solutions from B2:F2 to the relevant row in the range B20:F30.

In addition, we generate the objective variables for the different solutions in the range H20:I30 using the SUMPRODUCT operation. Choosing an appropriate column width or format, we obtain an acceptable display of the numbers (cf. Figure 17.6).

	A	B	C	D	E	F	G	H	I	J	K	L
1		I	M	E	R	L	Budgeting and Priority Setting					
2	x'	105.0	79.1	105.7	75.0	35.2						
3	Upper bounds	105	150	165	75	105	Usage		RHS			
4	Lower bounds	35	50	55	25	35	Ax		b			
5	Constraint1	0.5	0.5	-0.5	-0.5	-0.5	-15.9231	<=	0	I+M <= 50% of BE		
6	Constraint2	0	0	-1	0	3	7.62E-11	<=	0	E >= 3*L		
7	Constraint3	1	1	1	1	1	400	=	400	Budget expenditure(BE)		
8												
9	Objective 1:						Weights					
10	Income coefficients	8	5	2	8	6	Income					
11	Income	2258.15					1		Per-	Maximum value of		
12	Objective 2:								centage	the environment		
13	Environment coefficients	2	5	8	4	9	Environment		share	objective		
14	Environment	2068.00					0		80.00%	2585		
15					Environment constraint		2068 >=		2068			
16												
17	Weighted coefficients	8	5	2	8	6						
18	Weighted objective	2258.15										
19							120					
20							100					
21	Base situation	70.0	100.0	110.0	50.0	70.0	80					
22	Optimal budget allocation	105.0	79.1	105.7	75.0	35.2	60					
23							40					
24							20					
25							0					
26												
27							I	M	E	R	L	
28												
29							Base situation ···▲··· Optimal budget allocation					
30												

Figure 17.5   Priority setting with maximisation of the income objective and realisation of the environment objective of at least 80 per cent of the maximum objective value (exercise17a2.xls).

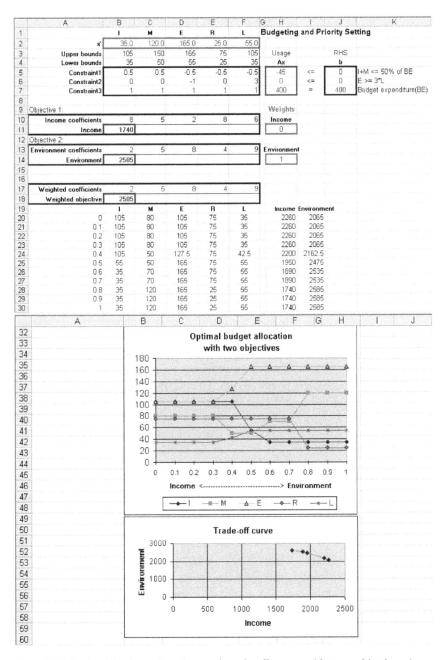

	A	B	C	D	E	F	G	H	I	J	K
1		I	M	E	R	L	**Budgeting and Priority Setting**				
2	x'	35.0	120.0	165.0	25.0	55.0					
3	Upper bounds	105	150	165	75	105	Usage		RHS		
4	Lower bounds	35	50	55	25	35	Ax		b		
5	Constraint1	0.5	0.5	-0.5	-0.5	-0.5	-45	<=	0		I+M <= 50% of BE
6	Constraint2	0	0	-1	0	3	0	<=	0		E >= 3*L
7	Constraint3	1	1	1	1	1	400	=	400		Budget expenditure(BE)
8											
9	Objective 1:						Weights				
10	Income coefficients	8	5	2	8	6	Income				
11	Income	1740					0				
12	Objective 2:										
13	Environment coefficients	2	5	8	4	9	Environment				
14	Environment	2585					1				
15											
16											
17	Weighted coefficients	2	5	8	4	9					
18	Weighted objective	2585									
19		I	M	E	R	L	Income	Environment			
20	0	105	80	105	75	35	2260	2065			
21	0.1	105	80	105	75	35	2260	2065			
22	0.2	105	80	105	75	35	2260	2065			
23	0.3	105	80	105	75	35	2260	2065			
24	0.4	105	50	127.5	75	42.5	2200	2162.5			
25	0.5	55	50	165	75	55	1950	2475			
26	0.6	35	70	165	75	55	1890	2535			
27	0.7	35	70	165	75	55	1890	2535			
28	0.8	35	120	165	25	55	1740	2585			
29	0.9	35	120	165	25	55	1740	2585			
30	1	35	120	165	25	55	1740	2585			

Figure 17.6 Optimal budget allocation and trade-off curve with two objectives (exercise17bc.xls).

Step 17.4 Now generate two charts. To do this, copy the names B1:F1 to B19:F19. Then select the range A19:F30, choose in the 'Chart wizard' the type 'Line with markers displayed at each data value' and generate the chart for the budget allocation with different weights. Figure 17.6 shows that there is a clear conflict between the objectives income and environment with respect to farm investment and agri-environment measures. Farm investment receives a higher budget at a higher weight of the income objective, but loses at a higher weight of the environment objective. The opposite applies for agri-environment measures. The conflict between the two objectives is not as pronounced for the other three policy measures.

For the trade-off curve in Exercise 17c you can use the above calculated objective variables in the range H20:I30. Use the chart type 'XY' with smoothed lines (cf. Figure 17.6). The chart shows the five calculated points of the trade-off curve.

Step 17.5 To solve Exercise 17d we have to set the value for the total budget to 300 in J7 (and 500, respectively) and calculate the Solver solutions for all weights according to the above parametrisation. The results are shown in exercise17d1.xls and exercise17d2.xls.

Step 17.6 The task can be simplified considerably by developing a macro. Macros are powerful instruments to handle parametrisation problems and to improve the analysis of complex policy problems, but using them is an 'art' that has to be learned. In addition, one has to be aware that macros can unfortunately be misused to spread and implement viruses.

We now want to develop a macro. To do this, go back to Exercises 17b and 17c. Copy the Solver solutions obtained in the range B20:F30 to K20:O30 to enable later comparisons and then delete the content in the range B20:F30. Now calculate the solutions for the parameter values 0.3 and 0.4 (cells A23 and A24), and record each step with the macro recorder.

To do this, proceed as follows: click on 'Tools', 'Macro', 'Record new macro' and start (with the macro name 'VectorOptimisation') by clicking on 'OK'. Each step will now be recorded.

Go to H14 and enter the formula = A23, activate the Solver and copy the solution values from B2:F2 to B23:F23 (next to 0.3). Go again to H14, enter = A24, solve with the Solver, copy the values from B2:F2 to B24:F24 and again click on H14. Then finish the recording with the macro.

Step 17.7 Delete the content of the cells B23:F24 and test your macro by clicking on 'Tools', 'Macro', 'Macros . . .' and then 'Run'. If everything works right from the start, you are lucky. It is more likely that an error message will appear in a visual basic window with which you may not be familiar. Close this window, thus stopping the debugger.

Open again the 'Visual Basic Editor' ('Tools', 'Macro' or by pressing the Alt-F11 key combination). In 'Visual Basic' click on 'Tools',

'References' and tick 'Solver.xla' and then choose 'OK'. It may be that you will first have to search for the Solver, for example, under C:\Program Files\Microsoft Office\Office\Library\Solver (or for Excel 2003, C:\Program Files\Microsoft Office\Office11\Library\Solver). Now click on your Excel model and run the macro again. Everything should now work. If this is not the case (e.g. the Solver has not been active), you should record your macro again, with the reference correctly set before and possibly with an open 'Visual Basic Editor' window.

NB: The references are linked to a single Excel file and dependent on the actual Windows installation; it is recommended that you check in advance. (If discrepancies exist, the macros in some files provided for Chapters 17 and 18 may not work. The macros will only work properly if the reference to the Solver is correctly set.)

General hint: After opening a file with a Solver-macro, address the Solver once before you run the macro.

Step 17.8 Have a look at the code of your macro in 'Visual Basic for Applications' (VBA) and try to understand the code. You will certainly recognise the two cycles, but we need 11 of these in the right order. Thus you have to complete the macro accordingly. To do this you can simply use copy and paste. You then have to edit the cell linkages in the code (from R[6] to R[16] and Range("B20").Select to Range("B30").Select). Test again the extended macro in your Excel sheet.

Step 17.9 The last disturbing thing is the result confirmation provided by the Solver. This may be suppressed by substituting the command SolverSolve with SolverSolve(True) in the Visual Basic code. Use 'Edit', 'Replace' and 'Replace all' (cf. Figure 17.7 and exercise17e.xls with the macro 'VectorOptimisation'). However, do not forget to 'Enable macros'; to set the 'Security' under 'Tools', 'Macro' to a medium level; and to check the reference for the Solver.

Step 17.10 For a total budget of 220 the model does not have a feasible solution, i.e. our macro misses a relevant error treatment. Convince yourself by opening the Solver manually. In Chapter 18 we will extend our macro accordingly and improve the programming.

```
Sub VectorOptimisation()
'
' VectorOptimisation Macro
' Macro recorded 16/05/2006 by jech
'


'
    Range("H14").Select
    ActiveCell.FormulaR1C1 = "=R[6]C[-7]"
    SolverOk SetCell:="$B$18", MaxMinVal:=1, ValueOf:="0", _
        ByChange:="$B$2:$F$2"
    SolverSolve (True)
    Range("B2:F2").Select
    Selection.Copy
    Range("B20").Select
    Selection.PasteSpecial Paste:=xlValues, _
        Operation:=xlNone, SkipBlanks:= _
        False, Transpose:=False
    Range("H14").Select
    ActiveCell.FormulaR1C1 = "=R[7]C[-7]"
    SolverOk SetCell:="$B$18", MaxMinVal:=1, ValueOf:="0", _
        ByChange:="$B$2:$F$2"
    SolverSolve (True)
    Range("B2:F2").Select
    Selection.Copy
    Range("B21").Select
    Selection.PasteSpecial Paste:=xlValues, _
        Operation:=xlNone, SkipBlanks:= _
        False, Transpose:=False
    Range("H14").Select
    ActiveCell.FormulaR1C1 = "=R[8]C[-7]"
    SolverOk SetCell:="$B$18", MaxMinVal:=1, ValueOf:="0", _
        ByChange:="$B$2:$F$2"
    SolverSolve (True)
    Range("B2:F2").Select
    Selection.Copy
    Range("B22").Select
    Selection.PasteSpecial Paste:=xlValues, _
        Operation:=xlNone, SkipBlanks:= _
        False, Transpose:=False
    Range("H14").Select
    ActiveCell.FormulaR1C1 = "=R[9]C[-7]"
    SolverOk SetCell:="$B$18", MaxMinVal:=1, ValueOf:="0", _
        ByChange:="$B$2:$F$2"
    SolverSolve (True)
    Range("B2:F2").Select
    Selection.Copy
    Range("B23").Select
    Selection.PasteSpecial Paste:=xlValues, _
        Operation:=xlNone, SkipBlanks:= _
        False, Transpose:=False
    Range("H14").Select
    ActiveCell.FormulaR1C1 = "=R[10]C[-7]"
    SolverOk SetCell:="$B$18", MaxMinVal:=1, ValueOf:="0", _
        ByChange:="$B$2:$F$2"
    SolverSolve (True)
    Range("B2:F2").Select
    Selection.Copy
```

Figure 17.7 Visual Basic code (derived from macro recorder) for multiple objective optimisation (exercise17e.xls).

```
Range("B24").Select
Selection.PasteSpecial Paste:=xlValues, _
    Operation:=xlNone, SkipBlanks:= _
    False, Transpose:=False
Range("H14").Select
ActiveCell.FormulaR1C1 = "=R[11]C[-7]"
SolverOk SetCell:="$B$18", MaxMinVal:=1, ValueOf:="0", _
    ByChange:="$B$2:$F$2"
SolverSolve (True)
Range("B2:F2").Select
Selection.Copy
Range("B25").Select
Selection.PasteSpecial Paste:=xlValues, _
    Operation:=xlNone, SkipBlanks:= _
    False, Transpose:=False
Range("H14").Select
ActiveCell.FormulaR1C1 = "=R[12]C[-7]"
SolverOk SetCell:="$B$18", MaxMinVal:=1, ValueOf:="0", _
    ByChange:="$B$2:$F$2"
SolverSolve (True)
Range("B2:F2").Select
Selection.Copy
Range("B26").Select
Selection.PasteSpecial Paste:=xlValues, _
    Operation:=xlNone, SkipBlanks:= _
    False, Transpose:=False
Range("H14").Select
ActiveCell.FormulaR1C1 = "=R[13]C[-7]"
SolverOk SetCell:="$B$18", MaxMinVal:=1, ValueOf:="0", _
    ByChange:="$B$2:$F$2"
SolverSolve (True)
Range("B2:F2").Select
Selection.Copy
Range("B27").Select
Selection.PasteSpecial Paste:=xlValues, _
    Operation:=xlNone, SkipBlanks:= _
    False, Transpose:=False
Range("H14").Select
ActiveCell.FormulaR1C1 = "=R[14]C[-7]"
SolverOk SetCell:="$B$18", MaxMinVal:=1, ValueOf:="0", _
    ByChange:="$B$2:$F$2"
SolverSolve (True)
Range("B2:F2").Select
Selection.Copy
Range("B28").Select
Selection.PasteSpecial Paste:=xlValues, _
    Operation:=xlNone, SkipBlanks:= _
    False, Transpose:=False
Range("H14").Select
ActiveCell.FormulaR1C1 = "=R[15]C[-7]"
SolverOk SetCell:="$B$18", MaxMinVal:=1, ValueOf:="0", _
    ByChange:="$B$2:$F$2"
```

Figure 17.7 continued.

Continued overleaf

```
    SolverSolve (True)
    Range("B2:F2").Select
    Selection.Copy
    Range("B29").Select
    Selection.PasteSpecial Paste:=xlValues, _
        Operation:=xlNone, SkipBlanks:= _
        False, Transpose:=False
    Range("H14").Select
    ActiveCell.FormulaR1C1 = "=R[16]C[-7]"
    SolverOk SetCell:="$B$18", MaxMinVal:=1, ValueOf:="0", _
        ByChange:="$B$2:$F$2"
    SolverSolve (True)
    Range("B2:F2").Select
    Selection.Copy
    Range("B30").Select
    Selection.PasteSpecial Paste:=xlValues, _
        Operation:=xlNone, SkipBlanks:= _
        False, Transpose:=False
    Range("H14").Select
End Sub
```

Figure 17.7 continued.

References

Albright, S.C. (2001) *VBA for Modelers: Developing Decision Support Systems with Microsoft® Excel*, Belmont, CA: Duxbury Press, pp. 13–25, 49–62, 171–86.

Guddat, J. (1979) 'Parametrische Optimierung und Vektoroptimierung', in K. Lommatzsch (ed.) *Anwendungen der linearen parametrischen Optimierung*, Berlin: Akademie Verlag, pp. 54–75.

Walkenbach, J. (2004) *Microsoft® Office Excel 2003 Power Programming with VBA*, Indianapolis, IN: John Wiley.

Winston, W.L. (2004) *Operations Research* (4th edn), Belmont, CA: Brooks/Cole, pp. 695–700.

18 Parametric analysis

Objective

In Chapter 18 we want to examine the importance of constraints for the discussed optimisation approach. By using appropriate parametrisation we will show how changes in budget or other constraints or coefficients affect the budget allocation and priority setting. Finally, we will explain how Excel models and VBA programs may be protected.

Theory

The importance of constraints for the solution of the optimisation approach, and hence for budget allocation and priority setting, is obvious. Changes in constraints will in most cases lead to a new optimal solution, which indicates the necessity of a more detailed assessment of the consequences of a change in a constraint for the optimisation result.

Figure 17.1 showed the solution values of the linear optimisation approach for different objective functions. Analogously, Figure 18.1 shows how an optimal solution is affected by different constraints. With the budget constraint R_1' we get BE_1' and BE_2' as optimal solution values. If the budget curve shifts to the left to R_1'', the set of feasible solutions reduces by the cross-hatched area, and we get BE_1'' and BE_2'' as optimal solution values. The change in the budget constraint thus leads to lower budget expenditure for the second policy measure and higher expenditure for the first policy measure.

This example shows that the consequences of a change in the constraints are difficult to assess even for a rather simple optimisation problem. The problem becomes more severe with an increasing complexity of the optimisation problem and constraints to be considered. This underlines the usefulness of linear programming in identifying and analysing such problems. The example also shows that simple recommendations and 'rules of thumb' for the adjustment of priorities as a response to changes in constraints often do not provide good answers to real problem settings. A popular example is the proposed linear cut of the budget for all policy measures under financial pressure. It is obvious that, given the

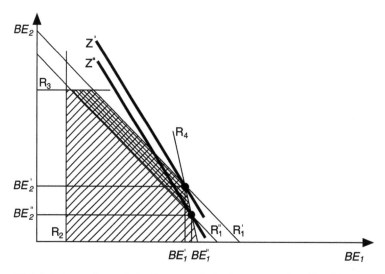

Figure 18.1 Solution values of the linear optimisation approach with different budget constraints.

complexity of real policy-making problems in budgeting and priority setting, such a recommendation is rather naive.

But how can we use linear programming to assess the importance of constraints and their changes for the optimisation problem? We have already mentioned that it makes sense to calculate different solutions for different values of the constraints. One example is to calculate the budget allocation to different policy measures for a small and a large budget; another example would be to show how different objective weights affect the optimal objective values under different budget constraints or the trade-off curve between the objectives considered.

A general problem of the linear programming approach is that it generates point solutions that could be different even for small changes in the constraints. It is not clear, for example, how stable a solution is for different budget levels. It is hence recommended to conduct a sensitivity analysis varying the constraints and evaluating how the solution values change.

Figure 18.2 outlines the approach. The example shows how a gradual decrease or increase of the available budget affects the solution value of the budget expenditure for a specific policy measure. We can see that the budget allocation to this measure is rather sensitive to a decrease in the budget, i.e. already, with a small reduction of the overall budget expenditure, the financing for this policy measure would need to be significantly cut. However, with further budget reductions expenditure for this policy measure seems to stabilise and remains constant. On the other hand, Figure 18.2 shows that only for a considerably higher overall budget the financial allocation to the measure considered would be extended.

The suggested sensitivity analysis may also be applied to other constraints (e.g. the parametrisation of the upper and lower bounds of budget expenditures

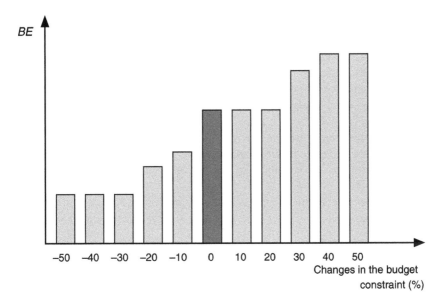

Figure 18.2 Budget expenditure for a policy measure with changes in the budget constraint.

for different policy measures). Moreover, a sensitivity analysis could also be conducted for the objective function by parametrising objective coefficients and/or weights. With respect to objective weights, we have already conducted a specific type of parametrisation as a sensitivity analysis in Chapter 17.

Such calculations and sensitivity analyses help us to assess the results of the optimisation approach for a specific problem setting and show the perspectives for the application. In fact, the approach should not be restricted to the calculation of 'point solutions'. The application should instead include some sensitivity analysis (e.g. analysing alternative scenarios with varying constraints and objective weights). Such additional calculations provide valuable insights into a specific policy-making problem and help to improve the quality of decisions.

Exercise 18

Let us again assume that a government wants to review the priorities of its rural development policy. Solve the following problems using the model developed in Exercises 16 and 17:

(a) Does it make sense to apply a budget cut from 400 to 300 as an equal linear reduction of the expenditures for all policy measures?
(b) Draw up a table and a chart to show how the priorities for rural development would need to be adjusted under a gradual reduction of the budget from 400 to 300.
    Solve this exercise using a macro.

(c) Improve the VBA code of your macro with a 'For . . . Next loop' and add to the macro an error treatment for the case that the model does not find a feasible solution.

(d) Using a sensitivity analysis, show how changes in the budget constraint from 100 to 600 affect the optimal budget allocation for the policy measures.

(e) Using a sensitivity analysis, show how the optimal budget allocation for the policy measures changes if the expenditure for agri-environment is x times (x varying between 0 and 5) as high as the expenditure for labour subsidies.

Solve this exercise using a macro.

Combine the three macros to parametrise the objective function, the total budget and the above value x in one Excel model for different sensitivity calculations.

Add a protection measure to your model and macro against modifications and access.

Solution

Step 18.1 Solve your model from Exercises 16 or 17 with the Solver assuming equal objective weights and a total budget of 400 and 300, respectively, and copy the solutions to an appropriate place in your table. Next, calculate the respective values for both objectives as well as their sum. Once you have multiplied the solution of the 400 (budget) version with 0.75 and you have also calculated the objective values, the remaining part of this exercise is only to develop a chart and interpret it (compare with Figure 18.3). Be aware that there is more than one optimal solution for the budget of 400, as explained in Step 16.5.

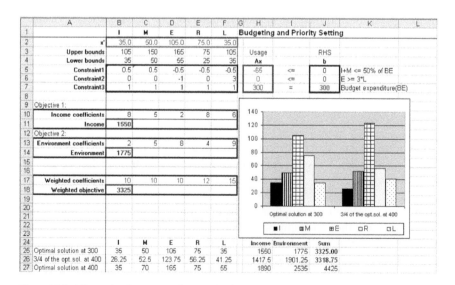

Figure 18.3 A linear budget cut and an optimal solution (exercise18a.xls).

The figure shows that a linear reduction in the expenditures for all policy measures by 25 per cent is not a sensible budget policy. In particular, the expenditures for farm investment and rural infrastructure should not be cut at all, while expenditures for the other three policy measures should be reduced by more than 25 per cent.

Step 18.2 To solve Exercise 18b we use model exercise17e.xls with the macro for the vector optimisation and the linked charts. Enter in this model the exogenous value 1 in the cells H11 and H14. Change the series in the range A20:A30 to 400, 390, . . ., 300.

Step 18.3 Next, edit the VBA code of your macro with the 'Visual Basic Editor' (Alt-F11 key combination). You should not change the weights (in cell H14), but change the value for the total budget in cell J7. Hence in the macro all character strings H14 have to be substituted by J7 and the cell references of R[6]C[−7] to R[16]C[−7] need to be adjusted, i.e. to be changed to R[13]C[−9] to R[23]C[−9] (cf. Figure 18.4).

Step 18.4 The new macro should also be renamed; for example, 'RHS_Parametrisation'. If the macro runs without any problems, we should get a result as shown in Figure 18.5 (cf. exercise18b.xls). You will realise the advantage of our modelling approach when you change the exogenous input data (e.g. the value of the contribution to the environment through farm investment in cell B13 (for example the value 8)) and restart the macro. In this way you can even visually follow the consequences of this change. The visualisation may be hampered by the high speed of modern computers. You can slow down the screen updating and improve visualisation by imposing an artificial time lag using a VBA code (cf. exercise18e_slow-down.xls).

In Figure 18.5 we have the optimal solution (55, 50, 165, 75, 55) for a budget of 400. The gradual decrease in the overall budget to 300 would not affect marketing support and rural infrastructure, but would quickly reduce the budget allocation for farm investment to the lower bound. Agri-environment and labour subsidisation initially would not be affected by a budget reduction, but would become increasingly reduced.

Step 18.5 In this and the next step we will, as required in Exercise 18c, improve and extend the macro. If you look at the code of the macro in Figure 18.4, you will recognise 11 similar cycles with only a few parts differing. It makes sense to use here a 'For . . . Next' command (see VBA-Online help), but you have to be aware of the syntax of VBA programming. You can see a solution in Figure 18.6 and in the file exercise18c.xls. This makes the program a lot shorter and concise while maintaining the same functionality.

Step 18.6 Parametrise the total budget from 100 to 600 (range A20:A30) and run the macro 'RHS_Parametrisation'. You will note that there is something wrong with the solutions. If you look at constraint 3 (in H7:J7) or open the Solver manually (e.g. for J7 = 600 or J7 = 100), you will see

```
Sub RHS_Parametrisation()
'
' RHS_Parametrisation Macro
' Macro recorded 16/05/2006 by jech
'
    Range("J7").Select
    ActiveCell.FormulaR1C1 = "=R[13]C[-9]"
    SolverOk SetCell:="$B$18", MaxMinVal:=1, ValueOf:="0", _
        ByChange:="$B$2:$F$2"
    SolverSolve (True)
    Range("B2:F2").Select
    Selection.Copy
    Range("B20").Select
    Selection.PasteSpecial Paste:=xlValues, _
        Operation:=xlNone, SkipBlanks:= _
        False, Transpose:=False
    Range("J7").Select
    ActiveCell.FormulaR1C1 = "=R[14]C[-9]"
    SolverOk SetCell:="$B$18", MaxMinVal:=1, ValueOf:="0", _
        ByChange:="$B$2:$F$2"
    SolverSolve (True)
    Range("B2:F2").Select
    Selection.Copy
    Range("B21").Select
    Selection.PasteSpecial Paste:=xlValues, _
        Operation:=xlNone, SkipBlanks:= _
        False, Transpose:=False
    Range("J7").Select
    ActiveCell.FormulaR1C1 = "=R[15]C[-9]"
    SolverOk SetCell:="$B$18", MaxMinVal:=1, ValueOf:="0", _
        ByChange:="$B$2:$F$2"
    SolverSolve (True)
    Range("B2:F2").Select
    Selection.Copy
    Range("B22").Select
    Selection.PasteSpecial Paste:=xlValues, _
        Operation:=xlNone, SkipBlanks:= _
        False, Transpose:=False
    Range("J7").Select
    ActiveCell.FormulaR1C1 = "=R[16]C[-9]"
    SolverOk SetCell:="$B$18", MaxMinVal:=1, ValueOf:="0", _
        ByChange:="$B$2:$F$2"
    SolverSolve (True)
    Range("B2:F2").Select
    Selection.Copy
    Range("B23").Select
    Selection.PasteSpecial Paste:=xlValues, _
        Operation:=xlNone, SkipBlanks:= _
        False, Transpose:=False
    Range("J7").Select
    ActiveCell.FormulaR1C1 = "=R[17]C[-9]"
    SolverOk SetCell:="$B$18", MaxMinVal:=1, ValueOf:="0", _
        ByChange:="$B$2:$F$2"
    SolverSolve (True)
    Range("B2:F2").Select
    Selection.Copy
    Range("B24").Select
    Selection.PasteSpecial Paste:=xlValues, _
        Operation:=xlNone, SkipBlanks:= _
        False, Transpose:=False
    Range("J7").Select
    ActiveCell.FormulaR1C1 = "=R[18]C[-9]"
    SolverOk SetCell:="$B$18", MaxMinVal:=1, ValueOf:="0", _
        ByChange:="$B$2:$F$2"
    SolverSolve (True)
    Range("B2:F2").Select
    Selection.Copy
    Range("B25").Select
```

Figure 18.4 VBA program for the parametrisation of the total budget.

```
    Selection.PasteSpecial Paste:=xlValues, _
        Operation:=xlNone, SkipBlanks:= _
        False, Transpose:=False
    Range("J7").Select
    ActiveCell.FormulaR1C1 = "=R[19]C[-9]"
    SolverOk SetCell:="$B$18", MaxMinVal:=1, ValueOf:="0", _
        ByChange:="$B$2:$F$2"
    SolverSolve (True)
    Range("B2:F2").Select
    Selection.Copy
    Range("B26").Select
    Selection.PasteSpecial Paste:=xlValues, _
        Operation:=xlNone, SkipBlanks:= _
        False, Transpose:=False
    Range("J7").Select
    ActiveCell.FormulaR1C1 = "=R[20]C[-9]"
    SolverOk SetCell:="$B$18", MaxMinVal:=1, ValueOf:="0", _
        ByChange:="$B$2:$F$2"
    SolverSolve (True)
    Range("B2:F2").Select
    Selection.Copy
    Range("B27").Select
    Selection.PasteSpecial Paste:=xlValues, _
        Operation:=xlNone, SkipBlanks:= _
        False, Transpose:=False
    Range("J7").Select
    ActiveCell.FormulaR1C1 = "=R[21]C[-9]"
    SolverOk SetCell:="$B$18", MaxMinVal:=1, ValueOf:="0", _
        ByChange:="$B$2:$F$2"
    SolverSolve (True)
    Range("B2:F2").Select
    Selection.Copy
    Range("B28").Select
    Selection.PasteSpecial Paste:=xlValues, _
        Operation:=xlNone, SkipBlanks:= _
        False, Transpose:=False
    Range("J7").Select
    ActiveCell.FormulaR1C1 = "=R[22]C[-9]"
    SolverOk SetCell:="$B$18", MaxMinVal:=1, ValueOf:="0", _
        ByChange:="$B$2:$F$2"
    SolverSolve (True)
    Range("B2:F2").Select
    Selection.Copy
    Range("B29").Select
    Selection.PasteSpecial Paste:=xlValues, _
        Operation:=xlNone, SkipBlanks:= _
        False, Transpose:=False
    Range("J7").Select
    ActiveCell.FormulaR1C1 = "=R[23]C[-9]"
    SolverOk SetCell:="$B$18", MaxMinVal:=1, ValueOf:="0", _
        ByChange:="$B$2:$F$2"
    SolverSolve (True)
    Range("B2:F2").Select
    Selection.Copy
    Range("B30").Select
    Selection.PasteSpecial Paste:=xlValues, _
        Operation:=xlNone, SkipBlanks:= _
        False, Transpose:=False
    Range("J7").Select
End Sub
```

Figure 18.4 continued.

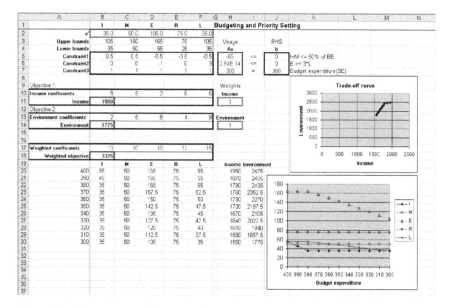

Figure 18.5 Consequences of a gradual budget reduction for the priority setting (exercise18b.xls).

```
Sub RHS_Parametrisation()
'
' RHS_Parametrisation Macro
' Macro created 16/05/2006 by jech
'
    For i = 0 To 10
        Range("J7").Select
        ActiveCell.FormulaR1C1 = "=R[" & (13 + i) & "]C[-9]"
        SolverOk SetCell:="$B$18", MaxMinVal:=1, ValueOf:="0", _
            ByChange:="$B$2:$F$2"
        SolverSolve (True)
        Range("B2:F2").Select
        Selection.Copy
        Range("B" & (20 + i)).Select
        Selection.PasteSpecial Paste:=xlValues, _
            Operation:=xlNone, SkipBlanks:= _
            False, Transpose:=False
        Range("J7").Select
    Next i

End Sub
```

Figure 18.6 VBA program for the parametrisation of the total budget with the 'For . . . Next' command.

```
Sub RHS_Parametrisation()
'
' RHS_Parametrisation Macro
' Macro created 16/05/2006 by jech
'
    For i = 0 To 10
        Range("J7").Select
        ActiveCell.FormulaR1C1 = "=R[" & (13 + i) & "]C[-9]"
        SolverOk SetCell:="$B$18", MaxMinVal:=1, ValueOf:="0", _
            ByChange:="$B$2:$F$2"
        If SolverSolve(True) < 3 Then
            Range("B2:F2").Select
            Selection.Copy
            Range("B" & (20 + i)).Select
            Selection.PasteSpecial Paste:=xlValues, _
                Operation:=xlNone, SkipBlanks:= _
                False, Transpose:=False
        Else
            SolverSolve
            Range("B" & (20 + i)).Select
            ActiveCell.FormulaR1C1 = "no solution"
            Selection.Copy
            Range("B" & (20 + i) & ":F" & (20 + i)).Select
            ActiveSheet.Paste
        End If
    Next i
    Range("J7").Select

End Sub
```

Figure 18.7 VBA program for the parametrisation of the total budget with a 'For . . . Next' command and handling of non-feasible solutions of the model.

that the Solver cannot find a feasible solution due to the upper and lower bounds (cf. Step 17.10). This problem can be solved through a clever use of the return value SolverSolve(True) of the Solver in the VBA code, which you will find in Figure 18.7 and exercise18d.xls. Through entering a character string for the case of non-feasible solutions in the relevant rows in the range B20:F30, the two charts may be interpreted accordingly (cf. Figure 18.8).

We have thus conducted the required sensitivity analysis (Exercise 18d) by defining the values of the range A20:A30 and applying the macro 'RHS_Parametrisation'. Analogously, you can examine parts of the different budget options (e.g. between 290 and 340 with an interval of 5).

Step 18.7 To parametrise the element x from the coefficient matrix (i.e. cell F6 of the constraint 2), proceed as in Steps 18.5 and 18.6. To maintain a clearly structured sheet, enter the start value 3 for x in cell M6 and write the formula = M6 in cell F6. As parameter values, enter the series 0, 0.5, . . ., 5 in the range A20:A30 (cf. Figure 18.9). You now only need to transform the macro 'RHS_Parametrisation' to a respective macro

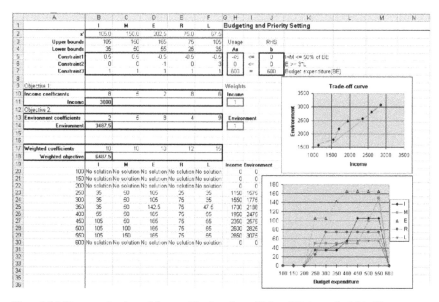

Figure 18.8 Parametrisation of the total budget from 100 to 600 (exercise18d.xls).

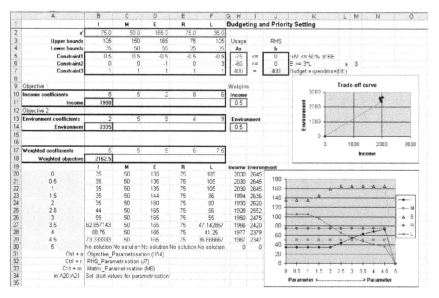

Figure 18.9 Sensitivity analysis of a model for budgeting and priority setting (exercise18e.xls).

'Matrix_Parametrisation' (cf. Figure 18.10 and the macro in exercise18e.xls). Then paste your macro 'RHS_Parametrisation' and another adjusted macro for the vector optimisation ('Objective_ Parametrisation') into it. At the beginning of the macros we automatically generate a part of the respective parameter values and at the end of each macro we enter the relevant start values for the parameter. To be able to open the macros quickly, we define certain key combinations as shown in Figure 18.9 (click on 'Macro', 'Macros . . .', 'Options . . .'). Finally, you have to choose suitable start values for the parameters in A20 and A21 and to run the respective macro.

NB: You should always be sure that you open the correct macro for the respective Excel file. This applies particularly if you have opened several Excel files with macros. Macros can be effective for different Windows programs and files.

The structure of the Excel model exercise18e.xls and of the time-lagged version exercise18e_slow-down.xls with these three macros may be extended and generalised. For example, it is possible to carry out a parametrisation of any coefficient of the constraint matrix, the right-hand side or the bounds for the variables. All possible data for parametrisation may be chosen through an indicator linked to specific IF functions (cf. Figure 18.11 and exercise18e2.xls). If the indicator has the value 1, the coefficient will be considered for parametrisation; otherwise the value is 0. Give it a try. You will possibly have to set a new Solver reference for the VBA code. You may now have realised that not all cells of the sheet are accessible. We have incorporated a password protection. We will explain how you can incorporate such a protection in the next (and last) step.

Step 18.8 Finally, we want to add protection to the model and the macros against unwanted changes. Let us first look at the protection of cells in our Excel sheet, which may be done in two steps. In the first step we format the cells by clicking on 'Format', 'Cells', 'Protection' and tick 'Locked' (and also on 'Hidden', if wanted). The default setting in Excel usually only includes 'Locked'. In the second step we protect the table with a password, which we can incorporate by clicking on 'Tools', 'Protection', 'Protect sheet . . .'. Note that you have to re-enter the password. The protection of the cells is now activated.

The activation of this protection implies, however, that all cells, which we want to access and change during the analysis, now need to be formatted as unlocked (i.e. without the two ticks). In our file exercise18e.xls this would apply to the ranges B2:F7, B10:F10, B13:F13, J5:J7, M6, H14 and A20:F30 (simply select and format all ranges with a pressed Ctrl key). This does not apply for the cell F6 and all other cells with formulas, for which we activate both ticks under 'Protection'.

```
Sub Objective_Parametrisation()
'
' VektorOptimisation Macro
' Macro created 17/05/2006 by jech
'
'    Range("A20").Select
'    ActiveCell.FormulaR1C1 = "0"
'    Range("A21").Select
'    ActiveCell.FormulaR1C1 = "0.1"

    Range("A20:A21").Select
    Selection.AutoFill Destination:=Range("A20:A30"), _
        Type:=xlFillDefault
    For i = 0 To 10
      Range("OF_Parameter").Select
      ActiveCell.FormulaR1C1 = "=R[" & 6 + i & "]C[-7]"
      SolverOk SetCell:="$B$18", MaxMinVal:=1, ValueOf:="0", _
          ByChange:="$B$2:$F$2"
      If SolverSolve(True) < 3 Then
         Range("B2:F2").Select
         Selection.Copy
         Range("B" & (20 + i)).Select
         Selection.PasteSpecial Paste:=xlValues, _
             Operation:=xlNone, SkipBlanks:= _
             False, Transpose:=False
      Else
         SolverSolve
         Range("B" & (20 + i)).Select
         ActiveCell.FormulaR1C1 = "no solution"
         Selection.Copy
         Range("B" & (20 + i) & ":F" & (20 + i)).Select
         ActiveSheet.Paste
      End If
    Next i
    Range("OF_Parameter").Select
    ActiveCell.FormulaR1C1 = ".5"
End Sub
```

```
Sub RHS_Parametrisation()
'
' RHS_Parametrisation Macro
' Macro created 17/05/2006 by jech
'
'    Range("A20").Select
'    ActiveCell.FormulaR1C1 = "300"
'    Range("A21").Select
'    ActiveCell.FormulaR1C1 = "310"
    Range("A20:A21").Select
    Selection.AutoFill Destination:=Range("A20:A30"), _
        Type:=xlFillDefault
    For i = 0 To 10
      Range("RHS_Parameter").Select
      ActiveCell.FormulaR1C1 = "=R[" & 13 + i & "]C[-9]"
      SolverOk SetCell:="$B$18", MaxMinVal:=1, ValueOf:="0", _
          ByChange:="$B$2:$F$2"
      If SolverSolve(True) < 3 Then
         Range("B2:F2").Select
```

Figure 18.10 Macros for a sensitivity analysis.

```
            Selection.Copy
            Range("B" & (20 + i)).Select
            Selection.PasteSpecial Paste:=xlValues, _
                Operation:=xlNone, SkipBlanks:= _
                False, Transpose:=False
        Else
            SolverSolve
            Range("B" & (20 + i)).Select
            ActiveCell.FormulaR1C1 = "no solution"
            Selection.Copy
            Range("B" & (20 + i) & ":F" & (20 + i)).Select
            ActiveSheet.Paste
        End If
    Next i
    Range("RHS_Parameter").Select
    ActiveCell.FormulaR1C1 = "400"
End Sub


Sub Matrix_Parametrisation()
'
' Matrix_Parametrisation Macro
' Macro created 17/05/2006 by jech
'    Range("A20").Select
'    ActiveCell.FormulaR1C1 = "0"
'    Range("A21").Select
'    ActiveCell.FormulaR1C1 = "0.3"
    Range("A20:A21").Select
    Selection.AutoFill Destination:=Range("A20:A30"), _
        Type:=xlFillDefault
    Range("A22:A30").Select
    For i = 0 To 10
        Range("M_Parameter").Select
        ActiveCell.FormulaR1C1 = "=R[" & 14 + i & "]C[-12]"
        SolverOk SetCell:="$B$18", MaxMinVal:=1, ValueOf:="0", _
            ByChange:="$B$2:$F$2"
        If SolverSolve(True) < 3 Then
            Range("B2:F2").Select

            Selection.Copy
            Range("B" & (20 + i)).Select
            Selection.PasteSpecial Paste:=xlValues, _
                Operation:=xlNone, SkipBlanks:= _
                False, Transpose:=False
        Else
            SolverSolve
            Range("B" & (20 + i)).Select
            ActiveCell.FormulaR1C1 = "no solution"
            Selection.Copy
            Range("B" & (20 + i) & ":F" & (20 + i)).Select
            ActiveSheet.Paste
        End If
    Next i
    Range("M_Parameter").Select
    ActiveCell.FormulaR1C1 = "3"
End Sub
```

Figure 18.10 continued.

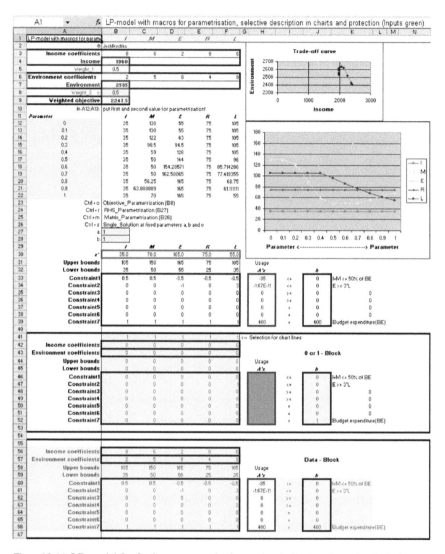

Figure 18.11 LP-model for further parametrisations using indicators (exercise 18e2.xls).

Once the sheet protection is activated, the Solver can no longer be opened via 'Tools', but the Solver can be activated using a VBA program. We have been quite lucky, as the Solver works without any problems with our three macros.

Furthermore, we can also protect the VBA code against unwanted access and changes. To do this, click in the Visual Basic Editor on 'Tools', 'VBA project properties' and 'Protection' and lock the program for viewing. You may use the same password as for the protection of the sheet. The protection is activated once you have saved the file and opened it again. The macros and the references will be shown only after the password has been entered. By the way, the password for our file exercise18e_protection.xls is 'exercise18e'. You may need the password to update the Solver reference (also take into account the note at the end of Step 17.7).

References

Albright, S.C. (2001) *VBA for Modelers: Developing Decision Support Systems with Microsoft® Excel*, Belmont, CA: Duxbury Press, pp. 63–105.

Frontline Systems Inc. (2005) *Standard Excel Solver – Controlling the Solver with VBA*. Available online at: <http://www.solver.com/suppstdvba.htm> (accessed 20 July 2006).

Nožička, F., Guddat, J., Hollatz, H. and Bank, B. (1974) *Theorie der linearen parametrischen Optimierung*, Berlin: Akademie Verlag.

Padberg, M. (1995) *Linear Optimization and Extensions*, Berlin: Springer, pp. 102–5.

Walkenbach, J. (2004) *Microsoft® Office Excel 2003 Power Programming with VBA*, Indianapolis, IN: John Wiley.

Winston, W.L. (2004) *Operations Research* (4th edn), Belmont, CA: Brooks/Cole, pp. 262–95.

Bibliography

Albright, S.C. (2001) *VBA for Modelers: Developing Decision Support Systems with Microsoft® Excel*, Belmont, CA: Duxbury Press.

Bowen, H.P., Hollander, A. and Viaene, L.-M. (1998) *Applied International Trade Analysis*, Basingstoke, London: Macmillan.

Chiang, A.C. (1984) *Fundamental Methods of Mathematical Economics* (3rd edn), Singapore: McGraw-Hill.

Chiang, A.C. and Wainwright, K. (2005) *Fundamental Methods of Mathematical Economics* (4th edn), Boston, MA: McGraw-Hill.

Corden, W.M. (1997) *Trade Policy and Economic Welfare* (2nd edn), New York, Oxford: Oxford University Press.

Edmonds, J. (1971) 'Matroids and the greedy algorithm', *Mathematical Programming*, 1, pp. 127–30.

Frontline Systems Inc. (2005) *Standard Excel Solver – Controlling the Solver with VBA*. Available online at <http://www.solver.com/suppstdvba.htm> (accessed 20 July 2006).

—— (1996) *Solver User's Guide*, Nevada: Incline Village.

Fylstra, D., Lasdon, L., Watson, J. and Waren, A. (1998) 'Design and use of the Microsoft® Excel solver', *Interfaces*, 28, pp. 29–55.

Guddat, J. (1979) 'Parametrische Optimierung und Vektoroptimierung', in K. Lommatzsch (ed.) *Anwendungen der linearen parametrischen Optimierung*, Berlin: Akademie Verlag.

Jechlitschka, K. and Lotze, H. (1997) 'Theorie und Anwendung eines Mehr-Markt-Modells zur sektoralen Analyse von Agrarpolitiken', *Zeitschrift für Agrarinformatik*, 5 (2), pp. 26–31.

Jensen, P.A. and Bard, J.F. (2003) *Operations Research: Models and Methods*, Indianapolis, IN: John Wiley.

Just, R.E., Hueth, D.L. and Schmitz, A. (2004) *The Welfare Economics of Public Policy: A Practical Approach to Project and Policy Evaluation*, Cheltenham, Northampton, MA: Edward Elgar.

Keller, H., Pferschy, U. and Pisinger, D. (2004) *Knapsack Problems*, Berlin: Springer.

Kirschke, D. and Jechlitschka, K. (2003) 'Analyse von Preispolitiken mit Excel', *WiSt-Wirtschaftswissenschaftliches Studium, Zeitschrift für Ausbildung und Hochschulkontakt*, 32 (10), pp. 582–9. Available online at <http://edoc.hu-berlin.de/oa/articles/re3C1x H26kQwk/PDF/29uPNywMfGpUI.pdf> (accessed 20 July 2006).

Kirschke, D., Odening, M., Doluschitz, R., Fock, T., Hagedorn, K., Rost, D. and von Witzke, H. (1998) *Weiterentwicklung der EU-Agrarpolitik – Aussichten für die neuen Bundesländer*, Kiel: Vauk.

Klein, M.W. (2002) *Mathematical Methods for Economics* (2nd edn), Boston, MA: Addison Wesley.

Koester, U. (2005) *Grundzüge der landwirtschaftlichen Marktlehre* (3rd edn), Munich: Vahlen (WiSo-Kurzlehrbücher: Reihe Volkswirtschaft).

Krugman, P.R. and Obstfeld, M. (2003) *International Economics, Theory and Policy* (7th edn), Boston, MA: Addison Wesley.

Mas-Colell, A., Whinston, M.D. and Green, J.A. (1995) *Microeconomic Theory*, New York, Oxford: Oxford University Press.

Microsoft, Original Handbooks and Microsoft Excel-help. Available online at <http://www.microsoft.com> (accessed 20 July 2006).

Nicholson, W. (2005) *Microeconomic Theory: Basic Principles and Extensions* (9th edn), Mason, OH: Thomson.

Nožička, F., Guddat, J. and Hollatz, H. (1972) *Theorie der linearen Optimierung*, Berlin: Akademie Verlag.

Nožička, F., Guddat, J., Hollatz, H. and Bank, B. (1974) *Theorie der linearen parametrischen Optimierung*, Berlin: Akademie Verlag.

Padberg, M. (1995) *Linear Optimization and Extensions*, Berlin: Springer.

Pindyck, R.S. and Rubinfeld, D.L. (2005) *Microeconomics* (6th edn), Upper Saddle River, NJ: Pearson Prentice Hall.

Powell, S.G. (1995) 'The teachers' forum: six key modeling heuristics', *Interfaces*, 25, pp. 113–25.

—— (1997) 'Leading the spreadsheet revolution', *ORMS Today*, 24 (6), pp. 50–4.

Stoer, J. and Witzgall, C. (1970) *Convexity and Optimization in Finite Dimensions I*, Berlin: Springer.

Varian, H.R. (2003) *Intermediate Microeconomics: A Modern Approach* (6th edn), New York: W.W. Norton.

von Lampe, M. (1998) 'The World Agricultural Trade Simulation System WATSIM', Discussion Paper No. 5, University of Bonn.

Wahl, O., Weber, G. and Frohberg, K. (2000) 'Documentation of the Central and Eastern European Countries Agricultural Simulation Model', Discussion Paper No. 27, Institut für Agrarentwicklung in Mittel und Osteuropa, Halle (Saale).

Walkenbach, J. (2004) *Microsoft® Office Excel 2003 Bible*, Indianapolis, IN: John Wiley.

—— (2004) *Microsoft® Office Excel 2003 Power Programming with VBA*, Indianapolis, IN: John Wiley.

Weber, G. (2001) 'Agricultural policy analysis in transition countries with CEEC-ASIM: who will lose, who will gain by the EU-accession?', in T. Heckelei, H.P. Witzke and W. Henrichsmeyer (eds) *Agricultural Sector Modelling and Policy Information Systems*, Kiel: Vauk, pp. 212–20.

Winston, W.L. (1999) *Financial Models Using Simulation and Optimization*, Newfield, NY: Palisade Corporation.

—— (2004) *Operations Research* (4th edn), Belmont, CA: Brooks/Cole.

Winston, W.L. and Albright, S.C. (2001) *Practical Management Science* (2nd edn), Belmont, CA: Duxbury Thomson Learning.

Winston, W.L. and Venkataramanan, M. (2002) *Introduction to Mathematical Programming*, Belmont, CA: Duxbury Press.

Zeleny, M. (1974) *Linear Multiobjective Programming*, Berlin: Springer.

Index